Joseph Philip Robson

Evangeline

The Spirit of Progress

Joseph Philip Robson

Evangeline
The Spirit of Progress

ISBN/EAN: 9783337005177

Printed in Europe, USA, Canada, Australia, Japan

Cover: Foto ©Thomas Meinert / pixelio.de

More available books at **www.hansebooks.com**

EVANGELINE:

OR,

THE SPIRIT OF PROGRESS;

TOGETHER WITH

A COPIOUS SELECTION

OF

MISCELLANEOUS POEMS

AND

SONGS,

SENTIMENTAL, HUMOUROUS, AND LOCAL.

BY

J. P. ROBSON.

NEWCASTLE-UPON-TYNE:
PRINTED BY J. M. CARR, 21, LOW FRIAR STREET.
—
1870.

INTRODUCTION.

J. P. Robson, the Author of several popular Standard Works, and, *par excellence*, *the* Bard of the Tyne, requires no introduction to the public, even from any of the bright stars in the literary firmament, far less, of course, from an unknown young man like myself. · Why, then, this preface? and, above all, why comes it from the present writer? To me, the most satisfactory answer is, that the Poet himself so willed it. Though painfully conscious of my own incapacity, our mutual friendship, combined with the high regard in which I hold the off-springs of his muse, forbade that I should decline the task. The duty, however, is light, because little need be said, and far from irksome, as my heart guides the pen.

Mr. Robson's years are not far short of the allotted span. He commenced life as a plane-maker, but his tastes lying in another direction, he afterwards followed the more congenial pursuits of a school-master in Newcastle, his native town, where he has lived all his days, with the exception of seven years spent in Sunderland. It is many years since he relinquished the ferule of the teacher, and devoted all his time to literary work. He has long been, and still is, a frequent contributor to newspapers and magazines. His weekly letter in the *North of England Advertiser*, written in the local dialect, under the *nom de plume* of "The Retiort Keelmin," has served greatly to increase and extend his reputation as a scholar, a wit, a sound thinker, a poet, and a man.

About five months ago, shortly after he began to prepare the present volume for the Press, he was attacked with a severe stroke of paralysis, from which he has partially recovered. Although his left arm and hand are still perfectly powerless, he is able again to attend to his literary duties, and, though, perhaps, not in a manner quite so satisfactorily and thoroughly as would otherwise have been the case, has succeeded in completing the work now given to the public. The "Selections," therefore, may be regarded as issuing from the bed-chamber of the poet, a fact, doubtless, which will, in the estimation of his friends and admirers, impart to them a peculiar interest and charm. While trusting that he shall long be spared to pay his devotions and render his eminent services to poetry, "the grandest chariot wherein king-thoughts ride," it may be thought, considering his advanced years and serious illness, that there is a mournful appropriateness in here reproducing his exquisite poem, "The Dying Poet," and that is done all the more willingly, as it has not been assigned a place in the following "Selections :"—

Hush, hush, wild throbbings of my aching breast,
　　And to my spirit yield fair Love's delight !
For I am weary of this world's unrest,
　　And wish on wings of death to take my flight.
What have I been that my poetic right
Hath from my genial heart been torn away,
　　And clouds of heaven that bore the silver light
Of seraphs' wings, have shut out every ray,
But what pale Genius lent to bless the dawning day

Oh, Poesy ! I've wandered in thy noon
　　Of glorious inspiration, like the lark
That steals the falling rainbows, as a boon
　　From mingled cloud-tears, ere the skies grow dark,
To drench with desolation Sorrow's moon.
Say, have I chanted Fancy's lays too soon,
　　That my poor voice, unused to tones of joy,
Dying in cadences of minor tune,
　　Feels in its strain the dross of earth's alloy,
　　And crucibles its hopes in flames too bright and coy

Remove the curtains from my dreary bed ;
　　Let the grand beam of glory on me shine !
Bring God's fair halos round my throbbing head,
　　For in His rays I feel Love's smiles divine !
　　I drink His Love as from a cup of wine !

Cling to me day-beams with an infant's glee,
  And lay soft kisses on these lips of mine!
Again I roam amid youth's valleys free,
  And soar o'er mountains high reflected in the sea!

What have I been that, like a rose-cheek'd child,
  On Nature's bosom I must fall asleep?
I that on storm and tempest only smiled,
  And with the dolphin danced upon the deep?
Why do I tremble now, and, childlike, weep
To part from loving faces round my bed?
  Have I a harvest still to sow and reap?
Am I to be with milk and honey fed?
No, no! my wayward spirit must by death be led.

Kiss me, my heart's young joy, and say "farewell!"
  I cannot see thee! Hath the day gone down
To the sea caverns, where the coral shell
  Murmurs my requiem? Hath night's cold frown
Deepened the shadows of my passing bell,
That gloomily my parting sighs shall tell
  To thee, sweet girl? Oh, kiss me, 'tis the last
Love-token from love's casket, from love's dell,
  Fragrant with love's own flowers, whence the blast
Of scorn shall fail to reach me till my doom is past.

And *then* the worm that lingers in my breast
  Will not bite keener than my faults appear
Huge as leviathan on ocean's crest;
  Pity will yield me all she can—a tear,
  And thou, kind girl, I know, with love sincere,
Wilt weep; but do not weep, thy grief restrain!
  Cast flowers of mem'ry o'er my humble bier;
Tears may fall gently, but they all are vain,
For thou canst ne'er bring back thy poet-love again!

Take thy red lips away, death claims me now;
  I go into a land of which no tongue
Hath ever uttered word. Ah, wipe my brow,
  And sing me, for the last time, my loved song.
  Alas, I hear thee not! The echoing gong
Were but a tinkling to my deafened sense.
  A crowd of shadowy beauties near me throng,
And beckon me to wander with them hence—
I die; farewell!—may God in death be thy defence!

Mr. Robson's home and heart experience has not greatly
differed from that of mankind generally, or that of the

Sons of Song in particular, for the cup of existence put into his hands has contained a large admixture of disappointment, vicissitude, sorrow and suffering. Not only have many of the best friends of his youth entered the Silent Land, but all his children, seven in number, have likewise been laid low in the grave. His own pathetic Muse best describes his desolate condition :

> I hae naebody noo ; for my bairns are a' gane,
>   And a' the day lang I sit subbin' alane :
> I hae naebody noo :—like a weed on the wave,
>   I am driftin' awa' to my bed in the grave.

But he is not altogether alone, for he still can count upon a goodly array of friends, tender and true, while by his side is to be seen her, so faithful and loving, who. through a long series of years, has been the helpful sharer of all his joys and sorrows.

There is good reason to believe that over-work has had much to do in bringing on the paralytic attack. The following list of his published works shows that he has never allowed his muse to slumber or his pen to rust :— "Wild Blossoms of Poesy," 1832 ; "Poetic Gatherings," 1839 ; "The Monomaniac," 1847 ; "Tyneside Songs," 1848 ; "Life of Billy Purvis," 1849 ; "Bards o' the Tyne," 1850 ; "Summer Excursions," 1851 ; "Poetic Pencillings," 1852 ; "Hermione, the Beloved," 1857 ; and "The Songs of Solomon, Translated into the Dialect of Northumberland," and "Lowland Scotch," for His Highness Louis Lucian Bonaparte, 1860, (only 250 copies of which were printed for private circulation). The following is a specimen of a poetic version of the Songs, in the Tyneside dialect :—

SOLOMON'S SANG.

PAIRT FIVE.

> Tiv maw gardin, maw sister, aw've come ;
>   Aw've raked up the marr an' the spice ;
> Honey-blobs aw ha'e lickt frae me thumb,
>   An' aw've suppt a' the milk an' wine nice.

Maw freen's, come, eat an' drink wi' me,
Drink, maw true love ; drink plenty, tee !

Aw sleeps, but maw heart's on the muve,
An' the cawl o' me luver aw hear ;
He says " Oppin, maw sister, maw luve !
Maw unspeckled duve, an' maw dear !
Maw heed wi' dew is fairly weet,
Wesht biv the rainin' o' the neet.

" Aw hae pat off the coat frae me back ;
Hoo ageyn can aw put me coat on ?
Aw ha'e wesht baith maw feet frae the black,
An' aw'll clag them wi' muck ef aw run !"

Maw luve then pat his neef inside
The hole what's i' wor dooer ;
Hoo cud aw lie, an' langer bide?
Aw let him in, for shure !

Tiv maw true-luve aw oppint the dooer,
An' maw han's wes a' cover'd wi' smell ;
Biv marr wes maw fingurs spreed ower,
That in drops on the lock-hancls fell.

Tiv maw luve aw the dooer oppint wide,
But maw sweetheart wes vanisht an' geyn,
Hoo aw trimmelt wheniver he sigh'd,
But maw luver had left me aleyn.
Aw tried te find him but aw fail'd,
Nor did he ansur when aw hail'd.

Biv the watchmen that shoot the toon roond,
Aw wes fand, an' they treeted me sair ;
For they ga'e me a verra bad woond,
An' they rove oot the curls o' maw hair.
Maw veil wes pull'd clean frae me feyce,
Biv the watchmen-rips aboot the pleyce.

O ye lasses o' Salem, teyk heed,
　　An' mind, ef maw sweetheart ye see,
That ye tell him aw's verra nigh deed,
　　An' to hurry, thereckleys, te me !
" O woman, that's fair 'mang the fair,
　　What's thaw luver owt mair nor the rest ?
For thaw sweetheart what cawl need we care
　　Ony mair nor the lads we like best ?"

Maw luver he's white an' he's reed,
　　Mang ten thoosan' he's chief o' them a' !
Like the finest o' goold is his heed,
　　An' his hair is as black as a craw.
His een like the cushat's appears,
　　When biv wettors ther' bonnily set ;
For ther' wesht biv the soft milky tears,
　　An' they shine like coal-di'mins o' jet.

Like twe beds o' fine spices, his cheeks,
　　Or the flooers i' wor gardins they are ;
His lips is like lilies that speaks,
　　Droppin' sweet smellin' ointmin' an' marr.
Goold rings set wi' di'mins that shines,
　　His han's elways seems te maw scet ;
Ow'r his belly, like ivory, twines
　　The glisterin' blue steyns complete.

Like twe pillars o' white marvel, set
　　On thor' sockits o' goold, is his knees ;
An' the feyce o' maw beautiful pet
　　Is as cumley as Lebanon's trees.
O sweet, verra sweet is his mooth !
　　A'thegither he luvesome appears ;
Noo, *this* is maw luve, in a' trooth,
　　An' maw freend, O Jerusalem dears !

These works are all out of print, and that fact
cannot fail to make the " Selections" all the more
acceptable. But it should be mentioned that, while the
volume consists chiefly of selected pieces, it also contains

several poems never before published. The opening poem, entitled " Evangeline ; or the Spirit of Progress," was specially written for the present work, and is dedicated to George Robert Stephenson, Esq., nephew to the great champion of progress, who may, I believe, be taken as the hero of this charming tale.

To show the versatility of Mr. Robson's genius, the introduction to a long unpublished Poem, on the "World of Waters" is here inserted. This Poem was written at the suggestion of the late Dr. Mordey, of Sunderland :—

ORBIS AQUARIUM ; OR, THE WORLD OF WATERS.

INTRODUCTORY.

War and its horrors, Death and Ruin wide*
    Stalk gaunt and grimly through the fertile vales
Of long down-trodden Italy. The haughty pride
    Of Hapsburg on his swart-plumed eagle sails.
France and Sardinia swell the ensanguined tide
    O'er welt'ring fields where stricken Freedom wails
Her thousands slaughtered—Glory's hecatomb !
Italia ! O Italia ! what shall be thy doom ?

My Muse sighs mournful as she looks on thee ;
    For O, she dreadeth lest the tyrant's might
Should sweep thy noble warriors, like the sea
    Big with its strength of storms, to death's long night !
Lest conq'ring France, to whom thou bend'st thy knee,
    Should fail to crown thy brow with wreaths of Right ;
For Gaul's proud eagles *have* been birds of prey,
And what they once secure hold fast beneath their sway.

O, that on earth, the footstool of Heav'n's King,
    Whose attributes are Mercy, Peace and Love,
The sons of men should dire destruction bring,
    And choose the rav'ning vulture for the dove :—

---

* Written during the Italian War.

The fierce tornado for the kiss of Spring !
  Why sleeps the lightning in the clouds above ?
Why let the despots live to strike the blow
That lays the aspiring crest of new-born Freedom low ?

From sick'ning scenes of gore-stained earth my muse
  Turns sighing to her limpid fountain cool,
Where balmy flowers exhale their grateful dews,
  And gentle zephyrs sport around the pool
On Helicon's fair hill.   'Tis there she woos
  Her Hippocrene, and far from wild Misrule,
And brazen-throated Rage, and streams of blood,
She quaffs th' inspiring draught from Aganippe's flood.

Nectar, insooth, art thou pure Element
  Of crystal Water !   Water, thou art life !
Thy springs, like veins of health with vigour blent
  In the heart's depths, rise beautiful, and rife
With all the charms of music and content ;
  Cooling to reason all the fires of strife,
And rend'ring nature gay and innocent.
  Blest be the blow that cleft thy mountain side,
  Parnassus, ever fair, whence living waters glide.

Water of Life, Amretsir ! where the sikh
  Laves his dark limbs on burning Hindostan,
And from thy waves immortal, pray'rful, meek,
  Comes forth a purified, regen'rate man !
O that thy balmy wings my brow and cheek
  And throbbing pulse of care might gently fan,
That, while I rested on thy fountain's brim,
My grateful voice might swell thy pilgrim-chaunted hymn.

· Water of Life ! long years should then be mine ;
  A genial Spring without the Winter's snow ;
When in the Ethiopian's sacred shrine
  With joy I'd leap ; then in thy deeps should glow
My cheeks with beauty adolescent, as the shine
  Of a pure unguent all my form would show !
Gay as the morning with no streak of gloom ;
Fragrant as vi'let's breath and redolent of bloom.

Or, with the Ammonians at the blush of day,
   When gentle throbbings of thy fountain, Sun,
On thy clear bosom, like soft mem'ries play,
   Ere the meridian chill thee into stone ;
. Or midnight boil thee into sultry spray,
   Let me, thy steps descending, seen by none,
Save the warm gale that floats on thy fair breast,
Bathe me in depths of Joy, like Psyche calmly blest.

Let rank, malignant streams be far from me !
   No Scythian fount my Hypanis to mar ;
Calm be my journey to Oblivion's sea,
   Unstained life's currents by the springs of Tar :
Hope's waters to the Future flowing free, ·
   And on their bosom shining Love's fair star,
Like some bright thought that makes a fairy bed,
In a smile's dimpling cheek, soft, rippling, ripe, and red.

E'en to thy stream Choaspes, near the fane
   Of Persia's Susa, with the kings of old,
My steps shall wander. From thy wave again,
   Despite the threaten'd doom, thy draughts of gold
My soul shall steep ; shall vivify my brain.
   By mummied monarchs free and uncontroll'd,
Water I sing ; life-giving boon divine !
Flow on, Choaspes, golden rills are mine !

    ✱   ✱   ✱   ✱   ✱   ✱

Ere Earth's creation out of chaos sprung,
   And shapeless matter 'mid dense darkness lay
Buried profound : ere the round lamps were hung
   In the vast vault to govern night and day ;
Ere tuneful stars their hymns melodious sung ;
   Or the wild comet shot malignant ray,
Thou wast, eternal element of might,
Shadowed, yet grandly dwelling in thy halls of light.

Life's glorious Spirit with creative breath,
   Lay brooding o'er thy vastness through all space,

When from the darkling robes of seeming death,
  Thou wast, in gloomy grandeur, to thy place
Determin'd by His will.   Rocks underneath
  And dark-peak'd mountains rose in kingly grace,
While o'er Earth's breast, outspreading wide, thy waves
Heaved, as from sleep, and spurn'd chaotic graves.

Then Light sprung flashing from the gates of Gloom !
  Night, that had reigned, proud, absolute and vast,
Brought forth an heir to heaven, as from Death's womb,
  A mystical conception of the Past !
Young Day was born, an infant of fair bloom,
  Crown'd by the rays of Beauty, long to last ;
He gazed on Earth's deep waters, waste and wild,
With the first beams of morning, like a child.

Far up in the high altitudes of calm,
  The Firmament appeared, divided now,
And soaring, like a novel world, in balm,
  With peaceful breast and majesty of brow,
From her late crypt of shadows ; the while psalm
  Of the rejoicing Planets trembled through
Heaven's throne of splendour radiate with new beams
That danced their first joy-measures on new streams.

In loveliness the gentle Moon was seen
  Walking the azure gardens of the skies ;
The new-crown'd Empress of the Night serene,
  And all the Earth gaz'd upwards with surprise.
The old rocks glistened 'neath her silvery sheen ;
  The Lotos woke and oped her wond'ring eyes ;
When, like a liquid desert, boundless lay
The WORLD OF WATERS 'neath her virgin ray.

*   *   *   *   *   *

While Mr. Robson, as a poet, may be said to enjoy a
national reputation, the planet of his fame shines most
brightly in his own beloved Tyneside.   His highest ambition, indeed, has been " to awaken the harp of old Tyne,"
and all know how effectively and sweetly he has done this.

But he also occupies an honoured place as a writer of Scotch lyrics ; nor will he soon be forgotten as the author of long poems, all admirably arranged, and containing noble aspirations, lofty thoughts, delicate touches and flights of the imagination, in which he never loses himself nor fails to fill the reader with rapture and delight.

An introduction to the Poet's "Selections" cannot be brought to a more suitable conclusion than by quoting his own beautiful verses, "The Poet's Request" (not included in this volume) which may be looked upon as the parting address of their favourite Bard to the people of Tyneside :—

When this hand that the harp of old Tyne oft awakened
  With lays rude and simple, lies low in the earth ;
When the angel of Peace to his bosom has beckon'd,
  And called him from Friendship, from Music and Mirth ;
Let the sunlight of Kindness in silence beam o'er him,
  And gild the dark spots on his mem'ry that lie ;
Let the radiance of Love to a rainbow restore him,
  And Hope spread her beautiful wings to the sky.

Let the strains that he warbled,—poor bird of the morning !
  Find echo in bosoms, the tender and true ;
And his spirit to earth in its gladness returning,
  In the Valley of Shadows his songs may renew.
O ye loved and true-hearted, forget all his errors !
  Clothe his mem'ry in robes of a penitent child ;
Let the grave where he slumbers be shorn of death's terrors,
  And Love's daisies shall bloom in their gentleness wild.

WM. FERGUSSON.

Newcastle-upon-Tyne, 1870.

CONTENTS.

Page

INDEX TO THE SONGS

TO WHICH AIRS HAVE BEEN ADAPTED BY THE AUTHOR.

EVANGELINE:

OR,

THE SPIRIT OF PROGRESS;

A POEM IN TWO PARTS.

EVANGELINE;

OR, THE SPIRIT OF PROGRESS.

'Twas at the holy eventide, the vesper hour of prayer,
Two children sat a brook beside ; the one a maiden fair,
A boy, the other, darkly pale, with black and shining hair,
Through yon grey mist now rising slow, 'mid balmy air serene,
The dwellings of the youthful pair distinctly may be seen ;—
The mansion of Evangeline,—the cottage of Eugene.
Wild flowers they had been gathering, and now with wearied feet,
Together on the bank they rest, to cull their treasures sweet ;
Simple as childhood were those flowers, their beauty fair, but fleet !
And was this child, of gentle birth, permitted thus to stray
With one of vulgar poverty mid wild-woods day by day ?
Did not the shades of misery fall—on this fair creature's play ?
Ask why the spirit dwells in earth ; why gems are found in dust ;
Why moonbeams rest on lowly flowers ; why poor men dare to
        trust !
Why the blest rain of heaven descends both on the vile and just !
Evangeline and this poor boy together oft were seen ;
She pitied him—he looked so pale,—though humble he was
        clean ;—
Her mother, too, had said she knew the parents of Eugene.
Her guileless heart, her trusting love, found pleasure in the boy,
For while he listened to her words his face seemed flusht with joy.
Could she, by scorn and petted pride, his bosom's trust destroy ?
" Come, let us make two wreaths," she said,—" the cowslip
        and the rose,
The daisy and the buttercup, and the blue flower that grows
So modest with its golden eyes, our garlands shall compose.
My mother is so fond of flowers ; she says their balmy breath
Falls on her heart, like memories of lov'd ones lost in death :
She is thinking of my father then—his nobleness and faith.
On the red field of Waterloo, Eugene, my father fell ;
Oh, it would make you weep sad tears to hear my mother tell
How, ere he died, his child he blest, and her he lov'd so well.

I love whate'er my mother loves, and so I love sweet flowers ;
Come ! I have cull'd and bound *my* wreath, say, shall I finish
    yours ?
Then we, at once, will haste away to those dear homes of ours !"
" Aw ha'e ne muther noo to please," Eugene, low voiced, replied,
" An' fether hates a' kind o' floors, sic things he thraws aside ;
Thoo cannet think hoo cross he's turn'd sin' maw poor muther died.
She kent thee well, Miss 'Vangeleen, an' yor bonny muther tee ;
She nurst thee when a little bairn, an' danc'd thee on her knee.
Oh dear ! aw miss her every day, she was se kind to me.
But, let's away, its gettin' dark ; hoo hungry now aw feel !
Aw's oftens fit to faint be want, aw'll drop before aw steal !
When aw can wark, mesel' aw'll keep, an' fether tee, as weel."
Evangeline in haste arose, her garlands now were made,—
" Come home with me, my mother kind will give you food," she
    said ;
" Come *every* day ! the Hall you know,—oh, dear to want for
    bread !"
Love sparkled in that boy's dark eye, yet honest pride was seen.
" Aw sure thoo is a darlin' lass, maw bonny 'Vangeleen !
But aw can niver bring maw mind to be a beggar mean !
" Aw needn't want for meat or claes—but aw mun say ne mair—
Aw see maw fether wiv a crowd afore the yell-hoose there.
Good neet, good neet ! an' think on me when thoo kneels doon
    to pray'r !"
Drear was the dwelling of that lad, no comfort there was seen,—
Straw was his pallet, on the boards, but seldom washed or clean :
Confusion, dirt, and hunger, were companions of Eugene.
No gentle hands his pillow smooth'd, no matron in her pride,
His form array'd in vesture trim, or wandered by his side ;
His was a life of misery, with none to cheer and guide.
The merry boys that sailed their boats, and waded in the peul,
Oft asked him why he could not read, and if he went to scheul ;
While some, more rude in speech, would say--" His faither is a
    ' feul !"
A kindling flush of boyish wrath would crimson brow and cheek,
To hear the bare-legg'd village lads, thus of his father speak ;
To turn against the foes were vain, he knew his cause was weak.
His father, heedless of the fact that ignorance in youth
Checks the fair growth of heart and mind, and chains the eagle
    Truth.

The wishes of his child repelled in language strange, uncouth.
" Scheul, scheul ! thoo's always crying, scheul ! wark first, and
scheulin' next !
D'ye want to be a preacher, lad, wi' white tie an' a text ?"
" Aw want to be like other lads !" Eugene replied, perplexed.
" Thoo's ganin seun to colliery wark, thaw daily keyk to eairn !
Just leuk at me ; aw cannot read, aw niver cared to leairn ;
Thoo's turned o' seven—thou'll wark the traps—aw'll keep ne
lazy bairn !
Thoo and thaw scheul !"—and, with an oath, the parent left his son.
His promised word in this was kept, for 'ere next day was done,
Eugene was stationed in the mine—and his first toils begun.
'Tis said that every mortal born, a guardian-angel hath,
That hovers round his bed of rest, and guides his noonday path,
To succour him in danger's hour, and still the storm of wrath.
Evangeline this angel proved, her placid face was seen,
To bend with beaming looks of love, upon the boy Eugene ;
For 'mid the colliers' wickedness, his thoughts were calm, serene.
And when the blessed Sabbath came, the lab'rer to release,
To quench the forge's roaring glow, bid thundering engines cease,
When thankful hearts breathed holy prayers of piety and peace ;—
Forth went Eugene with lightsome steps to join the village train ;
To mingle in the choruss'd hymn, devotion's sacred strain,—
To gaze on fair Evangeline, and hear her voice again.
And oft, at eventide, he strayed, and rested by the brook,
Where she would come, instructress young, with some sweet,
simple book,
And lead him onward through his task, by gentle word and look.
Oh, who can speak the mystic thrill that through his bosom ran,
When he had learned the saving words of Bible truth to scan ?
How angels had to earth come down, and converse held with man.
His hard, straw bed—his days of toil—his father's blows and
scorn,
Were all forgotten when he read of Him, in Beth'lem born,
Who had no place his head to rest—despised—rejected—lorn !
Patience he learnt, and bore reproof, though poor, his hopes rose
high ;
And many a stubborn task he fought—his books were always
nigh—
And thus six years of work and strife—struggle and toil, went by.
*   *   *   *

Rolling away, wave after wave—still ceaseless, rolling on—
Earth's seasons, like the billows, pass, with shadow, rain, and sun;
Sweet flowers awake, look gay and die, till beauty there seems
    none !
Bold winds, proud storms with wintry beards, on cloud-crown'd
    mountains reign ;
'Neath cold grey ice, streams lock their songs—snow-mantles
    robe the plain ;
Anon, the despots quit their thrones, and fragrance breathes
    again !
Years of fixt, patient industry, indomitably stern—
Unwearying assiduity—the will and power to learn,
Deeds, marvellously great, achieve, and fame's bright laurels earn !
As solid rocks, once grains of sand—the haughty waves defy ;
As oceans vast—but gathered drops—roll boundless 'neath the sky ;
So thoughts of man's determined mind, opposing rocks shall
    stand,
And Progress, like the gathered seas, spread glorious o'er the land.
Let knowledge forge the chains of soul, no time the links shall
    sever ;
Test them and strain them as ye may, they baulk each vain
    endeavour ;
Science still reigns omnipotent, and Wisdom lives for ever !
A change—arising after death—upon that cottage came,
New life was kindled in that home, and gaily glowed the flame.
A kind old matron, happy-faced, now ruled the miner's cot,
Where sweet contentment dwelt serene, and strife was all forgot.
The " callers" who aroused the youth for work at dawn of day,
The change remark'd, as to the pit, he went his willing way.
" Whie, lad, thoo's like a butterflee, thaw beyte-poke's white as
    snaw !
Aw shure thoo's thrivin' like a troot, luck's breezes surely blaw !"
In sooth, the breeze of fortune blew, and friendship rode the gale,
The balmy breath that opes the flower in life's secluded vale.
Bright was the eye, and rosy health, in fresh'ning bloom, was seen
To struggle through the pallid cheeks of the collier-boy, Eugene.
And when the hour of toil was o'er—the stains of coal removed—
Before his books intent he sat, and studied what he loved ;
While other youths to bowls and quoits, and alehouse-mirth
    would stray ;
Gainst ignorance he battled well, and conquered day by day.

Much had he suffered, poverty had been his teacher stern ;
Now with the wish the power increased, and aptitude to learn.
Tasks darkly strange he pondered o'er, till dawning wisdom came ;
As clouds the smiles of morning catch, and brighten in the flame.
Yet, ah ! how slow his progress seemed ; the little that he knew
Was but a step, and, what a maze he still must wander through !
Patience ! the spider Mind wove on—a line, and then the next ;
Though oft, mid warp and woof of thought, poor youth, he
    paused perplext.
" God helps us, when ourselves we help."—The village Teacher
    came,
A man of varied excellence, and yet unknown to fame.
Years of deep study mark'd his brow with intellect and grace ;
Though keen his look, a beaming glow of kindness lit his face.
Pleas'd with the progress of the youth, he led him gently forth,
By easy lessons, grave and gay, to books of ancient worth ;
Selecting, with judicious care, the useful from the crude ;
And with discrimination rare, the sprightly from the rude.
Rough was the gem, but time and care a polish soon bestowed ;
Here veins of beauty stole to view, there lines of lustre glowed :
Increasing pains the teacher's hopes and pupil's heart possest,
For 'mong the lads the village owned, it freely was confest
That " Eugey Train had scholarship, and manners far the best !"

    *   *   *

The last kiss of the blushing Day to Twilight had been given ;
And the pale star of Even stole from forth its house in heaven.
The moon awoke upon the lake, like holy thoughts of peace,
In vestal bosoms when the strains of vesper-anthems cease.
Clouds passed along the silent sky ; now fairy barges float
With white, silk sails and silver hulls, and then a beauteous boat
Would seem to skim the azure plain, like a swan with downy
    throat.
Still and serene the moonlight scene—the birds in silence rest ;
A silvery ray hath stolen away and found a linnet's nest,
Where leafy shades are lying soft, like dreams, upon its breast.
The trees are still, the flowers asleep—the butterflies repose,
With velvet cheeks and sunny wings soft cradled in the rose ;
While star-beams on the rounded leaves watch how the fair
    things doze.
Evangeline, the beautiful, her orisons hath said ;
Her warm, smooth cheek of sixteen suns is on her pillow laid ;
The chaste dream-spirit waves her wings above the sleeper's head.

She wanders in an Eden fair, where blight hath never been :
She looks on flowers that never fade, on rose-bowers ever green,
Where not a shadow lingers near the sunlight of that scene.
Birds sing sweet strains continually on amaranthine trees—
A perfume, like a seraph's prayer, exhales from every breeze ;
And not a single zephyr makes a ripple on those secs.'
A countless throng of happy hearts, young, innocent, and fair,
Sport o'er the meads with airy steps, wild roses in their hair ;
A tear their eyes hath never dimm'd, and sighs are strangers
     there.
Toil, Want and Care, and man's despair, are in this land unknown ;
There is no strife to vex his life, no grief to cause his moan ;
Love rules the myriads in these realms by happiness alone.
Peace hath a dwelling everywhere—in Castle, Hall, and Cot,
There Faction, Feud, and Jealousy, and Envy enter not ;
Each household hath its angel blest—this land is Love's bright
     spot !
Alas ! the scene grows faint and fades, like human dreams, away !
And sultry vapours gather round the dreamer in dismay !
A flickering flash lights up the room, as when the lightnings play !
Starting from sleep, Evangeline beholds red flames arise ;
Her chamber is one cloud of smoke, to shriek for help she tries ;
She faints and falls ; the windows crash as on the floor she lies.
A dingy form with face begrimed, and clothing scorch'd and rent—
A moment o'er the prostrate maid in terror's stupor bent ;
Then snatched her to his blackened breast, and through the
     windows went.
"She's saved ! thank God ! at last she's safe !" the village
     crowds exclaim.
" We never thowt a mortal man cud ever stan' the flame !
Oh, Eu', thoo's saved thaw bonny lass—but, marrows, where's
     her dame ?"
"Lost in the flames!" the maiden shrieked—"Eugene, oh,
     hasten ! fly !
How could you think of me, and leave my mother there to die ?
Help ! help ! my mother perishes ! Great Heaven ! I hear her
     cry ?"
Too late, alas ! was human help, the blazing rafters fell ;
Beneath a mother's form was found, but Life had sigh'd " Fare-
     well !"
And sounds of sobbing woe were heard, as knolled the funeral Bell !

PART SECOND.

Far from the village hath the Orphan gone,
To wealthy friends across the heaving main,
And poor Eugene toils sadly and alone,
His daily bread and learning's store to gain,
By nights of study, and by labour's pain ;
Still in his heart Hope rises with a prayer,
That he, one day, high honours may attain,
When by the side of her, the absent fair,
His days of toil may cease to kindle Love's despair.

She was the star to which his soul aspired,
Though far removed by birth from his estate,
Her watch-word, " Progress," was the charm that fired
His breast to battle, to be nobly great,
In spite of scorn, of poverty, and fate;
Yea, he would win her, like the knights of old,
And lead her, blushing, to his castle's gate ;
For though he lacked the needful spurs of gold,
His lance was Self-reliance, and his heart was bold.

His kind, old Teacher was a genius strange,
Of mind inventive, execution rare ;
With him "Mechanics" had the widest range,
Clocks he could make, Automata repair ;
Knew all the properties of Steam and Air ;
" Motions perpetual" he produced with pride ;
His changing pictures made the rustics stare ;
Organs with paper pipes he had supplied,
And flying vessels built to stem both wind and tide.

Latin and Greek, most scholarly, he knew,
Spoke French, like his own English, fluently ;
Music, and drawing, and Italian too,
He taught the gentles, oft for little fee,
Which much increased the teacher's poverty.
Alas ! and he made rhymes, and once, a book,
And " cast it on the waters " of the sea,
And though few golden fish e'er came to hook,
The printer's bill he paid, which some bards overlook.

Had he but known as much of human craft
And soul-deceit, as ancient lore and art,
He had been proof against the hostile shaft
With which the world delights to wound the heart,
And cause the tear of agony to start.
Poor, simple Man ! his unsuspecting mind
Dreamed not of guile, when Cunning showed his chart,
Confiding in lip-friendship, which seemed kind, ·
He thought not on the foes that dogged his steps behind.

But suffering and neglect had made him wise,
Wisdom that only came when he grew old ;
As silver clouds are seen, when daylight dies,
To robe the moon with vesture pale and cold.
His feet were standing 'mid the churchyard mould,
And he forgave the world its mock salute,
Which, Judas-like, his earthly freedom sold ;—
Complaint sat on his tongue in silence mute,
While lance-like feelings pierced his breast with stabs acute.

Eugene drew deep experience from the sage,
Whose golden lessons he in secret stored,
As diamonds gathered from the mine of age ;
In after years he used the precious hoard ;—
And though his tutor's fate he oft deplored,
Whose wit, invention, genius, manners, grace,
Had lent a lustre to the proudest lord,
He shunn'd all vagrant systems that displace
The laurels of Renown, and Fortune's wreaths deface.

The Mine was now forsaken, and the "Lamp"
Which oft has warned him in the hour of toil
Of that Fiend's presence in the shaft, Fire Damp !
Served now to hold th' illuminating oil,
While he essay'd a watch's spring to coil
Within the wheel-like box ; sore task to him,
Whose tools oft threatened patient skill to foil .
But though his eyes wax'd tired, and lamp-rays dim,
The works he saw complete, beheld the balance swim.

The village clocks by him are now made clean ;
The broken tube of weather-glass he mends ;—
The viewer wonders how the youth, Eugene,
Without pit-work among his people *fends !*
The lad seems clever ; but he hath no friends ;
Still industry and patience merit praise ;
Of learning, too, he hath some odds and ends ; —
One thing is certain ; he avoids the ways
Of those who drink their cash upon the fortnight-pays !

By constant, persevering, sleepless thought,
Eugene a man of local note became ;
Nor did he keep the knowledge he had caught
From bright Advancement's still increasing flame,
But gave to all who cared his help to claim,
Gratuitous, the boon Truth loves to yield :—
To bless his brethren was his noblest aim,
With all the fruits of wide Progression's field,
The rich man's best defence ; the poor man's safest shield.

Around him gathered men of speech uncouth ;
Unlettered miners, ignorantly strong—
Who ne'er had read a page from early youth,
And knew but little what was right or wrong :
Whose learning was comprised in some loose song,
Repeated oft, tiil memory, freely schooled,
Clung to its ribaldry, alas, too long !
This by Eugene was wisely overruled,
And useful precepts woke the jostling throng,
To know that sinful words to ignorance belong.

His pupils' thoughts were gradually led
From foolish notions to a love of sense,
Having Religion for its solid bed,
On which he built a structure of defence
Against the lawless bolts of impudence.
Examples of the good and great—the wise and bold—
Of ancient days, when learning scorned pretence,
This self-made teacher to his hearers told,
In short and simple phrase, which every heart controlled.

The young, who seldom listen long or well,
When first the voice of wisdom greets their ears,
Forgot to laugh at words they could not spell,
And ceased at last their winks and whispered jeers ;
For they beheld their mates of elder years
Look solemn, when Eugene, with earnest prayer,
Besought them, while his eyes were wet with tears,
To make improvement now their chiefest care,
And with their fellow-men the fruits of Learning share.

" Hard is your work, and nature needeth rest—
The body's slackened nerves anew to brace,
And fit you for the coming labour-test,
Yet Sloth should never dare to show his face,
Or claim within your minds a dwelling-place.
One hour of study, day by day, shall bring
The slowest runner in Progression's race,
In sight and sound of Wisdom's living spring,
Which patient Toil may quaff in comp'ny of a King !

" Oh, men !" he cried, " be sober and sincere !
Think on the dangers of the treach'rous mine !
Your wives, your household, and yourselves revere ;
And to the path of temperance incline.
A sober man in every grade may shine ;
While he who riots on destruction's brink,
And views the thunder-cloud around him twine
In sulph'rous folds, and still persists to drink,
Forges the bolts of wrath and severs mercy's link.

" And will ye dare th' Almighty Power to scorn,
And rise rebellious to His lifted hand ?
He who can smite ye to the earth like corn,
And leave ye scathed and scattered on the land,—
Blighted and blackened at His dread command !
Be sober, vigilant, by day, by night,
For, know ye not, ye may be doomed to stand,
Ere morning's dawn, before His awful sight ?
Then, oh, poor, sinful souls, how abject were your plight !

"List to my words. I am but of your class,
A poor, rude student in the school of Thought.
Let not my simple teachings idly pass,
As shadows vain that come and go to nought ;
Be faithful to your God, as all men ought,
Who, having souls immortal to be saved ;—
Souls ransomed—by a suffering Saviour bought—
Should look to Him, whose help was never craved
In vain from humble hearts, by tears of sorrow laved."

Well pleased, Eugene beheld Truth's tree begin
To tinge its branches with a verdant hue ;
A budding leaf was seen to break the skin,
Then other green companions stole to view,
And soon a little cluster struggled through
The rind, that erst appeared so hard and dry ;
Hope gathered then her arch of golden dew,
And Faith beheld this tree, now tow'ring high,
.With roots firm fixed in love, and blossoms 'mid the sky.
  *   *   *   *   *

Far into the night—the dark-robed night, Eugene was seated
 lone,
The clock's dull beat he heeded not, nor the lamp that flick'ring
 shone ;
Above him shadows, strangely danced, on the ceiling of his room,
Like shapeless ghosts in vapoury folds, that flit around the tomb.
Upon a book he sat and gazed, like one that dreamed a dream,
'Mid wheels and cylinders absorbed, and motive powers of Steam.
Did these wheels move ? these cranks revolve ? these pistons
 .fall and rise ?
There seem a fire and boiler there ;—behold ! what meets his
 eyes !
A huge, dark monster at his feet rose slowly in its might,
One round, red eye glowed 'neath its brow, its breath came thick
 and white.
.Panting along a path it moved, two shining lines between,
And as it turned its brazen neck, he marked one eye was green.
Away it sped through opening chasms of sable-throated rocks,
And as it passed the long green lanes white lambs rushed forth
 in flocks ;

Over the hedges leaping swift, and scudding o'er the plain,
Followed by others rapidly, like cloud-shades o'er the main.
Or, sometimes, you might fancy, when this monster hurried by,
That hundreds of white sheets were laid on the hedges low to
    dry.
Panting along, the sound grew faint, and as the form shot forth,
The round, red eye looked like a star, slow sinking to the earth.
Over the river—round the hill—the restless mammoth turn'd,
Whiter and brighter 'neath its brow its eye, like a meteor,
    burned.
Panting along—panting along—dark, huge, it loomed in sight,
Whirling its paws—snorting its foam, and thundering through
    the night.
Like a demon ship with flaming prow, and sails of foam and fire,
On, on, it rushed, while shrieked grim fiends their songs of
    mirthful ire.
Eugene awoke ! still shrieks and screams, and shouts of wildest
    woe,
Rose shrill and loud, while a gathering crowd, passed hurrying
    to and fro.
The pit hath blasted ! Oh, Eugene, what horror and despair !
What blackened heaps of miners dead ! what widows--orphans—
    there !
Had'st thou a foresight of their doom ?   Did angels write their
    fate,
And show thee all the names of those now lost and desolate ?
What pen can write—what artist paint the scene before us now ?
There matrons, frantic in their grief, before dead offspring bow ;
Warm lips pressed close in agony to lips that move no more ;
Words of endearment breathed to death—hearts bleeding at the
    core.
Children around dead parents clinging—screaming in dismay ;
Young widows, with white clasping arms, around their husbands'
    clay ;
Age, with long mournful cries of grief, and tears of abject woe,
Waiting above a household lost, death-blighted, scathed, and low !
But who is she that, 'mid the wreck of desolation, stands,
Like a fair angel minist'ring relief with gentle hands ;
Soothing the wretched in their woes, and uttering meek com-
    mands ?

The mild, blue eye, the sunny hair, the beauteous brow benign,
The sweet-toned language, soft and low, consoling, and divine,
All, all bespeak a seraph fair—the Maid Evangeline !

The pall of death was in each room—a coffin on each bed ;
Where mourning, woe, and wailing came—where floods of tears
    were shed ;—
That village was a catacomb ; each cot contained its dead.
Down to the churchyard's open gates, a mournful mile of woe—
A hundred coffins, placed in pairs, were drawn by horses slow ;
While the rain fell in big, warm showers ;—God's clouds were
    weeping so.
They for the dead wept not, but for the living desolate !
Who, 'mid the ruin of their hearths, must sorrow, want and wait
Till the old bell for them shall knoll, and ope the churchyard gate !
What have these poor in life to love ? the hand of help lies cold !
Deaf is the ear in which their tales of misery were told :
Destroyed are now their future's hopes—deep buried in the
    mould.
" Hath heaven its rainbows banished then ? is there no balm in
    prayer ?
Is God not yet the merciful ? shall demons rule the air ?
Kneel, oh, ye rent in spirit, kneel ! 'tis sinful to despair !"
" Oh, thou fair creature that hast come our sufferings to relieve ;
To pour the balsam of sweet hope to all that wail and grieve ;—
Evangeline, thou art our help ! we bow and we believe !"
" Dark as the gloom of death may be, let Faith these clouds adorn ;
The golden light of Love still beams, and Hope comes with the
    morn ;
The bosom of the earth is ploughed to make way for the corn !"

Hushed, as the dreams of sweet content, calm sleep these miners
    dead ;
The stars are shining on their graves, the moon looks on each bed ;
While memory waves her censer, where their blighted bones are
    laid.

Midway, and in a narrow lane where sunbeams rarely strayed,
An old house stood—unglazed in front—of rough stones rudely
    made ;
On a low bed in that dark house a dying man was laid.
Eugene was summoned to attend—and he the call obeyed.

"My time hath come!" the sage began, this world to bid adieu;
But ere the sand-grains in yon glass forever quit my view;
One word, Eugene, of love and truth I fain would breathe to you.
Work, watch and wait! the day shall come! be constant in thy
    toil;
Slack not the labour of thy mind; spare not the midnight oil!
Dig diligently; persevere! plough well Progression's soil!
Renown thy industry shall bless—let science be thy theme"—
The old man here exhausted paused—Eugene spoke of his dream;
On high the Teacher raised his hands, and cried "Eureka! *Steam!*
Give me those papers from that book!" to read in vain he tries;—
The film of death hath cast its gloom upon the old man's eyes;
Eugene the mystic scroll receives—the Village Teacher dies!
No tablet marks his place of rest; his genius hath no name;
He passed, as doth th' electric cloud that yields the lightning's
    flame.
Eugene the hidden fire possessed of future wealth and fame!
Years dig the graves wherein they sleep; as waves scoop out the
    sand
To fill the hollows with themselves; as sea birds seek the land,
And in the net o' the fowler, Time, die prisoners trepanned!
Years clasping years, the chains of life insensibly become;
Feeble at first; at last, how strong! the cradle and the tomb!
Brightest and best the middle links, the rings, Love, Peace, and
    Home!
Years worked Time's marvels in our tale; the collier-boy, Eugene,
With high-born nobles of the land, in free discourse was seen;
At table with great dukes he sat, in presence of his Queen!
One evening left him poor, unknown;—at morning he awoke?
The chains that held his genius down, he, by one mighty stroke
Of that huge hammer, Intellect, in a thousand fragments broke!
The dead man's scroll, like Merlin's wand, wrought transforma-
    tions strange!
The bosom of the wounded earth, seemed stricken by the change;
Lo! mazes of long iron veins through hills and valley's range!
Corn fields are ploughed by countless spades; an iron produce
    shines;
There's iron near the avalanche—and mingling with the vines;
Furrows of iron, everywhere, spread forth unnumbered lines.
The neighing steads at will may roam; the mail coach stands
    alone;

The driver cracks his thong no more; the guard's trump is
 unblown ;
The posting houses on the roads stand silent and unknown.
The roads seem books of ancient days—the histories of old ;
The finger-posts are lying ghosts, false mysteries they unfold ;
Oh, where are all the countless wheels that o'er these highways
 rolled !
Steam answers thus—" My iron steeds, on iron paths go forth !
Another race of chariots swift and travellers have birth ;
Railways are now the wandering veins and arteries of Earth !
The vision of our own Eugene Progression's brow hath crowned ;
With laurels of undying fame—the world is changed around ;
My Locomotive bears his name to earth's remotest bound !"
  * * * *

" Evangeline ! Evangeline ! my bride ! my sweetest—best !
The spirit that 'mid want and toil, fell light-like on my breast ;
In doubt thou wast my beam of hope—in fame thou art my rest.
Oh, beautiful, my own sweet wife ! Evangeline, for thee
My poor heart throbs in bounding joy, to know thou'rt all to me ;
Thou wast my angel of success—my love thou'lt ever be ?
Renown ! O Glory, Excellence ! how dim your noon-days shine
To thy bright face, love's sun, compared ! my own Evangeline !
Thou art the morn and noon of peace, O Excellence benign !"
" Eugene ! Eugene ! how I have loved, my tongue ne'er dared to
 say ;
But all the clouds to light have changed, and thou art Love's own
 day ;—
Pity that life an end shall make, and love-beams fade away !
Day after day—like wave on wave—we steal to that cold shore,
Where Age sits waiting on the rocks with dark clouds mantled
 o'er,—
To bind the sea-weeds round our brows, to cling there evermore !
Dost see yon rainbow ? how its hues, the golden, red, and green,
Have mingled into one bright arch—that arch is Love's, Eugene.
When that bow breaks—those hues will die, and be as ne'er they'd
 been !
They are but tears from balmy flowers—that bear their tints on
 high ;
Sorrows of infants—angel-painted, beaming in the sky ;
Oh, for the lasting arch of Peace that cannot fade or die !"
" Evangeline Evangeline ! of death we will not speak ;

Beauty hath no decadence yet in thy warm and glowing cheek !
Why dost thou, love, in rainbow hope the fear of sorrow seek ?
Let joy sit on thy bosom fair, and light beam from thy look ;
As suns dance on the fountains clear, and sparkle in the brook :
Why should a stain of sorrow blot the whiteness of Love's book ?
Come, my sweet wife, and with me stray : list how the nightingale,
Tells to the lonely Vesper star Love's oft-repeated tale :—
Come, we will wander, as of yore, through Tyne's fair flowery vale.
* * * * *

Two statues, in a Railway Square, of marble white are seen ;
A Locomotive is the base—one figure is Eugene ;
An angel bears a laurel crown above his brow serene.

POEMS AND SONGS ON ROBERT BURNS.

THE FOLLOWING WAS WRITTEN FOR THE CENTENARY OF THE
POET, JAN. 25TH, 1859, AND SENT TO THE CRYSTAL PALACE
FOR THE COMPETITIVE PRIZE:—

THERE are gatherings of all nations—there's a crowding on the
   earth ;
And mingling throngs of rich and poor, in festal joy go forth,
To hail the First Centennial of the Ayrshire Poet's Birth !
This Palace, like Jerusalem, rears high its Crystal Shrine ;
Here multitudes of pilgrims meet for one, vast, grand design,—
To honour Independence—Worth—and Intellect divine !
The name of Burns is breathed in balm by every wandering
   wind :—
'Tis uttered by unnumbered tongues—'tis graven on each mind ;—
The name of Burns ! a pearl of song in the hearts of man
   enshrined !
By the mighty Mississippi—by Niag'ra's thundering steep ;
On the vast, scorched plains of Hindostan,—by Ganges' sacred
   deep,
The Hundredth Birthday of their Burns the sons of Scotland
   keep !
Honour to Burns and to his name ! for him the Exile yearns,
And clinging to dear memories, like Love to Beauty turns,
Singeth aloud, i' the pause of grief, the strains of Robert Burns.
The Emigrant upon the deep forgets the dark dismay
Of roaring billows—distant home—wife, children, far away,
For he remembers Coila's Bard was born on this glad day.
The mountains of his native land are tuneful with his lyre ;
The woods repeat his melodies—the streams reflect their fire ;
His songs are prophet-canticles, that every soul inspire !
Great Preacher of stern homilies ; his lines live, breathe, and burn;
'Gainst Tyranny he dealeth death—'gainst Cant he hurleth scorn,
But with the poor oppress'd he grieves that " *Man was made to*
   mourn !"
Burns is the moon when Love's bright star the lay of Beauty
   sings ;

A fountain welling from the source of Pity's gentle springs ;
An eagle soaring near the sun with lightning 'neath his wings !
The simple daisy's modest flower, blooms fragrant in his breast ;
The mouse, " *Wee, tim'rous beastie*," sleeps as in a cushat's nest ;
While Maillie and the wounded Hare are to his bosom press'd.
Heaven's Virtues, like his mountain-lakes, around his genius
    flowed ;
Candour and Truth and Nobleness found there a warm abode ;
Humanity throbb'd in each vein—each pulse with passion glowed.
Philanthropy, with sleepless eyes, his suff'ring brethren viewed ;
His gen'rous mind, love-rectified, sprung forth refin'd—renewed,
And the deep fountains of his heart gush'd high in gratitude.
By Lugar's stream he mused and mourn'd, in sadness and dismay ;
Big drops of grief, like thunder's rain, were seen to shine and
    stray
From his large, lamping eyes, like stars that weep their light
    away.
Glencairn, his noblest friend, lay dead !—Glencairn, his hope, his
    pride—
The flaming pillar to his path, to bless him, guard, and guide ;—
Oh, Robert Burns, thy soul was rent when noble Glencairn died !
But the lark that lay with wounded wing, in agonizing pain,
Sings now before the gates of morn, his sweet and gladsome
    strain ;—
A sun-bow bright of merriment—an arch of golden rain !
Bask in his rays of jocund song, for, hark ! his social mirth
Rings, like loud bells, round happy hearts, and gladdens all the
    earth.
See ! Tam O' Shanter on his mare o'er Doon rides skelpin forth !
The mirth of Burns was Rapture's flood, and as he dashed along
Impetuous in his frolic glee, with feelings wild and strong,
He heeded not the cataracts that foamed beside his song.
Like a thron'd Monarch robed in joy, and laurell'd with his lays,
Burns reigns the King of Scottish strains ;—the world resounds
    his praise !
Burns is the ruler of all hearts—immortal through all days !
And now his Country's glory wakes, and calls him from her
    cloud !
The sword of eloquence he draws, to pierce the foeman proud ;
While " *Scots wha hae wi' Wallace bled ?*" the patriot shouteth
    loud !

Life's glorious elements of Air, of Water, Fire, and Earth,
In Burns have mystic photographs—in Burns have form and
   birth ;
Their majesty—magnificence—their music—madness—mirth !
Of *Air*—love's melting melodies, soul-breath'd in the gloamin'
   hour ;
Of *Water*—Ocean's songs of storm—of *Flame*—the volcanoes'
   power ;
Of *Earth*—the hymns of mount and glen, and strains from field
   and bower !
The moods of Genius—storm and calm, the revel and sad rest ;
Indignant scorn—repentant grief—devotion—thoughts unblest—
Recrimination—Love, Hope, Fear—alternate moved his breast !
Honour for ever be to Burns, who spurn'd all base control !
Sublime in God-like attributes—in the splendours of his Soul ;
Hail, intellectual racer bold, that gained th' immortal goal !
Arm'd with an independent mind, this Bard of Progress strong,
Battled for *"honest Poverty,"*—the Right against the Wrong ;
Heart-manliness his panoply—his conquering weapon, Song !
Oh, what to him Pride's tinsel show- the garter, star, and crown,
Divested of a heart and hand to raise mankind when down ?
The pageant of a fleeting name—the baubles of renown !
Man, in this glorious Minstrel's mind, was excellence supreme ;
The greatest, highest, *"noblest work,"* of Heaven's almighty
   scheme !
Let man prove honest—what were Rank ? an unsubstantial
   dream !
The ploughman-poet soared above vain, painted pomps of earth ;
Soul was Creation's priceless gem—man's Kohinoor, and worth ;
Oh, clay-made Dagons he despised—Burns claimed an angel's
   birth !
And yet no seraph pure was he—as erring man he fell ;
But shall your tongues his failings breathe—his human weakness
   tell ?
Bury his errors in the tomb—there let them ever dwell !
This day the Spirits of his loves commingle in this throng ;
Their wings unseen are hovering near, fair ministers of song !
Whisper 'gainst him no word of blame—e'en angels have done
   wrong !
The spirit of his *"bonnie Jean"*—the lass he lo'ed the best,
Such joy ne'er felt as on this day, in heaven, on earth she's blest!

How lovingly her wings she spreads, and leans on Robin's breast!
His Highland Mary, "*lingering star*," brings to this palace fair
The hallowed offerings of her love—the incense of pure prayer;
And to her harp celestial sings her minstrel's holiest air.
"*Oh, let us worship God!*" she breathes; then meek devotion
    kneels;
Affection lights her virgin lamp, as the Bible she reveals;
Then the solemn hymn for contrite hearts, 'mid fragrance sky-
    ward steals!
Now scatter your garlands gratefully o'er Scotia's poet's tomb;
Deck his cold marble monument in amaranthine bloom;
For the name and songs of Robert Burns defy change, time, and
    doom.

THE PEASANT BARD OF AYR.

A PLOUGHMAN by a mountain side,
Of stature noble, I espied,
Following his team with steps of pride,
      Like some bold bark at sea,
Casting the wavy furrows wide,
      In might and majesty.

Thick clouds roll'd slowly o'er his head,
Through which the sun dim lustre shed,
Like memories of wise sages dead—
      The ghosts of misty Fame,
Or like a troop of giants spread
      Around a beacon-flame.

And still the ploughman drove his team,
Entranc'd in some absorbing dream,
His thoughts, like shadows on a stream,
      Still passing—still to come—
Thronging, like angels, to the beam
      That marks their heavenly home.

The panting horses halted now,—
The ploughman rested on his plough,
Strange light o'erspread his spacious brow,
    And fired his lamping eyes ;—
High heaved his heart—outstretch'd his
    hand—
As if he grasped the earth's wide land,
And held all nature at command—
    Gaz'd on the arching skies.

Anon, the gloom the heavens had worn,
Grew brighter, as by radiance torn,
Then blushing came the maiden morn,
    With soft effulgence forth.
Day's golden garments clothed the plough,
A halo crowned the peasant's brow,
The soul of song had risen now
    To glorify the earth !

Bright tears of joy the ploughman shed,
By rapture's leaping fountains fed,
Celestial forms were round him spread,—
    Transfix'd he stood with awe :—
Bowed was his head to that Dread Power,
Who rules his first and latest hour ;
When at his feet a mountain-flower,
    Upturn'd and crush'd he saw !

He lifted up the " bonnie gem,
" Wi' broken leaves an' wounded stem ;"
No pearl from Beauty's diadem,
    Was aught to this compar'd !
For this poor daisy of the ground
Heart-eloquence he pour'd profound ;
Heart-pity gave the daisy's wound,
    And sympathy's regard !

And now the peasant's harp was strung.—
Of love, in varied strains, he sung ;
To love's warm heart he raptur'd hung,
    Like some endearing child,
Till woods and dales, and mountains rung
    With his love-measures wild.

He walked, like thunder, in his scorn,
Low laid the proud, like heads of corn ;
By him the robes of Cant were torn,
    And scattered with disdain ;
And yet he wept—" man made to mourn,"
    That wears the tyrant's chain.

The rock that braves the raging sea
Was not more firm in worth than he ;
His Spirit, like the ocean free,
    Unbounded and sublime !
A patriot King of Liberty,
    That dared the war of Time.

His brethren were the Sons of Toil ;
For them he pour'd Love's wine and oil ;
Oh, oft his songs have sooth'd the moil
    Of care-press'd, honest men,
Till Independence from the soil
    Rose, proud, erect, again !

Unmov'd he bore the zealot's ban,
Pursuing still his glorious plan,
To bind the heart of man to man,
    In Friendship's holy cause ;
To crush Injustice, and to scan
    With love, God's throne and laws,

And thus the Peasant Minstrel bold
The treasures of his mind unroll'd,
While he, alas ! lack'd needful gold—
    The Poet's fated doom !
For while he charm'd the young and old,
    The world prepar'd his tomb.

Neglect stood heedless of his moans ;—
He wanted *bread*—they gave him *stones*,
And monuments to hide his bones,
    Cold records of their shame !
They now would gladly yield him thrones
    To grace his deeds and name !

Unnumber'd altars now arise ;
To him Love offers sacrifice,
For him ascend Affection's sighs,
    From castle, cot, and hall !
His strains are echoed to the skies,
    The Song-king over all !

A hundred years have gone their round ;—
His fame with deathless glory's crowned ;
In every land his name is found ;
    To him the world now turns :
Behold him ! " Scotia's Bard," renown'd,
    The matchless ROBERT BURNS !

" A NICHT WI' BURNS."

" Orient Pearls at random strung."

THOUGH gloomy winter's gath'ring drear,
    We hail the season's snaw,
That brings the mem'ry of ane dear,
    The king amang us a' !
For Robie is our guest to-night ;
    His spirit here remains ;
Upon a beam of festive light,
    He smiles to hear our strains.

CHORUS.

Then we'll sing his sangs for auld lang syne,
    And drain the stoup by turns ;
For, while there's water in the Tyne,
    We'll hae " A Nicht wi' Burns !"

Oh, Willie brewed a peck o' maut,
    And merry boys are we ;
For cog or bicker has nae faut,
    Weel filled wi' barley bree !

Oh, barley rigs are bonnie things,
  When Lammas nichts are clear ;
For luve's a red, red rose that springs
  In beauty a' the year.

There's Duncan Gray come here to woo ;
  Wi' grey breeks sits Tam Glen ;
And Captain Grose is roarin' foo ;
  Scotch drink is guid, ye ken.
John Anderson, my Jo, John,
  You're cantie grown I see ;
Cock up your beaver, Jo, John,
  And tak' a drap wi'. me.

I see a form—I see a face,
  Wi' kind luve in her een ;
She weel may fill the fairest place,
  She is my bonny Jean.
And by her side sit mony mair,
  The pride o' ilka toon ;
My ling'rin' star in heaven sae fair,
  Sweet Mary Morrison.

Hech ! Willie Wastle—happy man—
  Your wife is weel, I hope ;
And does her clapper-tongue still gan' ?
  Hoot, gie the jaud a rope !
But beauty in the mornin' glows ;
  Aye, Willie swears that's true,
And d—ns the Linkumdoddie rose
  That turned sae sune to rue.

Oh, Tam ! oh, Tam ! the nappy's good ;
  The ingle bleezes bricht ;
Ye care na for the Doon's mad flood
  On sic a glorious nicht !
The Deil may cast his cantrips owre
  Puir bodies in the dark ;
But we, rejoicing, scorn his power,
  Shout, "Weel dune, cutty sark !"

Our hearts are now as blythe and free,
    As simmer days are lang ;
We still like ranting dogs maun be ;
    The best o' folk get wrang.
There's auld Rob Morris, doited chiel,
    To court the fule will gan' ;
But what can lassies do, the deil!
    Wi' sic a puir, auld man!

For naebody will we be sad,
    When we hae cash to spend ;
An' if we borrow to be glad,
    Ye'll no refuse a friend!
or syne the Bard o' Scotia deigns
    To mingle in our thrang,
Our hearts spring joyfu' at his strains,
    And hail his deathless sang.

The bluid-red rose at yule may blaw,
    An' simmer freeze the sea,
An' tender lilies bloom in snaw,
    Still Burns shall cherished be!
Though cauld his form sleeps in the tomb,
    His name, with glory crowned,
Shall flourish in undying bloom,
    Beloved — revered—renowned !

CHORUS.

And we'll sing his sangs for auld lang syne ;
    And, when this feast returns,
We'll celebrate, on banks o' Tyne,
    " *A nither nicht wi' Burns.*"

C

THE VISION OF ROBERT BURNS.

THE red star of night near the pale moon was beaming,
    And silence sat brooding o'er mountain and plain ;
As the Plough-bard of Scotia lay sleeping and dreaming—
    The dreams which the future proved *not to be vain !*
He saw the dark clouds which neglect had cast o'er him,
    Glow bright in the rays of the morning of fame ;
He saw gathered nations bend lowly before him,
    And heard strains prophetic thus honour his name.

"Oh, Caledonia, on thy breast
    The hallowed lights of Heaven recline ;
For Burns, thy bard, the sweetest, best,
    Shall, 'mid thy sterling glories, shine ;
Thy sylvan streams shall bear along
    His wild notes, like the mavis sweet ;
Thy woods shall oft his strains prolong ;
    Thy hills shall oft his songs repeat.

"The magic of his honored name
    Shall gather nations round his shrine,
Where beacon-lights of Love shall flame—
    Where Friendship's greenest wreaths shall twine.
The Don, the Dee ; the land, the sea ;
    The cot, the field ; the mount and grove ;
The Scottish peer, the peasant free ;
    The prince, the queen,—the world shall love.

"In every land—in every clime—
    The Songs of Burns response shall find.
A halcyon on the surge of time,
    In peace man's stormy soul to bind.
His natal day the earth shall hail ;
    Affection shall with Genius vie,
And rival songs of praise provail ;
    For, Burns, *thy memory shall not die.*"

The dream of the Poet hath fled as a spirit ;
He wakes in a frenzy of rapt'rous delight ;—
" Let me bear the world's scorn this renown to inherit,
The glory and greatness foretold me this night !
I have seen the dark clouds which neglect had cast o'er me,
Glow bright in the rays of a summer of fame ;
· I have seen gathered thousands bend lowly before me ;
Oh ! I heard Scotia's Genius exult in my name."

THE BRAW SONS O' BURNS.

OH ! " the braw Sons o' Burns " is my toast and my sang,
And as love-links maun ever to Robie belang ;
On the heart-chords o' nature affection maun fa'—
For in kissing the bairns we kiss Robie and a' !
Like saft flow'rets that cluster round sympathy's urns,
Devoted we cherish the braw Sons o' Burns !

As the bluid to the vein, as the pulse to the heart,
Wi' the Bard o' auld Coila we're parcel and part ;
We hae grown, as engrafted, in feelings the same,
Like lamps that are fed by ane fountain o' flame ;
And the faither and bairns we embrace in their turns :
Oh ! I wish that ilk house had a braw Son o' Burns.

When the Angel o' Death Robie, heart-broken, saw,
A tear gemmed the lance that inflicted the blaw ;
And e'er Ruin completed the wreck he designed,
This tear, Mercy's jewel, by Love was enshrined.
Through a' climes floats the Seraph, and tenderly yearns,
When he hears the glad strains for the Sons of her Burns.

Oh ! Robie and Jean, when frae skies ye look down,
And see your dear laddies enwreathed wi' renown,
If the chalice o' bliss ane drap mair could contain,
Ye wad na', though angels, frae weeping refrain.
Now the ills o' your lives seem but fleetin' concerns,
When removed by our love for the braw Sons o' Burns.

On a bonny green hill Scotia planted her pride,
And her branches outspreading encircle its side ;
Let us hail their green honours, that Coila may ken,
We hae sangs for her Minstrel, and feelings like men ;
And, as lang as the earth to its circuit returns,
We will toom friendship's cog to the braw Sons o' Burns.

ROBERT BURNS ON EARTH.

" Wha wad na' flee frae heav'n to see,
    Sic rantin' dogs an' sprightly ?
Faith, Robie's spirit mauna be
    Just spoken o' sae lightly !
The snaw is gane, an' spring will come,
    When lav'rocks carol clearly ;
Cast aff wi' me the winter's gloom,
    And hail my visit yearly !

CHORUS.

'' Sing, Here's to friends now far awa',
    And health to every crony ;
Sing, A' the airts the wind can blaw,
    To Highland Mary bonny.
That ling'ring star o' less'ning ray,
    Amang the leal she's happy !
Come, sing, this is my ain birthday,
    And tak' your fouth o' nappy !

" The devil's buckies o' this earth
    Wad fain hae scrimp'd my glory ;
But wha can smother honest worth ?
    It aye maun rise in story !
Ah, lad ! ye little ken the guile
    Puir Robie fand when livin' !
Now on their cantrips he can smile—
    They haud sma' fash in heaven ;

" Hech ! Robie was an awfu' man !
    Choke-fu' o' ilk transgression ;
But Mercy did na' tak' the plan,
    And damn like Courts o' Session :

The bigot coofs wi' a' their cant,
   Gat better kail to swallow ;
And Nick o' grease can no be scant ;
   He grasped baith hide and tallow.

I'm no just gangin' mair to tell ;
   'T wad mak' ye owre wisemen ;
But ae thing unco' queer befel—
   The deil gat nae excisemen !
Cock-sure was I auld clooties claws
   Wad gie their necks a nippin' ;
They brought ' Permits ' an' scorned his paws ;
   Else, wae betide the grippin'.

Oh ! aft I hear your praises loud,
   Mang sang and clav'ring clatter ;
An' if a spirit can be proud,
   Rob may be wi' your chatter ;
There's *ane*—but he has ta'en his leave—
   That in sic nichts delighted ;
Na, dinna for a moment grieve,
   I' th' lift joy's cogs we've plighted.

" The ' Haggis ' gars your lips to smack ;
   The glasses—how they jingle !
A merry nicht you're sure to mak',
   When friendly cronies mingle.
Lang be your lives wi' joy to craw,
   And, when deeth comes to free ye,
Remember Burns, and speed awa' ;
   In heaven wi' Jean ye 'll see me.

" Then, a' the airts the wind can blaw,
   Shall ne'er bring dool to ony ;
Then ye sall meet friends lang awa,
   And Highland Mary bonny ;—
That ling'ring star o' cloudless ray
   Amang us will be happy ;
And we will sing glad sangs for aye,
   And drink the nectar's drappie."

LAYS OF THE TYNE EXILE.

THE DEPARTURE.

Soft fell the light of dying day, on Tyne's fair flowing flood,
As on the shore, with burning breast, the hapless Exile stood :
To-morrow he must leave his home, his pleasures and his pride ;
Sad were his farewell strains of wo, as thus the mourner cried.

" Childhood's home, my lovely Tyne,
　　Heavy are the thoughts that grieve me,
When I know all beauty 's thine,
　　Yet, poor pilgrim, I must leave thee !
Leave my cottage, where, delighted,
　　Innocence and Love resided ;
Where the voice of Joy invited ;
　　Where the stream of music glided.

" Tell me not of eastern skies,
　　Where the landscape glows in splendour ;
Home is where true beauty lies,
　　Softly fair, beloved and tender.
What to me are diamonds shining,.
　　Where the alien stream is flowing ?
Tyne hath flowers round mem'ry twining--
　　Pearls transcendant in their glowing.

" Home, sweet pillow for the lorn,--
　　Home where hope reclines contented,--
Like a fondling babe, we turn
　　To thy bosom, love-cemented :
Like a wearied bird, at gloaming,
　　Winged with love, we hail thy river,
Where we rest from toil and roaming,
　　Dreaming of thy fields for ever.
Childhood's home, my lovely Tyne,
　　Heavy are the thoughts that grieve me,
When I know all peace is thine,
　　Yet poor pilgrim, I must leave thee !"

IN CHILDHOOD WE WANDER.

In Childhood we wander, unconscious and gay,
As a sun-glided cloud o'er the path of the day ;
And the flowers of the earth, and bright gems of the sky,
Seem made but for blooming, oh ! never to die.
Blest stars of our childhood, no longer ye shine .
Oh ! give me past pleasures by banks of the Tyne.

In Youth, when the heart is as bounding and free
As the vessel that gallantly skims the calm sea,
When fair Hope spreads her wings of delight to the gale,
And Fear with his rocks is unknown to prevail ;
Then Love and sweet Beauty, Youth's bosom entwine,
And moonlight wakes rapture on banks of the Tyne.

When Age, bending sad, like a blighted oak, bare,
His brow full of wrinkles and hoary his hair,
The light of his eyes, quenched in clouds of decay,
Views the scenes but in mem'ry now fading away ;
On his pillow he whispers, "This solace be mine :
I know I shall sleep by the banks of the Tyne."

FAREWELL! FAIR FIELDS.

Farewell ! fair fields I loved to wander ;
  Green memoried haunts of youth farewell !
Bright streams that, like our days, meander
  To stormy seas, where troubles dwell.
    Dear, happy, careless years,
    Cradled in hopes and fears,
    Lost now in sorrow's tears,
        Farewell ! ·

Farewell! true friends of times departed,
　Like stars that gem the brow of eve,
Shine on, amid the noble-hearted,
　Dark hours, with social light, relieve.
　　Friends of my boyhood's years,
　　Known to my hopes and fears,
　　Now in dark sorrow's tears,
　　　　　　　Farewell!

Farewell! my heart is sorely riven ;
　From home, friends, love, I'm doomed to go :
Oh! let my weakness be forgiven
　In this dread hour of bitter wo.
　　Love of my happy years,
　　First of my hopes and fears,
　　Drenched is thy kiss in tears,
　　　　　　Farewell! Farewell!

MAID OF MY BOSOM.

MAID of my bosom, farewell! I must leave thee ;
　Wide is my course o'er the path of the sea :
Let not my absence a moment e'er grieve thee ;
　Faithless, though exiled, I never can be.
Dost thou remember the vows we have plighted ?
　Doubt not the truth of a fond lover's heart ;
Fondly my hope with my grief is united—
　Hope that we'll meet again, never to part.

Lo! the grey morning from slumber is breaking ;
　Fast fade the stars from the depths of the blue ;
Wood, grove, and meadow, my sorrow partaking,
　Wave their green ringlets impearled with the dew.
Fare thee well! dearest ; my bark's on the ocean ;
　One fond embrace e'er I hasten away ;
Locked in my heart is thy treasured devotion ;
　Never, till death, shall my ardour decay.

BANKS O' TYNE.

BANKS o' Tyne! sae lo'ed and bonny,
Where I spent my childhood sunny ;
  Sair 's my heart, now laith to part
Wi' hame and friends—the best o' ony.
There my lassie, like a flower,
  By a tempest-cloud o'ertaken,
Droops within her lanely bower,
  Sad, dejected, and forsaken.

Banks o' Tyne! the moon is beamin'
O'er thy landscape siller streamin' ;
  Cauld the ray will flit away,
And leave thee in thy darkness dreamin'.
Silence on thy bosom lies ;
  Not a sound thy echoes waken ;
Hush, my sorrow-laden sighs,
  Rend nae mair a heart that 's breakin'.

Banks o' Tyne! the hours are stealin' ;
Morn is now thy scenes revealin' :
  I maun part ; my waefu' heart
Winna thole the tears concealin' !
Fare thee weel! the anchor 's weighed ;
  Links o' joy ! ye now maun sever ;
Why was luve sae sweetly made,
  To break the hearts o' a' that leave her ?

THE RETURN.

FROM wand'ring in a stranger land, an Exile had returned ;
And, when he saw his own dear stream, his soul with pleasure
    burned :
The days departed and their joys came bounding to his breast,
When thus the feelings of his heart in native strains expressed.

" Flow on, majestic river,
  Thy rolling course forever ;
  Forget thee I will never,
    Whatever fate be mine.
Oft on thy banks I 've wandered,
And on thy beauties pondered :
Oh! many an hour I 've squandered
  By bonny coaly Tyne.

" O ! Tyne, in thy bright flowing,
  There 's magic joy bestowing ;
  I feel thy breezes blowing ;
    Their perfume is divine.
I 've sought thee in the morning,
When crimson clouds were burning,
And thy green hills adorning ;
  Thy hills, oh! bonny Tyne.

" When stormy seas were round me ;
  When distant nations bound me ;
  In memory still I found thee
    A ray of hope benign.
Thy valleys lie before me ;
Thy woods are waving o'er me ;
My home thou dost restore me :
  I hail thee, bonny Tyne !"

CHORUS.

" Flow on, majestic river,
  Thy rolling course forever ;
  Forget thee I will never,
    Whatever fate be mine."

MISCELLANEOUS PIECES.

FIRST LOVE.

" Love, strong as death, the Poet led
To the pale mansions of the dead."
POPE.

THE spring's sweet flowers blossom,
    And summer comes again ;
But never can my bosom
    Forget its grief and pain.
To think that she I cherished
    Is lying cold and low ;
My hope's bright vision perished
    By fate's relentless blow.
I loved her from my childhood,
    And my love still glows the same ;
Though her grave is in the wildwood,
    My heart still bears her name.

Her face was fair as morning ;
    Her eyes like gems of night ;
Her lips seemed rubies burning ;
    Her teeth were lines of light :
Her lovely breast was seen to rise,
    Like snow upon the wave ;
Unheaving, motionless it lies,
    Cold, pillowed in the grave.
I loved her from my childhood,
    And my love still glows the same ;
Though her grave is in the wildwood,
    My heart yet bears her name.

When life's dull ev'ning closes
  Upon my mortal day,
And when life's pulse reposes
  In chill and lonely clay,
A blessed place remains for me,
  Where wo is ne'er descried ;
Where dwells a spirit fair and free,
  My spotless angel-bride.
I loved her from my childhood,
  And my love still glows the same ;
Though her grave is in the wildwood,
  My heart still bears her name.

WHEN WE WERE AT THE SCHULE.

I JUST maun chant a we bit sang,   ·
  An' play for ance the fule ;
An' tell the evils o' the days
  When we were at the schule.
Ah ! weel ye mind the wooden leg,
  An' think ye hear it stump : ·
Ye 'll no forget the "grey-mare, Meg ; "
  The name just gars me jump !

CHORUS.

When we were at the schule, my lads,
  We aft langed to be men :
We gat our wishes ; now we lang
  To be at schule again.

The Dom'nie lo'ed the "Quaker's wife"—
  The *sang*, I mean—fu' weel ;
He whistled as we sang for life ;·
  He drummed to mak' us squeel.
The dreadfu' " clog" fast to the ring,
  An' " Ginglesby," the sprite,
That in the garret waved his wing,   ·
  Filled a' our hearts wi' fright.

Ah! man, to kneel twa hours or sae
Upon a ruler round,
Was sic a pleasure in that day,
The like 's now seldom found.
An' then upon a desk to kick,
Gripped fast by leg an' arm,
Weel hammered wi' a clubby stick ;
It gared ye feel a' warm !

The maister was a canty chiel,
At ba' in schule he 'd play ;
He did na' heed the lads a deal,
An' what could callants say ?
He 'd fry us pancakes at a pinch,
An' clout our heads when dull ;
An' nip our lugs an' gar us flinch :
They were grand times at schule.

Methinks I see the bonny spot
Where pears an' apples grew ;
We did na' like to see them rot,
Sae kindly plucked a few.
Wow, lads, the maister kens it a' ;
Stuff bags down ilka back ;
An', if the cane should chance to fa',
Ye 'll never tent the crack.

Ye 'll no forget the " Washing-tubs " ;
The burn's " Green-water Pool " ?
Ye 'll maybe mind o' Tommy's rubs,
When ye cam' late to schule.
Your mem'ry o' the battle speaks,
When faes were doomed to fa' ;
Though Roman chiels, ye fought like Greeks,
But best ahint the wa' !

The days are gane ! but still we cling
To recollections dear ;
We haud the bee without the sting—
The thought without the fear.

Oh ! merry were the days o' yule,
  When our gude pastor came
Wi' grand prize-buiks an' cakes to schule,
  An' sent us dancin' hame.

Where is that honoured pastor *now ?*
  His fate was like the lave :
Time laid his cauld hand on his pow ;
  We bore him to his grave.
An', when his image meets our ken,
  The faithfu' tear is given ;
But—let us never weep again—
  He 'll no come back frae Heaven.

———

SONG OF THE CONVENT BELL.

OH ! happy am I, 'neath the clear, blue sky,
  As I swing to the perfumed air ;
The sound of my voice makes the soul rejoice
  When I summon pure hearts to prayer.
At *Prime, Tierce,* and *None,* they gladly own
  The charm of my ringing swell ;
And, with eyes bent low, to mass they go,
  At the sound of the Convent Bell.

What a meek face, see, and a bended knee ;
  'T is a Postulant, mildly fair :
And her costly dress and her flowing tress,
  Betoken an heiress there !
But the vestal vow is recorded now,
  And she biddeth the world " Farewell !"
She resigns, with delight, her long locks, bright,
  At the sound of the Convent Bell.

"Jubilate" they sing, "Jubilate" I ring ;
  And the chorus of praise is loud :
And angels attend while the tale I send
  To the prostrate, suppliant crowd.

Oh ! my iron-breast is a holy nest,
   Where devotion loves to dwell :
Sinner and saint alike have confessed
   There was hope in the Convent Bell.

Misguided Zeal fain had spoiled my peal,
   When it hurled my grey turrets low ;
My song and sound were but seldom found,
   And my tongue was mute in wo ;—
But the morning broke, and my voice awoke
   To the strains I knew so well ;
And Love shone forth to the sons of earth,
   And again peals the Convent Bell.

THE OLD ABBEY TOWER.

OH ! the Old Abbey Tower that for ages hath stood,
The stranger's sole refuge, the home of the good ;
Where the poor found relief, where the weary reposed,
Where the gates of Benevolence never were closed.
Lone, lone thou art now ; all thy glories are gone ;
Still our hearts, like the ivy-green, cling to each stone :
Though the fall of thy grandeur we live to deplore,
Still we love thee, Old Tower, in thy loneliness more.
      We love thee, Old Tower !

When, Old Abbey Tower, the " Angelus bell,"
Like a lark, woke devotion in dingle and dell ;
When the " *Lucis Creator* " of vespers was borne
On the wing of the zephyr ; what bosom could mourn ?
Hushed, hushed are the voices of cantor and choir ;
The grand pealing organ no more can inspire !
Now the bleak winds of winter thy solitude wake ;
Will none sing a *requiem* but *them* for thy sake ?
      Alas ! Abbey Tower !

Adieu, Abbey Tower ! thou a ruin must fall ;
Yet eloquence breathes from each chink in thy wall :
Though the owl and the bat to thy niches have fled,
Thou art great in decay, and, though dying, not dead.
Peace, peace from thy altar's crushed fragments bestow ;
Let the Cross of Salvation bid Charity glow ;
Let Hope breathe her halos through each painted pane,
For thy now crumbling walls may, ere long, rise again.
    Thou shalt rise, Abbey Tower ?

THE FALL OF THE AVALANCHE.

The Sun is exulting on throne of light ;
 Geneva is crowned with gold ;
And the peak of Mont Blanc, in stainless white,
 Sits calm as a giant old :
Abroad is the Rhine with her glitt'ring gems,
 And the Rhone with her winding flow ;
And the Avalanche, bathed in his diadems,
 Looks proud on the vales below.

Showers of music fall sweetly on air,
 And the bells, like glad hearts, ring out ;
Lucerne seemeth void of bewild'ring care,
 For, hark to the laugh and the shout !
The Youth, with his train, the Bride, with her swain,
 Come thronging the beautiful way ;
Pass on, with a kiss, to the church and to bliss ;
 Joy ! joy is their portion to-day.

Down, with a thundering sweep, descends
 A thousand years of snow !
" The Avalanche falls ! the Avalanche falls !"
 Hark ! hark to the shrieks of woe.
The Avalanche falls, like a sea of foam,
 Hurled vast from the vaulted skies ;
And, buried beneath her long-loved home,
 The Bride of the village dies !

THE AULD WIDOW'S LAMENT.

I HAE naebody now ; for my bairns are a' gane,
And a' the day lang, I sit sabbin' alane :
I hae naebody now ; like a weed on the wave,
I am driftin' awa' to my bed in the grave.
When weary wi' weepin' I sink to a slum,
I dream that my bairns to their mither hae come ;
And I feel their saft lips and their tears fa' like rain,
But I wauken to find that the tears are—my ain.

I hae naebody now, as in days o' lang syne,
When Robie was wi' me—ah ! wha could repine !
Then the lang simmer days cam' as blythe as could be ;
Now Robie is gane, and a' 's winter wi' me !
Ah ! there hings his bonnet, but law lies his head ;
His staff canno' guide his cauld feet frae the dead ;
And his auld elbow-chair to decay maun sune fa',
Oh ! in grief now it moulders—its maister's awa'.

I hae naebody now ! I 'm a puir helpless thing—
Like a tree in the desert, forsaken by spring :
I hae naebody now to console my heart's cares ;
E'en the breeze whistles past as it lifts my white hairs.
The cloud on the hill, wi' its dark-mantled brow,
In the smile o' the mornin' shall bonnily glow ;
But the gloamin' that shadows a lane widow's day,
To darkness increases that lingers for aye !

I hae naebody now ; a' my joy's in the tomb ;
Like a lamp, I am wastin' mid silence and gloom :
I hae naebody now to enkindle its flame ;
A' is cheerless and mirk in my heart an' my hame.
But my time sune maun come—for my spirit is wae,
And langs for its pillow o' death in the clay ;
Oh ! it langs for the land where my bairns now abide—
Where the tear of the heart-broken mourner is dried.

ALE! ALE!   ALL ALE.

I 'LL sing you a song, with a voice as bold
  As the lion in the wood,
While I quaff a cup, of the brown and old,
  And it glows in my brain and blood.
Oh, how a fish I 'd love to be,
  If the ocean were good Ale ;
Among the foam, right merrily,
  I 'd gambol like a whale.

CHORUS.

Singing, Ale, all Ale ! my boys, all Ale !
  There 's nothing like Ale can be ;
Regale, regale on the home-brewed Ale ;
  And, a jolly full pot for me !

Oh, ever since the world began,—
  Some say long before,—
Good Ale was dearly loved by man,
  Who drank it in galore ;
For Sampson strong had never been ;
  Each fox had kept his tail ;
And Gaza 's gates we might have seen ;
  But the strong man loved good Ale !

King Pharoah loved a chirping cup,
  As it plainly doth appear ;
For he strove to drink the Red Sea up,
  As it looked like good old beer ;
But, unto his *tee-total* cost,
  He found it *rayther* small ;
So he dam'd the water where he was lost—
  Cars, horses, men, and all.

Hurrah ! for the Saxon days of yore,
  When the wassail cup went round !
When the barons pledged of healths a score,
  To the ladies fair renowned !

Each dauntless warrior feared no foe ;
He 'd doff his coat of mail ;
For the devil a soul could stand his blow,
When he sharped his steel with Ale.

Queen Bess was in her glory quite,
To see her yeoman bold !
For they fed on beef, and drank all night
Deep draughts of the brown Ale old !
" O give me none of your water men,
With their faces lank and pale !
For the boys that can cut and come again,
Must quaff whole butts of Ale ! "

Hurrah ! what a sight is the tankard bright,
When the sun is glowing hot !
A pound for a pull of the cool delight,
And three cheers for foaming pot !
'T is a fountain of joy in seasons all ;
'Tis hope when your prospects fail ;
For the heart can never droop or fall
When its blood 's well warmed with Ale !

This Knight, Sir John, is a rare old cove,
Quite honest in his way ;
And many a maid he 's coaxed to love,
On a Christmas holiday.
He bids the tender bosom burn,
And Cupid's darts prevail :
Oh, a fine, brave soul is Barleycorn ;
Let us pledge him now in Ale !

So, prate no more of your cogniac,
Nor your teeming skins of wine ;
Let me of " heavy " have my whack,
I 'll never once repine !
I 'd meet the devil in the dark,
And cut his swingeing tail ;
And quench of brimstone every spark—
Why, we 'll drown him in good Ale !

The Cockneys may boast of their Porter-fame
  And deem their " Stout" divine ;
But they never can claim the glorious name
  Of the Ale on the Banks of Tyne !
Like that fine stream—clear, old, and good—
  It was never known to fail ;
Nay, kings have enriched their regal blood
  By draughts of Newcastle Ale !

So now, my brave boys, my song is done,
  Come listen to my toast !
" May every one who loves the *sun*,
  Contrive to *rule the roast !*
May Trade, in every form increase ;
  May Commerce spread her sail !
May fortune crown the brow of Peace :"
  Hurrah ! for the good old Ale !

MY BONNY BAIRN.

OH ! dinna greet, my bonny bairn nor look sae sair at me ;
I canna ease, my bonny bairn, the pains that torture thee !
Night after night, my bonny bairn, I sit an' watch thy bed ;
I daurna sleep, my bonny bairn, I 'd wake an' find thee dead.

Sae constant hae I, night an' day, gazed on thy sickly face,
That naething but thy features wan in ither things I trace ;
That heavy eye, thy rolling head, thy low and piteous cry ;
My bonny bairn, I 'll watch thee still, resigned to Him on high.

Five years are gane, my bonny bairn—ah ! weel I mind the day—
When thou wast born, my bonny bairn, thy father dying lay :
He took thee in his thin, white hands, an' clasped thee to his breast;
He kissed an' blessed thee, bonny bairn, an' sunk for aye to rest.

Five years are gane, a lanely widow, wi' her babe, was cast,
Unpitied by the heartless warld, to bear the keenest blast.
Wae's me ! wae's me ! my bonny bairn, an' now I 'm left alane ;
My bairn, my bonny bairn, is dead, an' a' my hope is gane !

THE CONTENTED PLAYER;

" OR, WHERE'S THE ODDS ?"

I was turned o' saxteen, wi' a head half demented ;
Wi' play-buiks an' play-folks my heart was contented :
I stormed like a baillie an' louped like a laird, man,
An' spent muckle mair than my pouch ever shared, man.
Swats a' the day, an' at night reamin' toddy,
Rantin' just wud, on the floor to ilk body ;
Dancin' an' fencin', or toomin' the nappy,
Hech ! aften fou ! where 's the odds ? I was happy.

The minister preached o' my state frae the pu'pit,
An' damned the profession as awfu' an' stupid ;
Vowed that the stage was the sink o' a' evil,
An' banged Willie Shakspeare and me to the devil.
" Cannie," quo' I, took my staff in my hand, then ;
Left my auld daddie to spier for the grand then :
Croonin' my speeches, whiles takin' a drappie ;
Like a dog frae a rope I was canty an' happy.

My name is young Norval, on hills o' the Grampian ;
For " a horse," as crooked Dick, I rin shoutin' and stampin ;
But ae night, as Macbeth, when I crept to kill Duncan,
Man ! I fell on the knives, wi' the whisky I'd drunk in :
" On to the beach," I screamed out, as King Harry ;
Black as Othello, " most potent," I tarry ;
Like " a fool i' the forest," I looked but a sappy ;
But where 's a' the odds ? I was cosy an' happy !

My auld, doited granny gat tent o' my station,
Sae she trudged to the playhouse to see her relation ;
I was Hamlet that nicht, an' my father was speakin,'
When on popped puir granny, her lost laddie seekin :
" Angels o' heaven, i' mercy defend me !"
" Sandy," quo she," did ye think I no kened ye ?
Wi' your out-landish kilts an' the wig on your tappie :"
I was mad ; where 's the odds ? when my granny was happy.

To mak' matters fit, a young lassie I courted ;
Miss Randolph wi' Norval sune verra weel sorted :
Desdemona I smothered ; Ophelia I wedded ;
Jane Shore, as my wife, was nae blate to be bedded ;
Queen Kate took her aith that she lo'ed me sincerely ;
Joan o' Arc, though a witch, was the queen I lo'ed dearly ;
Wi' Romeo, my Juliet sipped poisonless nappy .
Where 's the odds, then, for names ? wi' them a' *I* was happy.

But my Haller proved fause, sae I played her the "Stranger :"
My debts were unpaid, and my dresses in danger.
The "bond" I had signed, so I tried to be waggish,
Instead o' the *flesh*, why I left them the "*haggish*."
Railways are handy, and strollin' aft dreadfu' ;
Starrin', I went, an' I sune bagged the needfu' :
Here I hae come to mak' friends wi' ilk chappie,
And the odds 'll be queer, if we are no' a' happy.

MARY HAY.

Oh ! where, tell me where, has my bonnie lassie gane ?
  I 've come, frae waesome travel, hame.
    An' mony a bloody fray ;
  I 've warstled sair for Scotland's fame ;
    For my hope was Mary Hay.

Oh ! where, tell me where, has my winsome lassie gane?
  She was my dearest, treasured thoucht ;
    A star to cheer my way :
  Nae wish o' wardly gear I sought ;
    My wealth was Mary Hay.

Oh ! where, tell me where, has my artless lassie gane ?
  Her cherry mou', and rosy cheek ;
    Her locks, like gowden day ;
  Her saft blue een—but wha can speak
    O' the charms o' Mary Hay ?

Oh ! where, tell me where, has my bonnie lassie gane ?
  Oft, on a simmer's afternoon,
    I 've listened to her lay ;
  And, when her witchin's sang was dune,
    I 've kissed sweet Mary Hay.

Oh ! where, tell me where, has my fairest lassie gane ?
  Last time we met, wi' luve my head
    On her warm bosom lay ;
  I vowed that till my heart were dead,
    'T wad beat for Mary Hay.

Oh ! where, tell me where, is my bonny lass laid ?
  Farewell ! ye dreams o' blissfu' life ;
    A hapless wretch I stray !
  I wadna hae a queen for wife,
    Sin' I lost loved Mary Hay.

THE DIRGE OF THE SHROUD.

DEATH sat at night in a church-yard lone,
Mid a grotto of graves on his charnel throne :
The silently mould'ring Past was there ;
Monarch and serf—the false and fair.
A hearse-plume waved o'er his hairless head ;
A pall was the mantle round him spread :
At his feet lay a form, like a slumb'ring cloud ;
'T was his regal dress—the snow-white shroud.

He fled, from his seat of clay-wrapt doom,
To a flower of life that dared to bloom ;
Oh ! the fair one's eyes with love grew bright,
But he breathed on her brow his mildew blight.
Pale grew her face, and her limbs grew weak,
A hectic flame marked the maiden's cheek ;
With anguish the parents' hearts were bowed,
For death wrapt that maid in his snow-white shroud.

He gathered the spears from a thousand bands ;
The mighty he scattered o'er distant lands :
From the victor he snatched the wreath of fame,
And left him to vultures without a name !
'Mid thunder and shouting, the spoiler rushed ;
The waves with the shame of murder blushed :
Down in the deep sunk the poor and proud,
And the ocean's foam was their cold, white shroud.

On a hallowed hill, a form was seen
Of a mortal mould but of Godlike mien.
Death stood aghast when his blow was given ;
Dark grew the sun, and the rocks were riven.
The sepulchre closed—and all was still ;
Death smiled at his power, that mocks earth's will ;
But the God awoke, like light from a cloud,
And burst the chill bands of the Tyrant's shroud.

Woe, woe to the day when the first shroud came,
A snow-wreath to chill the heart's pure flame !
When the madness of earth first smote the good,
And forth poured the innocent Abel's blood !
Since that time of dismay, as leaves they descend,
And wrap stricken forms of foe and friend :
Yea, the moment shall come, when the world's wide crowd
Shall sleep, side by side, in a mouldering shroud.

"MY NATIVE HILLS."

My native hills again I see rise o'er the heaving foam ;
Oh ! let me breathe the balmy gale that bears me to my home.
My wand'ring feet no more shall stray from thee, my dearest isle ;
The tears I've shed are passed away, with Hope again I smile.

My native shores again I hail ; my heart is bounding free,
And flutters like the joyful gale that spreads its wings for me :
I never dreamed, that such delight would gild my clouds of woe ;
Oh ! tears of peace now bathe my sight, home-raptures now I know.

BEWILDERED BEAUTY;

A PARODY.

SHE wore an old straw bonnet
  The first time that we met ;
She had no ribbons on it ;
  Her pockets were "to let ;
Her eye it squinted beautiful--
  Alas ! she had but *one ;*
But that was *very* dutiful,
  Much better far—than none.
I saw her in the gin-shop ;
  Methinks I see her now,
With her cap all torn in pieces,
  And hanging o'er her brow.

Nor hat nor cap, when next we met,
  Upon her head she wore ;
Her *only* eye was marked with jet,
  Still squinting as before :
Her nose—though of the *turn-up* race—
  Seemed drooping, sad, and blue ;
And sundry scratches scored her face,
  Tho' why—no stranger knew.
I saw her in the gin-shop ;
  Methinks I see her now,
With her hair, like carrots, hanging
  In bunches o'er her brow.

But what a plight I saw her in,
  When last I crossed her way ;
Oh ! she had swallowed too much gin,
  And on the ground she lay.
Her gentle form, by blue-coat men,
  Was raised and quickly borne
To that "keep" from which "disorderlies"
  Must pay ere they return.
I saw her safely carted ;
  And methinks I see her now,
In the pride of tipsy beauty,
  With a *coal-sack* o'er her brow.

OH ! I'LL NEVER FORGET.

Oh ! I'll never forget when I roamed with my love,
    With a bosom as light as a feather :
Tyne's woods waving green o'er a beautiful scene,
    In the eve of the sweet summer weather.
In love's tranquil hour we sat in the bower,
    Above us the moon brightly beaming ;
Not a throb in the breast that could give it unrest,
    Or rob it of fancy's wild dreaming.

The day seems as bright as that time of delight,
    And the bower's still fresh in its gladness ;
But my footsteps are lone, for my Ellen is gone,
    And left me to wail her in sadness.
Oh ! why do ye bloom, painted things of perfume,
    When Affection's sweet rose-bud hath perished ?
Let your green leaves be wet with the tears of regret,
    For departed is all that I cherished.

The sweet smile of Spring no comfort can bring,
    Nor Summer can happiness waken ;
The hope that is fled, the joy that is dead,
    The heart that beats lorn and forsaken.
O'er moorland and lea my wand'ring shall be,
    Till Death's icy fingers shall bind me ;
With my Ellen I'll sleep in a grave cold and deep,
    Where the Angel of Pity may find me.

HOMEWARD BOUND.

(This incident was recorded in the "Newcastle Chronicle,"
January 20th, 1844.)

The gallant ship from Afric's shore,
    With streaming colours at her mast,
Across fair England's channel bore,
    And hailed her snowy cliffs at last.
The flaunting "Union" marked her homeward way,
Like sunshine dancing to returning day.

Aloft, in haste, young Henry flies,
   And grasps the flag with eager hand ;
" Cheer, cheer, for home, my lads !" he cries ;
   " Behold, once more, your native land !
Again our charming girls' sweet lips we 'll press ;
Again our spouses shall their husbands bless."

As soars the lark on joyful wings,
   With lay melodious cleaves the sky ;
When lo ! the heartless sportsman brings
   Its bleeding form on earth to die !
So Henry, by the fresh'ning breeze o'erta'en,
Falls from his station to the heaving main.

Oh, piteous sight ! the struggling, brave,
   And wounded sailor, to behold :
In vain he stems the briny wave,
   The rope slips from his grasping cold !
His sinking form the British flag enshrouds,
Like day enveloped in eve's purple clouds.

Oh ! Mary, Mary, watch no more
   For Henry, thy fond lover true ;
He dies in sight of that dear shore,
   Where last he waved a kind adieu :
Beneath the surging billows of the deep,
An endless watch thy lover cold must keep.

ISABEL.

Oh ! did ye ken my Isabel,
   The pawky queen sae darkly sweet ?
The lassie's charms I fain wad tell ;
   She is the bonniest thing ye meet.
She has twa een that, like a dirk,
   Jist rin ye through if ye dare gaze ;
They seem twin stars o' e'enin' mirk :
   Her hair in jetty ringlets strays.

I wadna gie the miser's grip
O' countless stores o' warldly gear,
For ane saft kiss o' her red lip—
To breathe her breath o' luve sincere.
The ring-doo builds a cosy nest ;
The lambkin's bed is snug and warm ;
But my lo'ed lassie's snaw-white breast
Yields to my cheek a safter charm.

Oh ! far abune her graces a'—
As skies are clearer by their height—
Her mind nae cloud o' ill can knaw ;
Her soul is kindness bathed in light.
Then blessin's fa' in ceaseless showers ;
An' Hope's bright iris gild the rain ;
An' may the blossom frae sic' flowers
Be claimed by Beauty as her ain.

THE WAIL O' THE FALLEN.

I CANNO' come to thee, mither ;
My hame I daurna seek :
I ken no' where to flee, mither ;
My heart is like to break.
The pet I was o' a', mither ;
The youngest wean o' ten ;
An' why I fled awa', mither,
I wish I didna ken.

The warnin' an' the dree, mither,
Like snaw upon the flood,
Were wasted things to me, mither ;
My ears were deaf to guid.
But the bird is sure to fa', mither ;
That spreads a wilfu' wing ;
The snare or vulture's claw, mither,
Destruction sune maun bring.

Wi' slae-black, glitt'ring een, mither,
    The tempter smiling came,
Ca'd me his winsome queen, mither,
    And whiled me frae my hame :
The silken gowns and gowd, mither,
    Uncounted, were my ain ;
An' though he fondly wooed, mither,
    My spirit sunk in pain. ·

I thoucht o' hame an' thee, mither,
    As tears gushed frae my een ;
My love proved fause, to me, mither,
    As ithers aft had been.
I wake as frae a slum, mither ;
    The gowd and gems are gane :
Thy words o' truth hae come, mither ;
    I 'm dyin' here alane !

I canno' come to thee, mither ;
    My weary limbs are weak :
The grave my hame maun be, mither ;
    What ither dare I seek ?
My brow is red wi' shame, mither,
    That ance was pure as snaw :
Oh ! how can I come hame, mither,
    That broucht disgrace on a' ?

SUMMER HATH COME AGAIN.

Summer hath come again ;
    Banish thy care and pain,
    Wander the flowery plain,
        Mary, with me.

Sweetly the warblers sing,
    In the wood gathering ;
    Welcome and joy they bring,
        Mary, to me.

Come, in thy loveliness ;
Come, in thy beauty's dress ;
Come, and my bosom bless,
　　　Mary, to me.

Come, as the rosy day
Chases the clouds away ;
Come, as the merry May,
　　　Mary, to me.

Days are departed love,
When through yon balmy grove,
Happy I used to rove,
　　　Mary, with thee.

Oft hath my bosom beat
Sadly, with deep regret,
Musing, with eyelids wet,
　　　Mary, on thee.

Still, when on danger's stream,
Thou wast my cheering beam,
Bright as an angel's dream,
　　　Mary, to me.

Joyfully now I come
To my sweet maiden's home,
Never again to roam,
　　　Mary, from thee!

———

THE SEASONS.

WHEN Spring, a maid, in beauty buds,
And verdure decks the fields and woods ;
When streamlets, freed from bonds of snow,
Like Childhood, in their gambols flow ;
Oh ! then, sweet girl, I think on thee,
Lone, wandering o'er the dewy lea ;
When thoughts, in gentle currents, run
Beneath Affection's glowing sun,
　　　　　　　　　Sweet Emily.

When Summer, in her ripened bloom,
Smiles on her pillow of perfume ;
And Flora twines a garland fair,
To wreathe her wanton, waving hair ;
Oh ! then, dear maid, I think on thee,
When musing 'neath the hawthorn tree ;
And when small birds their music wake,
I join them for thy mem'ry's sake,
     Sweet Emily.

When Autumn, with her golden corn
And gushing grapes, salutes the morn ;
When songs, of rustic joyance, rise ;
When " Harvest-home " rings to the skies ;
'T is then, loved maid I think on thee,
When twilight lingers on the sea ;
And when love's lamps adorn the sky,
My thoughts to thee in silence fly,
     Sweet Emily.

When rill and river stand aghast,
Beneath stern Winter's howling blast ;
When Want bends to the driving hail,
And pours to heaven his piteous tale ;
'T is then, dear girl, I think on thee—
Thou who art softest sympathy ;
Thou canst not see the wretched mourn ;
Thy voice wilt soothe his breast forlorn,
     Sweet Emily.

A NIGHT WITH A JOVIAL SET.

A NIGHT with a jovial set—
 A song with a merry crew ;
For Odd-fellows here are met
 In the bands of friendship true.
Let the miser grasp his gold,
 Let the tyrant boast his might ;
Leal hearts we can still behold,
 Like stars, in our Lodge to-night.

The sea, with its ceaseless roll,
  The gale, with its silent wing,
Are figures of Friendship's soul,
  Whence secret charities spring.
Like a rock our Order stands
  'Mid contending billows foam ;
A beacon to straggling bands ;
  A guide to our Lodge's home.

As dew on the blue-bell's lip,
  Or balm from the rose's sigh,
Are the honied sweets we sip,
  When the hive of our hope is nigh.
Oh ! a love-bound band are we,
  Like a mercy-moulded chain ;
Odd-fellowship then for me,
  And hurrah for his golden reign !

HAIL, HAIL TO THE ORDER !

HAIL, hail to the Order—the honest and free,
Where Truth, Love, and Friendship united must be ;
Hail, hail to the craft that Odd-fellowship steers,
'T is a bark, braving danger, outliving all years ;
A temple of feeling—the brightest and best—
Where love lies enshrined in her truth-covered nest ;
Where malice, nor falsehood, nor evil is shown ;
For each Lodge claims sweet mercy its G. M. alone.
Far, far from our band is all jealousy borne,
We treasure no tares in Odd-fellowship's corn :
Sweet, sweet are the buds that from Unity blow ;
Hail, hail to that tree everlasting to grow !

The P.G's we honour, as days that are fled,
That twined golden wreaths of delight round each head;
We love them, like childhood, that mem'ry brings back,
And from N.G. to V.G. we see the bright track.

Oh ! blest be that mortal, undying his fame—
Let songs of true gratitude blend with his name—
Who first, in earth's creatures, bid charity glow ;
Who raised leaping gladness from darkness and wo !
Hail, hail to the Order, the honest and free,
Where Truth, Love, and Friendship united must be ;
Hail, hail to the craft that Odd-fellowship steers,
'T is a bark, braving danger, outliving all years.

SONG OF THE PRESS.

RAISE high, raise high, in marble might,
  Old Caxton's glorious form,
And wreathe his brow with living light,
  As he smiles amid the storm !
Let moon-beams rest on his placid breast,
  And the stars with love look down ;
For, so long as they shine from their towers divine,
  The Press-King shall wear his crown.

From a cave in the depths of the earth I came,
  And the Fire-kings bound me fast ;
And they rode on their steeds of blood-red flame,
  And my form was scorched by the blast :—
But soon, like a giant, strong I grew,
  And 'scap'd from the Fire-kings' den ;
And the world rejoiced when my strength it knew,
  And the Press was the pride of men.

Let the Hieroglyphic scrolls of yore
  From the mummied shrines depart !
Let the Sybils now lament no more
  The rejected books of their art :
For the Press with his mystic hand, can raise
  The voices of seers long dead,
And bring on a car of rainbow days,
  The memories of glory fled.

Hurrah ! for the song of Caxton old !
  Hurrah ! for his *Chapel's* lore ;
Hurrah ! for his *impress* black and bold,
  O'er which men love to pore !
See, how sage Wynkyn spreads his *forme,*
  To the Press's rolling might !
See, Genius-stars, from Lethe's storm,
  Come bursting into light !

Behold ! unconquered Steam comes on,
  And the eye can scarcely wink,
When the wizard-spell breaks the phœnix-shell,
  And the soul appears in ink !
Let Memphian pillars fall to dust,
  And mountains waste away ;
But so long as Time on his bell can chime,
  The Press shall not decay !

Then raise, raise high, in marble might,
  Old Caxton's glorious form,
And wreathe his brow with living light,
  As he smiles amid the storm !
Let moon-beams rest on his placid breast,
  And the stars with love look down ;
For so long as they shine from their towers divine,
  The Press-King shall wear his crown.

THE POET'S CONSOLATION.

One summer morning straying
  Along my native river's side,—
The banks sweet flowers displaying,
  In Nature's wild and artless pride,—
A form of loveliest feature
  Stole on my vision, like a dream ;
She seemed an aerial creature—
  The guardian spirit of the stream.

Her shining locks fell gracefully
  Around her bosom white as snow,
Which am'rous zephyrs, roving free,
  Revealed—then gently hid from show.
Her eyes, like love stars, shining,
  Seemed di'monds in dark vi'lets set;
Her lips seemed coral, lining
  A pearl-enamelled cabinet.

Her fairy feet stole peeping,
  Like bashful lilies, to and fro ;
Her vestures' folds fell, sweeping
  The verdant mead, like wreathing snow.
She moved in Music's motion,
  A summer cloud of floating light ;
Or, as o'er slumb'ring ocean,
  Glides the meek orb of peaceful night.

Now to my side advancing,
  (The air I felt with perfume blow) ;
And on me mildy glancing—
  Her words might charm the soul of woe.
" Fear not," she said, " my coming,
  For thou to me art not unknown ;
Thy strains, though unassuming,
  Find in my breast responsive tone.

" Thy dawning mind delighted
  'Mid wild poetic shades to flee ;
And oft have I invited
  Thy roving steps to dwell with me.
And oft, when dewy morning
  Rose on the hills of bonny Tyne,
I've seen thy bosom burning
  To celebrate its praise and mine.

" Yes ! when my river flowing,
  Thy raptured heart with ardour fired,
I came, and joy bestowing,
  Thy welcome strains of home inspired.

Cease not, dear Bard, thy singing,
　　Though heartless fools thy music scorn ;
Though round thee thorns are springing,
　　Receive this rose *without a thorn.*"

I took the balmy blessing
　　That just had left her bosom's bliss,
And fondly vowed, carressing
　　Its blushing beauty with a kiss,
That, till my mem'ry perished
　　In Nature's ruin and decay,
This rose should e'er be cherished,
　　And ever bloom a child of May.

Now, 'mid the worldly sorrow
　　That bears the mortal to the earth,
My rose I bid "good morrow,"
　　And love it for its artless worth.
To me it proves a treasure
　　Bequeathed by beauty to my mind ;
And, yielding fragant pleasure,
　　With poesy it is enshrined.

THE MINERS' DOOM.

'T WAS evening, and a sweeter balm on earth was never shed ;
The sun lay in his gorgeous pomp on ocean's heaving bed ;
The sky was clad in bright array, too beautiful to last,
For night, like Envy, scowling came, and all the scene o'ercast.
'T is thus with hope—'tis thus with life, when sunny dreams
　　appear ;
The infant leaves the cradle-couch, to slumber on a bier ;
The rainbow of our cherished love we see in beauty's eye,
That glows with all its mingled hues—alas! to fade and die !
'Tis dark, still night ; the sultry air scarce moves a leaf or flower ;
The aspen, trembling, fears to stir in such a silent hour ;
The footsteps of the timid hare distinctly may be heard
Between the pauses of the song of night's portentous bird.

And, in so drear a moment, plods the Miner to his toil,
Compelled refreshing sleep to leave for labour's hardest moil ;
By fate's rude hand the dream of peace is broken and destroyed ;
The savage beast his rest can take but *man* must be denied.
And why this sacrifice of rest ? did not the Maker plan
The darksome hours for gentle sleep?—the day for work by man ?
Yes ! but the mighty gods of earth are wiser in their laws ;
They hold themselves with pride to be *their creatures'* first great
    cause.
The Miner hath his work begun, and busy strokes resound ;
Warm drops of sweat are falling fast ; the coal lies piled around.
And what a sight of slavery ! in narrow seams, compressed,
Are seen the prostrate forms of men, to hew on back and breast ;
Fainting with heat, with dust begrimed, their meagre faces
    see,
By glimmering lamps that serve to show their looks of misery.
And oft the hard, swollen hand is raised to wipe the forehead's
    dew ;
And sighs are heaved for labour's close, but toil they must renew :
And manly hearts are throbbing there, and visions, in that mine,
Float o'er the young and sanguine soul, like stars that rain and
    shine.
Amid the dreariness that dwells within the cavern's gloom,
Age looks for youth to solace him—waits for his fruits to bloom.
Behold ! there is a careless face bent from yon cabined nook ;
Hope you may read in his bright eye—there's future in his look ;
Oh ! blight not then the fairy flower, 't is heartless to destroy
The only pleasure mortals know—anticipated joy !
Oh, God ! what flickering flame is this ? see, see again its glare !
Dancing around the wiry lamp, like meteors in the air.
Away, away ! the shaft—the shaft ; the blazing ruin flies :
Confusion—speed ! the lava stream the lighting's wing defies !
The shaft—the shaft ! down on the ground, and let the demon
    ride,
Like the sirocco on the blast, volcanoes in their pride.
The *choke-damp* angel slaughters all—he spares no living soul ;
He smites them with sulphureous brand—he blackens them like
    coal !
The young—the hopeful, happy young—fall with the old and
    grey ;
And oh, great God ! a dreadful doom, thus buried—to decay

Beneath the green and flowery soil whereon their friends remain;
Disfigured, and, perchance, alive, their cries unheard and vain!
Oh, Desolation! thou art now a tyrant on thy throne;
Thou smilest, with sardonic lip, to hear the shriek and groan!
To see each scorched and mangled corse to raining eyes displayed;
For hopeless widows now lament, and orphans wail dismayed.
Behold thy work! The maid is there her lover to deplore;
The mother wails her only child, that she shall see no more :—
An idiot sister laughs and sings—oh! melancholy joy—
While bending o'er her brother dead, she opes the sightless eye.
Apart, an aged man appears, like some sage druid-oak,
Shedding his tears, like leaves that fall beneath the woodman's
    stroke:
His poor old heart is rent in twain; he stands and weeps
    alone;
The sole supporter of his house—the last, the best is gone!
This is thy work, fell tyrant! this the Miner's *common lot;*
In danger's darkling den he toils, and dies lamented not.
The army hath its pensioners; the sons of ocean rest,
When battle's crimson flag is furled, on bounty's downy breast.
But who regards the mining slave, that, for his country's wealth,
Resigns his sleep, his pleasures—home, his freedom and his
    health?
From the glad skies and fragrant fields he cheerfully descends,
And eats his bread in stenchy caves, where his existence ends.
Aye, this is he that masters grind, and level with the dust;
The slave that barters life to gain the pittance of a crust!
Go read yon pillared calendar, the record that will tell
How many victims of the mine in yonder church-yard dwell.
Hath Honour's laurels ever wreathed the despot's haughty brow?
Hath Pity's hallowed gems appeared, when he in death lay low?
Unhonoured is his memory—despised his worthless name;
Who wields in life the iron rod, in death no tear can claim.

———

THE TRAPPER-BOY'S DREAM.

SILENCE was in the lowly cot; the Trapper-boy reclined
Upon his clean, though humble, couch, prepared by mother kind;
And near him sat the matron form, as fearful to molest
The slumber which she thought partook of dreaming and unrest.

For, see ! he starts—he mutters words, breathed from his lips of
    fear ;
And drops of sweat, upon his brow, like shining beads, appear.
And now he lifts his trembling hand—he holds his burning brow ;
" Save me ! oh, save me !" loud he cries ; he wakens wildly now.
" Oh ! mother, such a dreadful dream ; a cup of water, pray."
How eagerly he takes the draught ; his cheek is cold as clay.
" Oh, what a dream ! I would not sleep to see again that sight,
For all the gold that earth contains ; oh, horror and affright !
I thought that at my post I sat, upon my duty bent,
When suddenly there came a sound, as if the mine were rent ;
And then the earth rocked to and fro : I strove for help to call,
For o'er my head a mass of coal hung ready for to fall ;
·It swayed— it tottered, still it hung, as held by secret power ;
And, as I gazed, such horrid faces seemed on me to lower !
Grim demons looked, with scowling eye, and nearer then they
    came ;
They smote me—dashed me to the earth, and turned my heart
    to flame.
I felt my bones were ground to dust—my carcass mangled lay ;
My head I found was crushed ; the brains were mingled with
    the clay ;
And yet the state of sense was left ; the terror of the heart
Was vivid, and I thought how blest if I from life could part.
I saw, as 't were, without my eyes, and reasoned without brains;
I felt a death that dying man ne'er felt in worst of pains ;
Without a tongue, a voice I found, and called on God to save :
Oh ! mother, did I ever think so earnestly to crave ?
God heard me, and I dream no more ; but do not let me go
Again within the dreary mine ; I 'm warned to shun the blow !
You weep, my mother, and I know what you would wish to say,
That I am foolish to regard a dream that fades away.
Oh ! do not weep, and I will chase this vision from my brain ;
'T is for *you*, mother—we are poor—I go to work again."
'T is done, and he obeys the dictates of fond love ;
For 't is alone by sacrifice affection we can prove.
'T is done, and now the shapeless form reclines on that same bed ;
Where late it dreamt—from which it rose—on which it lieth
    dead ;
Proclaiming to the selfish world, that labours to destroy
The better feelings of the poor : *this was a Trapper-boy !*

SONG OF THE COAL-MINE SPRITE.

DEEP in Acheron's pitchy fume,
My palace in stench, my throne in gloom ;
Horror around me dismally grim,
Shown by the flare of the Davy dim ;
Pick, pick, pick, hack and hew,
Moiling and toiling all the week through !
Miners, or slaves,—the meaning is one,—
Haggard and worn, keep labouring on.
Pick, pick, pick, hack and rend,
Sunday to Sunday, toil without end ;
Sunday to Sunday, let them toil,
My engines want steam and their wheels want oil.
Let not the pick in your hands get cold !
The ships want freights, and our masters—gold ;
The beads of sweat are their pearls of gain ;
Their coffers are swelled by the bleeding vein.
Tired backs may ache, strained eyes may start,
And arteries gorged may burst the heart ;
Muscle and fibre, sinew and vein,
And the maddening leap of the feverish brain,
May tear and torture—rend and rave—
Pick, pick, pick ! toil on, thou slave !

Sons of oppression ! Christian slaves !
Though I give ye not food, I *give ye graves !*
Leap in my bucket and clutch my rope ;
Hurry to darkness, heart and hope :
Kiss not your children ere you go ;
Orphans they 'll be ere long, I know.
Send that young, fondling wife away ;
A widow she 'll be ere break of day !
Thou silly old man ! I 've spared thee long,
Keep from the crowd of the hale and strong !
Hoar locks in my mine are seldom seen ;
Besides, my prey is the young and green.
Down to your dungeons—rend and hack—
Crowd in your caverns, breast and back ;
Horror surrounds ye dismally grim ;

The flickering spark of the Davy dim,
Lighting no more of your broad domain
Than to show where Toil and Misery reign.
Labour by Fate was given to man ;
Labour is Poverty's boon and ban !
Shall he repine and cease the stroke,
And cast from his neck the galling yoke ?
Though scorned and flouted, toil he must ;
What is poor man but vulgar dust ?
Where are his houses, lands, estates ?
No gilded car his pleasure awaits ;
Nor gold, nor silver plate hath he,
Nor vassal to bend the pliant knee ;
What title hath he reward to seek ?
Mute let him toil, nor dare to speak !
Low let him crouch at the despot's throne ;
What rich man heeds the poor man's moan ?
Let him go labour, faint, and die ;
Thousands are left his pick to ply !
Pick, pick, pick ! work the mine ;
Ye have leave to toil but not to repine !
Call me a tyrant ! what do I heed ?
Toil is my motto—my master's creed.
Many, through ignorance, brand my name ;
Who is the cause of my blackened fame ?
Who is the tyrant ? Say ? Not I !
Ask Wealth—ask Pride ! What ! no reply ?
Then gather the dust of a thousand years,
Mingle its grains with Affliction's tears ;
Fashion the clay to a giant grim ;
Give it a spirit—life and limb ;
Give it a tongue ! and ask if I
E'er doomed the mining wretch to die ?
Agent of Ruin I 've been too long ;
Scourge of the *weak* when oppressed by the *strong !*
Effect of destruction—not the cause ;
A tyrant compelled by the tyrant's laws.
When prisoned 'mid sulphur and choked to death,
Gasping and writhing for lack of breath,
I asked but the common boon of air,
They mocked my moans and scorned my prayer :

Imploring and threatening—'t was all in vain !
Ha—ha ! but I burst my bonds in twain !
Raging with fury and vengeful fire,
I strode the pale horse of deadly ire ;
Blighting and blasting I swept along,
Mangling, destroying the old and young ;
Changing to ashes the mortal mould,
Leaving the doomed of creation cold !
Then the pick was silent ; no hands to hew :
" 'T was Pride who slaughtered, not I who slew !"

HARTLEY'S SACRIFICE.

MORNING rode high among the hills that cluster in the skies,
And in her car of pearl and gold, near noon, was seen to rise ;
The mists fled from the mountain peaks ; the ocean, bathed in
    light,
Lay, like some conq'ror, armour-clad, and dreaming of the fight.
And there was joy in many hearts on God's grand orb of earth,
Aye, e'en beneath the thrones of pride, pleasure had breath and
    birth ;
Toil, for a season, dreamed of peace, of heavenly air and rest,
And freedom wrapped her mighty wings around the miners'
    breast ;
'Tis " changing time " at Hartley shaft ; the welcome cage
    descends
The " set " to bear from dens of gloom to home and loving
    friends.
The coal-grimed miner leaves his seam, prepares for bank to
    start,
Eager his wife and bairns to see, and clasp them to his heart.
As seamen cast on islands drear, amid the treach'rous main,
Hail with delight the ship's dim form that bears them home
    again ;—
So joyed our miners when the cage swung looming into sight,
'Twas like a rising from the grave to liberty and light.
Up, up, like larks, on high they soar, their songs float on the
    gloom,
Alas ! it is the dirge of death, the prelude-notes of doom !

For ere the cage a third time pass'd from darkness into day,
Down crashed an iron avalanche, and changed their form to clay.
A pond'rous beam, like some huge fiend, plunged down the
    yawning caves,
And now the subterranean gulf becomes the miners' graves ?
Horror of horrors ! men and boys, Two Hundred and a Score,
Are buried 'mid the choke-damp fiends in earth's most dismal
    core !
There is no second friendly shaft ! no outlet from their fate !
Poison is now the air they breathe—their doom is desolate !
Say, why was not a " rising shaft " in this dread dungeon seen ?
Hath harsh neglect or avarice the ruthless murd'rer been ?
Shall love of gold, or niggardness, prove still the miner's bane ?
Shall man's immortal soul be staked for owner's greed and gain ?
Give to the slaving serfs below the means from death to fly,
And then no blame shall blot the name of wealth when poor
    men die.
Above, on bank, strong, willing arms, and noble hearts are found,
While mighty Science struggles hard to clear the gulf profound.
Giants in nerve and energy, to save their " marrows, " toil,
They work as if they dug for gold, all eager for the spoil !
Urged in their labours by the " jowl" of voices far beneath,
They shrink not from the deadly gas that chokes their panting
    breath.
With cheering words they strive to hush fear's agonising wail,
For struggles, gaspings, screams for help, in that vast tomb
    prevail.
The bright-eyed angel-stars look down with pity in their eyes,
And veil their faces in dismay to hear the suff'rers' cries,
Morning comes forth—high Noon appears, and Evening, bathed
    in grief,
Beholds the noble pioneers whose toil brings no relief ;
The " jowling " answers from the mine are hushed as marble
    death ;—
The catacombs are echoless—and voiceless Ruin's breath.
The work of heroes still proceeds from rise to set of sun ;
From frowning night till morning's blush the toil of love goes on ;
And lab'ring thus, day follows day, and long dark nights are
    pass'd,
Till death's sad slaughter-field of woe stands full revealed at
    last.

Brave hearts ! God bless ye all ! Let angel-fingers twine
A wreath of sweet, unfading flowers to crown your deeds divine!
A nobler vict'ry ye have won than patriot-warriors claim,
Let trophies rest on every breast, and glory gild your fame.
Imagination spreads her wings, and with a downward sweep,
Pierces the stenchy, stygian dens, and views the coaly deep ;
When, God of Mercy ! such a scene of horror meets her eyes,
That in affright she speeds her flight and gains her native skies.
But O ! the abject misery—the crowding of despair—
The hurrying of unnumbered feet—the shrieks that rend the
    air—
The agony of breast and brain—wild, anguished bitterness,
Of fathers, mothers, children, wives, what language can express?
Hope wrecked and shattered on a rock—the life-boat far away—
Love wailing for her slaughtered young, to Indian fiends a prey—
Sorrow on battle's sanguine field when storms of winter yell—
Fail far the dreadful doom to show that on New Hartley fell !
Come, then, ye mourners, leave this scene of soul-subduing woe,
And, like your gen'rous, widowed Queen, relief's best gifts
    bestow ;
Join the grand host benevolent—who nobly have employed
The surest solace time can yield for hearts and homes destroyed—
Share what your bounty can afford ; let none the suff'rers
    slight—
With gold let Riches prove his love—the poor bestow their
    mite ;—
Thus may the orphans cease their wail—the widow's tear be dried,
And for the Hartley Miners Lost a lasting boon supplied.

THE MINER'S MOTTO.

"Let us live by our labour," and never forget—
    Though our destiny weaves us a troublesome chain—
When the worth of our labour is generously met ;
    The pleasure will balance the weight of the pain !
'T is oppression that only can injure the peace,
    And rob the young heart of its joy and content ;
For who would be happier, were tyrants to cease
    To laden the back overburdened and bent ?

We care not for riches ; our children supply
  Every treasure of price with affection and love :
And we care not for honours—the great and the high ;
  The *honours we* sigh for, are *faithful* to prove !
Yes, faithful to *all* who, like *men* and not *slaves*,
  Shall hold us, though humble in station, to be ;
But when, by hard grinding, they treat us as knaves,
  Our bosoms are roused, and we vow to be free !

We are lowly ! but shall we be spurned by the great ?
  Omnipotence honours the rank of the *soul*,
And heeds not the mock'ry of splendour and state,
  But weighs *the kind feelings* of man as a *whole !*
We are men, and possessed of God's image and spirit ;
  In the eyes of our Maker as great and as high,
As the butterfly creatures that soar without merit,
  Though wing'd, but poor *worms* that with maggots must lie.

Then blame not the Miners, who wish to secure
  The *right of the workmen—the worth of his toil ;*
Who shrink not from danger nor death to procure
  Teeming coffers of gold from the womb of the soil.
Let our masters proclaim us the rudest of men ;
  Let them scurrilous epithets foolishly give ;
But, oh ! let them *never withhold what we gain ;*
  " For we live by our labour ; we labour to live !"

THE DIAL OF LIFE.

"Come like shadows, so depart."

THE BELL STRIKES—ONE.

" Haud your whist, ye squallin' brat !
  Ken ye what ye wad be at ?
Here ye are, an' here maun stay,
  Till a' the sands o' Life decay.
Bide ye, bairnie ; tak' your rest,
  Snugglin' in your mither's breast ;
Drinkin', sleepin', wakin'—then
  To drink, an' sleep, and wake again !"

TWO.

" Creepin' now, but sune ye 'll gan ;
Mind your head, my bonny man !
Tak' your time, an' hae a care
How ye grip your father's chair !
Gie 's your hand, ye stach'rin' dunce !
Walk awa', a man at ance ;
Lauchin', toddlin', but an' ben ;
Bairns hae pride as weel as men."

THREE.

Sabbath morn.   The claithes are new :
Never winked the hale nicht through !
Pond'rin' o' the tartan frock ;
Countin' ilka weary clock :
Jumpin' up an' squattin' doon ;
He thinks it morn—but 't is the mune !
" Whist, daft callant ! hear the rain ;
The auld duds ye maun wear again."

FOUR.

Kate an' Jock are wilfu' weans,
Just acquainted wi' their teens ;
Ane, a lassie jimp an' sma' ;
T'ither callant, crouse an' braw ;
Wand'rin' by the banks o' Clyde,
Emblems o' its passing tide ;
To pu' the gowans o' the glen,
They 've both played " wag " frae schule ye ken !

FIVE.

Stars are cheaper than the gas ;
Ilka lad can court his lass :
Nane to turn the tap an' say,
" Come, be aff—for light we pay !"
Sae fand Jock, when by the door,
Croonin' Cupid's sonnets o'er ;
Whisp'rin' luve to Kate sae plain,
She bade him sing them owre again.

SIX.

"Kate, my darlin', joy is ours ;
Happy moments fa' in showers :
Blest wi' health, an', what is mair,
Linked to thee, my lassie fair.
Prospects brighten to my view ;
Not a speck to blot the blue :
Not ane thoucht o' wae to ken ;
Kiss me—for I'm king o' men !''

SEVEN.

"Kate, my lassie, fret nae mair ;
Nane but fules are fashed wi' care :
Tent nae grumblin' landlord loon ;
Crack his head wi' half-a-croon !
Gawkie millers scratch their pows ;
Bairns, puir things, maun hae their brose :
Cash is unco short we ken,
But better days will come again !''

EIGHT.

"Katey, lass, the day is dune,
Youthfu' times o' feckless fun !
Passed the dafflin' courtship hours ;
Withered lie the orange-flowers !
Still o' luve I'm naething blate ;
'Deed, I think I'm dafter, Kate !
But a' 's weel enough in men ;
Better luve as loot, ye ken.''

NINE.

"Wae 's me, but you 're looking auld,
An' my pow is gettin' bald !
Deary, but your haffit 's thin ;
Still ye wear a bonny skin !
Care 's a buckie, lass, to bite ;
Beauty feels its powerfu' spite ;
Teeth fa' oot, an' lips gae ben ;
Gums maun tak' a spell, ye ken !''

TEN.

" Heaven be praised, our bairns look green !
Spierin' now what we hae been ;
Lads wi' sneeshen, guard, an' watch ;
Lassies wi' their gowns to match.
The turtle-doo maun hae a nest ;
Let the young folks' hearts be blest !
Kate, ye 're but a tappit hen,
An' I'm no sae young, ye ken."

ELEVEN.

" Kate, the news can no' be true ?
The dowpie wean is buckled noo !
Jock has twa, an' Sandy five ;
Bless the bairns, I hope they'll thrive.
White 's my head an' weak 's my feet ;
I feel easier when I sit :
Ance, I 'd jump wi' ony men ;
Noo, I 'm eighty-sax, ye ken."

TWELVE.

" Kate, speak louder ! do ye hear ?
Fit my trumpet to my ear ;
This weary cough ! mind what I say ;
I 'm deaf an' blind—ah, well-a-day !
Blind an' deaf, an' lame an' auld ;
Sune the mools maun be my fauld ;
Calm I 'll dee, for weel I ken
Jock shall join his Kate again !"

———

TO THE SKYLARK.

BEAUTIFUL warbler, bird of the sky !
Glad be thy bosom, now soaring on high.
Sweet is thy singing, artless thy strain ;
Breezes are bringing thy music, like rain.

Rain of pure melody, music's soft dew,
Full of rich sweetness, sparkling and new,
Mellowly teeming ripe from thy throat ;
Sounds that are beaming with bliss as they float.

High o'er the palace, far from the bower,
Mingling with heaven, and praising its power.
Whither still flying ? Hark ! 't is thy tone,
Louder, undying, thy flight speeding on !

Dim is my vision, aching mine eyes ;
Ah, man ! how unsuited to gaze on the skies.
Lo ! thou appearest ; welcome thy form ;
Go to thy dearest ; soothe her and charm !

Now thy tired pinions cleave to thy breast ;
Speeding, like lightning, down to thy nest,
On the green meadow, cheerful and gay ;
Thy callow young feeding, and murmuring thy lay.

Beautiful warbler, bird of the sky !
Glad be thy bosom, when soaring on high.
Sweet is thy singing, artless thy strain !
Up—up thou art springing, warbling again !

A NIGHT SCENE.

" 'T is night, dead night ; and weary Nature lies
So fast, as if she never were to rise."
                                        A. LEE.

Low sinks the sun ; the evening clouds
Troop slowly in their garbs of gloom ;
Castle and village church wax dim,
Hiding their summits in dark night.
Now comes the full-orbed moon amid
Her company of glittering stars,

E

Like a fair bride upon her couch,
Amid her tending maids, that smile
With lovelier looks to see her joy.
The Ocean bids his dancing waves
Salute her with uplilted hands,
And catch upon their jewelled brows
Her chastened glow.   The wakening hills
Disrobe them of the clinging mist,
And deck their fronts with yellow light,
While the slow-nodding forests spread
Their leafy branches to the moon.
  Hark ! how mellifluous Music takes
Her perfumed flight ; like a young soul
That sin-untainted, seeks the skies.
Ah ! modest Philomel, 't is thou
That melt'st the heart to melody ;
And, by an alchemy of tone,
Dost fuse its feelings into gold.
Cease—cease, rapt bird, thy eloquence !
Lest angels, wandering from their orbs,
Grow jealous of thy arguments,
And yield their harping minstrelsy
To win thy magic powers of song !
  'T is night !   How charming is the deep
And dreaming night !   The placid lake
Clasps to her mirrored breast the moon,
The stars, the skies, and the dim hills,
And folds them in her gleaming robe.
The winds are resting, like a babe,
Wearied with murmuring, asleep,
So silently, that their sweet breath
Fails to bestir a single leaf,
That, shadow-like, upon the tree,
Lies motionless.   The clouds
Float noiseless o'er the firmament ;
While glade, and glen, and sylvan stream,
Seem steeped in poppied lethargy.
Again the love-birds' fairy's note
Steals to the ear, with steps so faint,
So whisp'ringly, that Echo dreams
Unconscious of a sound.   The night !

How lovely is the night ! The world
Hath cast its sorrows, like a vest
Unmeet to wear ! The stars look down
Benignly meek, as if their gleams
Were but the lowly glow-worms' lamps,
And not the bright, mysterious orbs
That shame in vast rotundity
Our sphere below. The bosom's pulse
Beats calmly regular ! while Hope
Looks upwards to the star-paved dome,
Blessing her sisters in the sky.
    Blest Comforter, sweet Hope ! to thee,
Amid this elemental war
Of battling storms, volcanic fires,
Simoons that blast, and gales that fieeze ;—
Midst all the troubles that surround
Mortality, thy cheering voice
My drooping bosom cheers, and dreams
Invest my sorrows with thy charms !
Then, like refiners' crucibles,
Life's bitterness as dross appears ;
The sterling metal of the mind
Yet unconsumed remains.
                Perchance,
Ambitious, I have sought the mount
Parnassian, and have boldly drawn
The breath of Inspiration ! still
If I have never smote the string
That Vice delights to hear, my verse,
In noble minds, shall bear no scorn ;
For, like thee, Moon, my course hath been
A wanderer through the clouds of life ;
And many a dark and sullen spot
My struggling ray hath dimmed ; but now
The evil waning hour hath passed,
And day by day, Hope's crescent fills
To make Anticipation glow
An orb of Friendship beautiful !

FORGET AND FORGIVE.

"To err is human ; to forgive divine."
                                        POPE.

THIS were a merry world and wise,
If man would mark with milder eyes
His brother's failings as they rise,
    And not give scandal birth.
The human heart might heave unriven ;
Care's clouds from comfort would be driven ;
Cancelled man's crimes—his faults forgiven,
    And all sweet peace on earth !

But how the happy scheme arrange ?
Who shall effect the cheering change ?
For man is stubborn, strong, and strange ;
    To heartless laws he clings.
Hail ! blest Utopian land indeed,
Where fruit spontaneous knows no seed ;
Where flower of Eden fears no weed
    To choke it as its springs.

As one grand chain of Friendship vast,
O, man, thou shalt thy form outlast ;
Leaving thy greatness unsurpassed ;
    The model of mankind !
But first, all haughty hate forego ;
Deem not thy fellow-worm thy foe ;
To erring clay sweet pity show ;
    So shalt thou mercy find !

Forget that better words were spoken ;
Forgive each dark and scornful token ;
Forget that Friendship's ring was broken,—
    Forgive e 'en Slander's tone !
Forgive ! as dews to heaven exhale,
Adorning night when stars prevail !
So, Pardon, on a perfumed gale,
    Shall rise to Mercy's throne !

Behold ! Day's dazzling fount on high,
In whose bright breasts the seasons lie,
To which vast worlds unnumbered fly,
    To bathe their brows in light !'
To glad their moody moons, and make
Dark planets happy for their sake ;
That, when Earth's wretches weeping wake,
    They may not deem it night !

" Oh ! Care and Crime, with temples torn,
Bewildered, banished, and forlorn ;
Come, ye have long stern Justice borne,
    To Mercy wake and live !"
'T was thus a Saviour's mandate mild
Reclaimed a weak and wand'ring child,
And Jewish rage to peace beguiled,—
    How Godlike to forgive !

CHANGEFUL KINDNESS.

My love's a lively lass and strange—
    A cloud of light and rain,
That passes with a cheerful change,
    Like shadows o'er the main.
My love's a lily 'mid the flowers,
    Just tinged with rosy bloom ;
A sunbeam shining 'mid the showers,
    And laughing at the gloom.

My love looks lamb-like when I sigh,
    And imitates my sorrow ;
Sometimes, in silence, steals me by,
    Nor breathes a sweet " good morrow !"
Strange witching eyes I watch, that rest
    Upon her blushes burning ;
And still, I think she loveth best
    The face that bears her scorning.

Her footsteps, like the the thistle's down,
  Float through the mazy dances ;
She ever wears the Graces' crown—
  Still bashful are her glances.
Her eyes—twin diamonds dipped in dew—
  Their glitt'ring glow increasing ;
Shooting my poor heart through and through,
  With arrows aimed unceasing.

Her smile—Love's palace in the skies,
  Where dimpled Joy is seen,
Clothed in the gems of Paradise,
  Seraphic and serene.
Her laugh—the lark's melodious lute ;
  A silver timbrel sounding ;
A tone that holdeth Envy mute,
  All jealousy confounding !

I had a dove that lack'd his mate ;
  Long days he sat deploring ;
She soothed him in his saddest state ;
  Her care his life restoring.
Oh, oft I wished that bird to be,—
  To sleep 'neath her caressing ;
Still sidelong stole her eyes on me ;
  My jealous bosom blessing.

My rival died ; my sweetheart's tears
  Fell on the dead bird shining ;
The hope that held my heart for years,
  Now round my love was twining.
I wept to see her weep so sore,
  E'en for a dove departed ;
My eyes, like cups of grief, ran o'er,
  For love so tender-hearted.

I know not ; but the fate fell out,
  That, grieving thus together,
Our tears commingled—little doubt—
  Like rainbows in fine weather.

And yet my love 's a changeful thing :
　Three seasons in a minute ;
Autumn, and Summer, and young Spring ;
　But never Winter in it !

THE "BOOK OF SCOTTISH SONG."

OH, what a coronal of flowers is here !
The balmy blossoms of the loved and dear ;
Rich, rainbow-tinted beauties of the mind ;
Music's aroma, rarest of its kind !
But do ye, perfumed spirits, still exhale
Your grateful essence to the lingering gale ?
Doth your green freshness still the world delight ?
Or, are ye things that long have born the blight
Of Winter's coldest breath, and now are come,
Bright visitants from Lethe's misty gloom,
To glad again the noble of the earth,
And bless the Muses with a second birth ?
Why have ye slept in dark, oblivious caves ?
Did ye not buffet Life's tumultous waves ?
Did ye not slow consume the lamp of mind,
And break your hearts to leave a name behind ?
Welcome, sweet flowers ! again ye shall not die !
Here ye shall bloom to immortality.

Oh, Poesy !—bewitching syren !—thou
Deceitful gild'st th' aspirant's youthful brow
With rosy chaplets ; and with whispers soft,
Woos the too sanguine soul to soar aloft !
Genius ! thou art an eagle ! near the sun
Thy heavenward race forever must be run !
Heed, soaring bird ! though Jove-descended, heed ;
Behold th' envenomed shaft, with lightning's speed,
Hurries to dip its thirsty beak in thee !
'Twas thus with Burns ; a genius frankly free !
'Twas thus with Ferguson and Tannahill !
'Tis thus with every sterling bard, and ever will !

Then why bright gems of uncreated mind,
Give ye these "pearls of price" to base mankind?
Why do ye heap the precious gold of song?
What earthly dross to poets can belong?
Are ye not poor—despised—the jeer of men—
Your works rejected, as a worn-out pen?
And *still* ye deck and ornament the world?
Ye raise the tower, and from its height are hurled!
"O glorious death!" me thinks I hear ye say;
" Immortal honours crowd the minstrel's way!
Though poor an earth, his verse a wealth bestows
Which no crowned king or titled noble knows!
Away, ye grov'ling herd! we cannot fall;
The blissful heaven of glory waits us all!
Our deeds superior to the wreck of Time,
Live on, uninjured—deathless, and sublime!"

SPEECH OF CROMWELL,

(Dissolving the Long Parliament, 1652.)

CROM. (*aside*).
          'Tis well! the time is now mine own!
Let me encounter scowling arrogance;
Shall it move Cromwell's soul?
          (Addressing the house).
                    The motion, sir,
Before this house, hath, in my plain conceit,
Such baneful bearing that I cannot brook
A moment's longer pause to speak my mind.
For what a crouching knave I were and base,
Unworthy of the dignity of soul,
To stand, mute as a sculptured effigy,
When, to my sight, the crimson edge of crime
Reeks with its fell and bloody purposes.
What are ye all?   Say not, that heaven defends
The dark designs of arbitrary power!
Say not, that high Divinity doth hedge ye,

When ye, blasphemers, to His footstool bring
Your venal offerings of blackest deeds!
Do ye not turn His even-handed scales
By your flagitious laws? What are ye all?
Blood-spillers of a prostrate nation's heart!
Do ye not bondage-bind the valiant men
That, in the fiercest of the contest, fight,
Ready for death, that freedom may be won?
Why do ye seek to rack the English code
Of legislation by your lawyer's wheel?
To vex, to goad, and tear the Constitution
By your infernal Presbyterian scourge?
And all for what? but to perpetuate
The viper-brood of hell-begotten power!
To glut, with drossy ore your empty purses;
Empty with riot and debauchery;
Empty with largess of your wicked bribes;
Empty—but no! I may not speak the rest!
For now the time hath come!
          The Lord disowns,
And hurls ye, howling, from his angry sight!
And He hath chosen, in his providence,
Vessels more pure and fitter for his work!
Ye are no Parliament! Your reign is o'er!
Nay, hiss not through your grinding teeth the words
Ye dare not speak! I say *your reign is o'er!*
And you, Sir Harry Vane! Oh Harry Vane!
The Lord deliver me from Harry Vane!
Honest Sir Harry! Juggling hypocrite!
A parliament, forsooth! a precious set
Of drunkards, knaves, extortioners! Behold,
With bloated carcase, like a dropsied whale,
Sits Challoner, besotted and asleep!
And there's another with adult'rous paunch,
The veriest semblance of a common sewer!
But why, with words like these my tongue defile?
Ye gape aghast! yet the bold deed is yours!
By day, by night, have I the Lord besought
That he would slay me ere this hour arrived;
But he would not. What say'st thou, craven wretch!
"My conscience might prevent it!"

Guards, advance!
Secure the peculator that dare prate
To me of conscience! aye, away with him;
Away with *all!*   Let not a tongue be moved
In foul aspersion of my embassy;
Examine well each harqebuss: be firm
And do your duty, if one Philistine
Shall dare to rail against the chosen one,
Or turn rebellious 'gainst the Lord's appointed.
Here, give me that fool's bauble—gilded toy—
Befitting kingly wisdom.   This I hurl,
And all such impious images of Baal
To dark oblivion!   Now my task is done.

———

STANZAS WRITTEN IN SICKNESS.

THE church-bells are ringing,
Their sweet music winging,
And holy thoughts bringing
  To hearts of delight;
But vain is their warning
To me, lonely mourning;
For sorrow's returning
  Like clouds of the night.

Oh! lost is each pleasure;
Denied is the treasure,
That fills, without measure,
  The bosom of peace.
In sickness repining,
I sit, with grief twining,
Fate's links undesigning
  My hope of release.

Ye sounds now ascending,
On seraphs' wings bending;
Let suppliant sighs blending,
  Be raised to the throne;

Let tears of contrition
Embalm my petition,
And blot each omission,
    That grace may be shown.

The blood that flows nearest
My heart—to me dearest ;
Oh, God !—thou that hearest—
    All is thine to be free.
Once more to be kneeling
At thy alter, revealing
My soul, and appealing
    For mercy from Thee !

BETTER TIMES.

"Then Hope again to me appeared and waved her golden wing."

LET not the stricken heart despair ;
    'T is folly to repine !
To-day the sun dark clouds may wear ;
    To-morrow he may shine.
The ocean, with vexation rife,
    To-day a giant wild ;
To-morrow—where is all his strife?
    He slumbers like a child.
Then let this proverb ever cheer,
    With bee-note sweetly humming,
" Though bad times mark the present year,
    The better season's coming."

And let not poor men sigh for wealth ;
    Enough is kindly given ;
If they possess the treasure—health,
    · They bear a gem from heaven.
But had they all that gold can give,
    'T would fail true peace to buy ;

Then let them good and honest live,
  To-morrow they may die :
Then shall they find this proverb clear,
  When death their souls shall summon,
"That bad times are but trials here,
  For better seasons coming."

The poor man, when by cares beset,
  Sits murm'ring all the day ;
As if complaints and vain regret
  Would drive the ills away !
Up and be doing ! Try again :
  Who knows, but you may rise ?
The baffled ant still drags the grain,
  And labour crowns the prize :
For is my maxim not quite clear ?
  Come, Resolution summon !
" The present season's only here—
  The better times are coming."

And, if the worst should come that *can*,
  'T is manly still to hope ;
How mad must be that drowning man
  That clutches not the rope.
Though want and poverty be thine,
  And sickness unto death,
Still to a blessed hope incline ;
  Submissive yield thy breath :
Then shall these accents to thine ear
  Float with angelic humming,
" Though sorrow marked each mortal year,
  God's kingdom bright is coming !"

"LITTLE DOTH THE POOR GOOD."

ONCE roaming through a bonny field,
  Where summer flow'rets grew,
I heard a rustic maiden sing
  A strain unfeigned and true :

Upon her knee a babe was laid,
　And thus she lulled her pet,
" Oh ! little doth the poor good,
　And little do they get."

Thought I, there's simple truth contained
　In this young nurse's song,—
For often have the poor complained
　Of burdens borne too long.
But what's the use of sitting down,
　And nursing vain regret ?
If little doth the poor good,
　A little still they get.

I'd sooner be a rambling rill,
　To steal along the glen,
Than be a torrent's roaring flood,
　And buffet with the main.
I'd sooner low and happy be,
　Than in a palace fret ;
Though poverty might pester me,
　My little still I'd get.

The rich man hath no greater claim,
　Upon the bliss of heaven,
Than he who bears the humblest name
　That e'er with want hath striven ;
Save when he yields spontaneous aid
　To man in mis'ry set ;
Then stands he, as an angel, made
　To cancel Mercy's debt.

God, who created rich and poor,
　Determined their estate ;
All stars shine not with equal light,
　Nor move with equal rate ;
Yet cheerful glows each spangled speck,
　On Night's wide robe of jet !
Bless him, ye poor, and grateful take
　The little ye may get !

USE THE MEANS.

I Saw a fisher in his boat,
  Rocked by the restless wave ;
All night his nets had been afloat,
  - Yet fortune nothing gave.
The morning found him fishing still,
  Though hunger pained him sore ;
Dark doubt came oft, his heart to chill ;
  Hope whispered, "give not o'er.".
And now he draws, with willing hand,
  His nets, large shoals possessing ;
He used the *means*—you understand,—
  And God had sent the *blessing !*

A farmer owned a spacious field,
  And long untilled it lay ;
Nor fruit, nor corn, it deigned to yield :
  He sold it on a day.
The buyer wisely ploughd and dressed—
  Enriched it with manure :
Of all his land it proved the best ;
  Its crops were ever sure.
And still he drained—the clods he bruised ;
  Its produce still progressing ;
For well he knew, when *means* are used,
  God fails not in the *blessing.*

I saw a mild and holy man
  To sinfulness appealing,
With gentle and persuasive plan,
  Religion's truths revealing.
And long rebelled this infidel,
  Love's precepts disregarding ;
Till flashed conviction's hallowed light,
  The pastor's zeal rewarding.
Unwearied still he kindly came,
  Till man, bowed low, confessing
That, through a Saviour's powerful name,
  Descends Salvation's blessing.

The gathered moments make the hour ;
　Years are but hours repeated :
Time slowly seems to waste his power ;
　Still time is soon completed
The loftiest spire had but one stone
　To form its first foundation ;
But, stone by stone, the work went on ;
　Behold in skies its station !
Thus man, by constant virtuous deeds,
　Feels not earth's cares depressing ;
But, like the spire, on high proceeds
　To speak of God's own blessing !

FADED BLOSSOMS.

Composed whilst sitting on a Tombstone, in St. Nicholas' Church
Yard, Newcastle.

FADED blossoms around me are lying ;
　Cherished flowers in silent decay :—
Soft the breezes around them are sighing ;
　Tread as light o'er the graves as you may.
Fairest cheeks lose their beautiful roses ;
　Sparkling eyes are here lustreless grown ;
Gallant Manhood forever reposes ;
　Glory's stars sunk in darkness unknown.

Sunny Hope in her zenith is clouded ;
　Fondest Love by the canker-worm dies ;
Visioned home is by Sorrow enshrouded ;
　Here the last of the stranger's dust lies.
Full of years the old Temple remaineth,
　Like a tower in the midst of the deep ;
Nor of age nor decay she complaineth,
　But watches the dead as they sleep.

THE SPIRIT'S REVELATION.

Scorn not the tales I tell, nor yet the way
I tell them, for, believe me, they are truth !
My eyes, accustomed secrets to survey,
See with the clearness of an optic youth ;
I view thick darkness as bright noon of day ;
Nor can cemented sepulchres, forsooth,
Hide e'en *their* histories from my piercing ken,
For like a book I read the hearts of men.

I live, yet am invisible to all ;—
  High on the cold caps of the Appenine,
As in the sea-maid's coral-covered hall,
  I dwell. The record of past worlds are mine.
This earth, before my sight shall shrink and fall,
  And other planets, in her place, shall shine !
Earth, stars, and suns are but as lighted waves,
Succeeded still by others from their graves.

Yon nebulæ, like diamond-dust in air,
  Countless as sparkles in a world of seas,
Shall, every one, with our big sun compare,
  Claiming their satellites to roll at ease ;
Pale, friendly moons, that will be thought as fair
  As is our own, growing by small degrees,
To the round fulness of their orbits, to decay
In their rotundities—and pass away !

And thus, in endless newness, shall the light,
  Like fruits and flowers, spring forth, bloom, fade and die ;
Thus Day shall ever rise, and thus shall Night
  Succeed, to fall, that Day may walk the sky,
An emblem of the glorious Maker's might !
  A heart of life that shall for aye supply
Matter and motion with a ceaseless round
Of infinite perfection, grand—profound !

The scrolls of antient kingdoms I unfold ;
    Decypher the dim symbols of the Past,
And make intelligible themes of old ;
    So that e'en children may peruse the vast
And ever-during hieroglyphics rolled
    Round mould'ring mummies, long ignobly cast
'Mid Memphian pyramids. I speak a lore
That long hath slept mute in Oblivion's core.

Kings, that seem wreathed with haloed crowns of light—
    Shrouded with amaranthine holiness—
Whose names, too long, were spell-words for the Right
    To waken Liberty, shall, in a motley dress,
Appear foul-hearted with their deeds of spite ;
    While masquerading bigots shall confess
That they were merely mockers of the just,
Deserving Hate to spurn their worthless dust.

Warriors shall stand before ye ; men, renowned,
    (Whom strumpet Fame belied by calling good),
Not with the victor's trophied-laurel crowned,
    But dripping with a nations' dearest blood !
Men, bartering Christian thousands for the sound
    Of Glory's vaunting voice ; who poured a flood
Of reeking gore to saturate the ground,
That lisping sycophants and knaves might run
Shouting, " *This chief a hundred battles won !*"

And classic climes shall cast their mighty dead
    Resuscitated on this earth again,
To be adjudged and in the balanced weighed !
    Then shall be scanned the Poet's lauding strain,
And Truth, once more, in spotless robes arrayed,
    Uplift her voice ; nor shall her words be vain !
Popes, potentates and priests shall there assemble,
The just shall weep for joy—the wicked tremble.

Patriots shall leap from out the hidden mound,
    And, trumpet-voiced, arouse the nation's ire ;
Imperial knaves, in horror at the sound,
    Shall quail before their elocution's fire ;—

Hampdens, and Tells, and Kossuths shall be found
    Clad in the mail of Freedom's bright attire.
I will awake the Evil and the Good,
And they shall roll before me as a flood !

Aye, and the uncomplaining poor, the scorned—
    Whose deeds, whose memories, never found a tongue
To sermonise the tyrant, shall be mourned ;
    Then shall the earth deplore the *cause of wrong*,
And scoffs reproachful bitterly be turned
    Against th' oppressors, who delighted long
To trample, maim, destroy the minds that rose,
Superior to their own, 'mid want and woes.

To gorgeous mansions and to hovels drear,
    To glittering state and abject Poverty,
Oh, Man, I will conduct thee ! and thine ear
    Shall drink from mingled fountains ; thou shalt be
A dweller with the peasant and the peer ;
    Weep with the sad, rejoice amidst the free ;
To-night upon a silken couch to lie,
To-morrow freezing 'neath a wintry sky.

I hear thee whisper, " tell me what thou art ?"
    My misson's one of kindness, mercy, love !
To heal the wounds that fester in thy heart ;
    The myst'ry that besets thee to remove ;
To make the Evil wince beneath the smart
    Of conscious guilt ; with fervor to reprove
Whatever tends to chain the champion Mind,
That should be free to rove as wave'or wind.

To tell thee what I *am,* or whence I *sprung,*
    Or e'en my *destination,* when my goal
I've gained, hath been denied a seraph's tongue :—
    When *thou* shalt know what forms *thy* secret soul,
Or tell the cause why God permits the wrong
    To sway man's heart, and e'en His grace control,
Thou, from thy alchemy, may'st then unfold
A wisdom greater than creating gold.

But hark ! our sister Spirits wake their lyres ;
   And while the purpling Iris yields her tone
To the chromatic preludes of their wires,
   The golden strings give cadence all their own :—
Now Inspiration lights her holy fires,
   And perfumed censers of sweet thoughts are thrown ;—
Silence hangs list'ning, while her waving wings,
Motion the time to which each Spirit sings.

SONG OF THE SPIRITS.

FIRST SPIRIT.

DEEP within the ocean lies
Light that floated o'er the skies ;
Slumber hangs o'er half the earth,
Soon to pass and give Care birth ;
Grief and Sorrow, Madness, Pain,
Bringing to mankind again !
   Haste, ye Spirits of the Night,
Shed your visions calmly bright ;
Sooth the wretched heart and head ;
Hover kindly round his bed ;
Lend him pleasure in his sleep,
Do not let him wake to weep !

CHORUS OF SPIRITS.

Mortals, slumber, and inherit
Joys that crown the happy spirit.

SECOND SPIRIT.

I must to yon cradle lone,
   Where an infant's lying ;
Wave my wing and sooth its moan,
   While its mother's dying.
Then I'll to the murd'rers cell,
   Where its father slumbers ;
Soon he'll hear that prison-bell
   Which his moments numbers.

CHORUS.

Mortals, slumber, and inherit
Joys that crown the happy spirit.

THIRD SPIRIT.

Trembling from Despair I flew,
    There foul shades abide !
Rage his wife and infant slew,
    Sunk a suicide !
One bright coin their lives had saved,
    But a miser near
Grasped the pittance they had craved—
    Death bestowed a bier.

CHORUS.

Mortals, slumber, and inherit
Joys that crown a happy spirit.

FIRST SPIRIT.

Haste then, Guardians of the Night,
Morning comes with smiling Light !
Then our mission *we* begin,
Battling with the chiefs of sin.
Rankling Envy, boasting Pride,
Lust and Anger, Fratracide !
Hypocrites we must behold ;
Superstition, madly bold ;
Zealots crouching to the base ;
Men, that savage wolves disgrace,
Mingling with the pure and good,
Pois'ning Mercy in the blood.
Hope with Frenzy, Joy with Sadness ;
Love with Hatred, Mirth with Madness ;
Evil hearts with saintly speech ;
Tongues that would e'en heaven impeach !
    But my mission is below,
    Guardians of the Gloom, I go !

CHORUS.

Mortals, wake ! and, by your merits,
Earn the guidance of just spirits.

KIND WORDS AND HARSH WORDS.

LIKE the footsteps of angels that gild as they go,
Are the accents of kindness, sweet, tender and low ;
Falling soft as the breath of Æolian sighs,
Changing tears into rainbows of peace in the skies.
Harsh words are like thunder, they fill us with dread ;
The dark brow is scowling, the eye flashes red ;
While the weak, erring mortal, bereft of reply,
Sees pity evanish, like light from the sky.

Kind words are like morning, with pearls on her brow ;
To the infant, like beautiful roses, they glow ;
They bring gladness to childhood, and honor to youth ;
Oh, blest be that speaker with love in his mouth !
Harsh words are volcanoes all lava and flame,
Desolating Love's garden in ruin and shame ;
Kind words flow like music when stars gem the hill,
Or, like oil on life's ocean, bid fury "be still !"

Oh, 'tis not the tempest that wakens our love !
'Tis the smile of the Iris, the voice of the dove ;
'Tis the whisper that leads to sweet home and its hearth ;
Gives the wanderer rest, and the sorrowful mirth !
If to poise a steel needle on water to swim,
Needs the delicate fingers and firmness of limb ;
So to place a young mind on Truth's waters to move,
Needeth care the most gentle—a parent's best love.

We wind up our watches with vigilant care,
As their balance of motion is ruled by a *hair ;*
Some tenderly turn our loved offspring in youth,
By the *key of affection*, to honor and truth.
For, as snow-flakes descending insensibly grow,
Till they form a huge barrier—a mountain of snow ;
So words of unkindness make ice of the heart,
For the streams of life's sympathies freeze and depart.

Let your chidings be spoken in blandness of breath,
As though you were seated near sickness or death ;
Consid'rate and kindly ; still weaving that chain,
Which may link blessed hopes to the murmurs of pain.
Yes, speak gentle words, for, like infants, we creep
To gather wild flowers by the brink of a steep ;
One word of loud anger, we startle and fall,
But the sight of Love's bosom our doom may recal !

THE HEAVENLY HAME.

THE day was just closin',
For the sun was reposin'
On his low crimson couch wi' its fringes o' flame ;
When my lo'ed bairn was lyin',
Pale, wasted an' dyin',
Just wearin' awa' to her heavenly hame.

Oh, I mark'd her face brighten,
Like clouds when they lighten,
Her lips faintly murmured her ain mither's name ;
Her white hands were lifted,
Like snaw newly drifted,
An' her looks were fast fixed on her heavenly hame.

Oh, your een wad hae glisten'd
Wi' tears, had ye listen'd
To words, that like stars through the broken clouds, came ;
They were saft, sweet and tender,
Just as angels might render,
When penitent sighs reach their heavenly hame.

There was balm in their breathin',
Like incense-clouds wreathin',
An' fauldin' wi' fragrance the censer o' flame ;
They were Faith's surest token,
An' the last that were spoken :—
"*I see a licht, mither! I'm no far frae hame!*"

THE NORTHUMBERLAND LIFE-BOAT.

GOD speed the brave Northumberland,
   Let honor crown his name ;
Let heart and hand, on sea and strand,
   His noble deeds proclaim.
Now gallantly we mount the brine,
   The sinking ship to gain ;
And we float in his boat
   O'er the wild and stormy main ;
Though surges lash, we onward dash
   O'er the wild and stormy main.

Let tempests rage around us,
   Let mountain-billows sweep ;
Our Boat's a Northern Diver bold,
   And skims the rolling deep.
The howling waste of boiling foam,
   Bursts over us in vain ;
As we float in our boat
   O'er the wild and stormy main ;
When surges lash, we onward dash
   O'er the wild and stormy main.

Cheer up, ye drooping mariners
   That crowd the found'ring wreck !
The Prize-Boat of Northumberland
   Shall snatch ye from the deck !
Tear down that signal—hush your cries—
   Your cannon's roar restrain !
As we float in our boat
   O'er the wild and stormy main ;
Though surges lash, we onward dash
   O'er the wild and stormy main.

Long hath the tyrant Ocean
   Warred 'gainst the pilot-crew ;
E'en when the stranded bark was cleared,
   Their Life-Boat overthrew !
Now, thanks to brave Northumberland !

These dangers we disdain ;
  While we float in his boat
    O'er the wild and stormy main ;
We hold the Chart from mighty Art,
    On the wild and stormy main.

Ye hardy Sons of Neptune,
    Ye dwellers on the deep ;
Ye fishermen who win your bread
    While thousands soundly sleep ;
Ye wives and children of the brave,
    Raise high the grateful strain !
While we float in our boat
    O'er the wild and stormy main ;
While rescued throngs join in your songs
    On the wild and stormy main.

————

ROWING AGAINST THE CURRENT.

Ah, many are the boatmen
    Upon the stream of life ;
And few escape the currents
    Of trouble, care and strife!
To buffet breeze and billow,
    And stem the rushing surge,
We must forsake the pillow,
    And bravely onward urge.

'Tis morning.   On the waters
    Yon heart-linked pair behold !
The maid, fair as Love's daughters,
    Her boatmen, young and bold.
Wild is the gale and blustering ;
    The current rough and strong;
Still tugs and toils the boatman,
    'Gainst wind and tide along.

Fear chills the maiden's bosom ;—
　Upon the scowling skies,
While trembling at the tempest,
　She turns her tearful eyes.
Mute is her tongue of music ;
　Her quivering lips, apart,
Grow paler, as sad sighings
　Come bursting from her heart.

Urge on, urge on, young boatman,
　The promised land's in view !
Yonder's the village steeple—
　Cheer up ! Be gallant—true !
Wearied !　Nay, do not falter !
　One lusty effort more,
Brings thee to Joy's bright altar,
　To bliss unknown before !

Gain'd is the goal !　Oh, rapture
　Swells now the maiden's breast !
The storm is soon forgotten—
　Two faithful hearts are blest.
Come then, down-hearted neighbour,
　Thou hast been idle long ;
Take Hope's good oars and labour,
　Like the boatman of my song.

SAILING WITH THE STREAM.

'Tis Evening ; and the rainbow
　Bears up the bending sky ;
The waves are gently creeping ;
　The winds in whispers sigh.
The clouds, with blushes glowing,
　Swim reflected on the tide ;
As down the stream are going
　The boatman and his bride.

Her looks have lost all sadness ;
   Her lips breathe sweetest balm ;
Her bosom glows with gladness :
   Her brow is smoothly calm.
Cheek to warm cheek is lying ;
   Heart throbs to heart as one ;
Truth to fond Love replying—
   Thus they go sailing on !

Look on those happy creatures,
   Amid the tranquil scene !
Thou saw'st the morn's stern features,
   Thou know'st what gales have been.
But the winds have stilled their roaring,
   The stream steals smooth as oil ;
The maid sighs not deploring ;
   The boatman knows no toil.

The fond pair list the cooing
   Of cushats in the wood,
And imitate their wooing,
   Calm sailing with the flood.
While Day is slowly wending
   His journey to the deep ;
And the moon's the vault ascending,
   To guard the lov'd in sleep.

Life thus presents its changes,
   And emulates the moon ;
Now sorrow joy estranges,
   Now pleasure glows like noon !
On the deep flood of chances,
   Like wandering barks we seem ;
Now lab'ring 'gainst the current,—
   Then sailing with the stream.

PADDY'S VALENTINE.

ARRAH, Judy, ye sint me a beautiful letther,
   Wid cuckoos an' pigeons, an' hearts bladin'red ;

Bud yoursilf is a creathur thin Vanus much betther,
   Becase you're alive, an' the t'other is dead !
Fait, ye blarney me, Judy ! you're takin' me aff, now !
   To flatther my looks when you know that I squint ;
Bud my voice is delightful—that's barrin' my cough, now ;
   Shure, why did ye put Paddy's faturs in priut ?

Och. Judy, I love yees much betther thin roses ;
   (I'm fander ov praties than tastin' the flowers);
They may sarve for to tickle the gintlemen's nosés,
   Bud their breath's not so swete as thim red lips ov yours.
The moon's a big lanthern sit up in the sky, now ;
   The stars are bright buttons that give a bit glame ;
Bud your face Judy, darling —widout e'er a lie, now—
   Has more hate in one smile thin the comets ov flame.

My heart fell to batin' the first time I view'd ye!
   The hair down your neck stramed like shadows on snow ;
I was clane out ov breath at your dancin' dear Judy !
   Och ! I lost my *cross looks* wid delight at the show !
For you're nate, little feet, like white rabbits, kept playin'
   At huntin' the slipper from under your skirt ;
In the wet, rainy weather my coat I'll be layin',
   Jist to keep your soft trotthers, luve, out ov the dirt !

Heaven smooth the white pillow you're restin' your cheek on !
   An' blist be the blanket that covers ye warm !
Och ! I am dead wid the ague, bud cure I am seekin'—
   Let me feel your soft neck on the thick ov my arm !
Fait, content would I live jist your bed powl to be, now,
   To stand the long night lookin' down on your face ;
Though I doubt wid the mattress I wouldn't agree, now—
   I'd be lavin' my *post*, and be takin' its place.

I'm no fist at the pothooks, so, Judy, be aisy !
   Take my spells as ye git them—they're honest, like Pat ;
I wasn't ordained wid much larnin' to taze ye ;
   Och, sildom the scholards can iver git fat !
Bud I'm not to be kicked, though my eyes aren't twins, now ;
   I can carry the monkey wid lime up a spout ;
Thin take me on thrial, and show your fine sinse, now,
   Och ! an' if I don't plase ye—thin bundle me out !

THE WIDOW'S SON OF NAIN.

There's a sound of loud wail at the portal of Nain,
And a widow laments in the fulness of pain ;
For the hope of her bosom lies stricken and cold,
Her son, her last hope, she no more shall behold.

And the tears of the people are streaming in grief,
But none can afford the poor widow relief ;
For her son hath departed ; they bear him away
To his rest in the tomb, to his couch in the clay.

And his mother in wretchedness waileth aloud,
While a moan of pure sympathy thrills through the crowd ;.
She clasps her pale fingers and holds them on high,
And wearies with praying the pitying sky.

The Scribe and his daughter are weeping to see,
And tears wet the cheek of the proud Pharisee ;
And the soldier-centurion looks on with a sigh,
For *he*, too, hath sons, and *his* children must die.

And the virgins are sobbing with sadness sincere,
For the youth lying cold to their bosoms was dear ;
He was faithful to goodness, and fair to the eye,
And they sorrow to know that e'en Virtue must die !

Why rolls back the crowd like a wind-broken wave ?
What arrests the sad progress of death to the grave ?
Who is *he*, with meek beauty, now seen to appear ?
See ! he lifts his white hand ; he approaches the bier !

Hushed as night is that throng, and the bearers stand still ;
" *Arise* !" speaks His voice ; death departs at his will ;
Lo ! the son of that widow, like morn from the gloom,
Awakes and arises from night and the tomb !

Oh, who can depicture the heart-bounding joy,
When the widow embraced the warm form of her boy ?
She wept with delight ; kissed her son now restored,
And blest the great mercy of Jesus her Lord !

TO ELIZA COOK.

ELIZA ! now thou can'st not veil thy face :
  I gaze upon thee, and thy piercing eye,
  Soul-fraught, look'st purest Posey !
Thy forehead calm, with intellectual grace ;
Thy artless tresses o'er thy cheeks I trace :
Thy lips compressed, where sorrow's sombre shade,
Trembling to dwell, a dimpled nook hath made.
  Methinks, I see thy Mother's arms around
Thy lovely neck, and thee, with fondest look,
Each eye-tear-filled and shining like a brook,
  Clasping her neck in turn ; as flowers are found .
Mingling their balmy petals wet with dew :
Like flower and leaf—the child and parent true,
Whisp'ring their fragrant loves which seem forever new.

TO FRIENDSHIP.

THERE is a glorious link in Nature's chain,
  That binds heart, soul, mind, feeling, into one
  Magnificent delight. 'T is when the sun
Of regal Friendship holds his golden reign,
  And triumphs in the splendour of his sway :
'T is when the kindred leaping of the vein,
And the responsive breast, beat free from pain.
  Oh, is there ought in this dull waste of clay
Like goodly Friendship ? 'T is the welcome Spring
  Amid the desert of departed fame ;
'T is the warm, downy plumage of Hope's wing
  That fans to life Joy's just-expiring flame !
Friendship, thou art a stream that wanders free,
Bright with the glow of immortality !

TO MUSIC.

"Oh, give me Music, for my soul doth faint!"

MUSIC! thou art to me a healing balm,
    So sweetly soothing that I'd walk with Grief,
    That thy sweet charms might yield again relief.
MUSIC! I love thee, in the storm or calm—
    In the faint murmur of the dying breeze,
Wafted in perfume o'er the mirrored lake;
    Or, in the tumult of the raging seas,
When the loud, bursting thunder-tones awake,
    Rolling the chorus mightly along,
'Till mount, and rock, and echoing welkin, shake
    With the deep laughter of the boist'rous song!
MUSIC, I love thee! wilt thou grant to me
Thy soothing strains when sick and low I be?
Yes, give my soul the kiss of melody!

TO A POET'S WIFE.

THE pen is but a feeble engine of the heart,
    For Love, like Truth, lies in our breasts concealed;
    'T is but the di'mond's lustre, half revealed,
Failing the gem's bright substance to impart.
    Fain would I sing of *one*, with eloquence,
And find rapt sounds to wing it from my soul;
But oh! words are but breathings of the whole;
    Dim rays of what we love; the moon's pretence
For telling how the sun can burn and glow;
The semblance paper beareth to the snow,
    Which seemeth pure until the snow is shown:
    So pen and tongue must let my love alone.
That I do fondly, truly, dearly love, I vow;
And that my fondest, truest, dearest wife, art thou!

THE RAILWAY KING!

THE Railway King is the king for me!
As the light on the hills, as the foam on the sea ;
As the wing of the eagle, outstripping the gale ;
As a meteor, he darts o'er the sounding rail !
His coursers rush, panting, with burning vein,
Unchecked by the mountain, uncurbed by the main ;
Like a bolt of red lightning, from clouds they spring,
Snorting their joy to the Railway King !

Oh! the Railway King, like his sire, old Time,
Worketh wonders on earth with his steeds sublime ;
He rendeth the rocks that had Time defied,
Humbling the hills in their cedared pride.
Your Cæsars—your Hannibals—what were they ?
Poor plodders to fame, by a weary way !
Their elephant-armies would now take wing,
By the outstretched plumes of the Railway King.

The desert's dry waste and the dread simoom,
Where the camel-borne Arab finds tent and tomb,
Are terrors that soon shall cease to appal,
For the King of the Rail shall conquer all.
The precipice steep and the dark ravine,
A smooth shaven surface shall soon be seen ;
The chamois and ibex to plains shall cling,
And leap at the bell of the Railway King.

Ye forest majestic ! your hearts shall quail,
As ye bow to the throne of the mighty Rail !
He cometh ! ha ! ha ! for his giants behold,
Sunning their locks with the summer's gold !
His dominion the earth shall proudly know,
Till man shall be summoned with Time to go :
But we heed not the sage while this song we sing,
Hurrah ! long life to the Railway King !

STANZAS.

Ah, cruel Fate !
That hold'st in captive chain
The desolate,
How dare I tell my pain ?
How dare I say to thee, I love,
When the cold world will disapprove ?

Yet, what to me
Are worlds without thy smile ?
Sad misery,
That hope can ne'er beguile !
For how can Hope in me remain,
When Love, its spirit, lives in vain ?

Ah, gentle Fair,
Why did thine eyes prevail ?
Delusive snare !
My bosom wears no mail,
To turn the darts that leave thy bow,
Empoisoned with the sweetest woe !

No magic spell
Have I the thrall to break !
If *thou* can'st tell
How I may conquer, speak !
Alas ! I fear thy words can never
Dissolve the charm they bound for ever !

Thy snowy hand
The mystic pen can wield ;
Thou may'st command
Thy slave to fly and yield
His wounded heart to other arms,
While he will kiss thy written charms.

Oh ! that mine eyes
Thy face had ne'er beheld !
For burning sighs
My bosom since have swelled ;
Yet sighs and tears are balm to me,
When they are breathed and shed for thee !

NEVER SAY YOU ARE POOR.

To succeed in this world, do you know
That appearance wins half of the prize ?
You must strive to maintain a good show,
And *seem* to be great'in men's eyes.
The book when most splendidly bound,
Though bereft of all wisdom and lore,
Hath often more countenance found,
Than the volume whose clothing is poor.

The nightingale's song gives delight,
When the ravishing bird is unseen ;
But bring the enchantress to sight,
And the critic despises its mien :—
While the beautiful Paradise-bird
For its plumage is held in great store ;
Thus dress to true worth is preferred—
Take the hint—*never say you are poor !*

The flippant, the empty—the vain—
Bedizen'd with jewels and gold,
More esteem from the affluent gain,
Than the wise with his garniture old.
A plague-spot is seen on the cheek—
There's infection in poverty's core ;
Let man write as a seraph would speak,
He's contemned when he's found to be poor.

'Tis true, there are men on the earth,
Who from poverty never have turned ;
But how few pay a tribute to worth,
Till the loss of his genius is mourned.
Some may laud his sweet music in life,
Still they leave the sad wretch to deplore ;
They have heard with the world he's at strife,
And forsake him because he is poor !

He is dead ; now conviction appears !
Now his works bear the multitude's praise ;

There's a torrent of counterfeit tears—
    The whole world is in love with his lays.
" Let the marbles his lineaments save ;
    " Let his fame spread the universe o'er !"
Oh, mock not the bones in his grave !
    Don't you know that their owner was poor !

THE WEARY LADDER OF LIFE.

I'M sittin', dear Phil, an' I'm dolefully chimin'
    O'er the poverty-throubles that bother love's smiles ;
Don't I see ye, poor sowl up the ladther slow climbin',
    Wid a hodful ov lime for the man on the tiles ?
Och hone! grammachree! bud this life's a quare ladther,
    Which ivery clay-morthal's compill'd to ascind !
The furder we rise, sure, the road becomes sadder,
    An' are we not weary before the stips end ?

Fait, the nobles git up to the tap widout trouble ;
    Because their *hod's* impty—an' sometimes their *head*—
Bud the poor man has loads both of sinse an' pains double,
    An', wid lashins ov work, on peraties is fed.
Niver heed, Philic, boy ! there's small faut to your risin' ;
    Your high ilevation no morthal can blame ;
For the stips yees be takin' I'm far from despisin',
    God grant that grand haroes won glory the same !

I fancy young luvers life's ladther is tryin ;
    How they smirk wid clane joy as their journey begins !
Bud sorrow will come ; as they mount they'll be cryin',
    "Bad luck to cross fortune, we're breakin' our shins !"
Arrah, see, to the crowds of deludin', proud craturs,
    The bashful an' beautiful fall at their feet ;
Would ye think, now, to gaze on the gintlemen's faturs,
    That the devil could musther sich imps ov desate ?

Now down your *own* ladther, dear Phil, ye are craepin',
    Wid the lime on your timples—that's age wid its snow—
Thin, again on your shouther fresh morthar you're heapin',
    That's the turf on your breast whin they bury ye low.
Come, keep up your heart, Phil, the priest's often told us
    That a ladther, like Jacob's, has rest in the sky ;
I trust it's a strong'un, at onct, Phil, to hould us—
    Though, *when we get wings*, to the tap we can fly !

THE LAZY FRATERNITY.

AMELIA'S a girl of good looks,
    But her eyes wear a dull, stupid haziness ;
She's fond of no work, and her books
    Are dispatched in the hurry of laziness.
Her sister, Maria, sits still,
    Her excuse is oppressive obesity ;
She does nothing, for work makes her ill,
    So to idleness clings with tenacity.

Her brother is always asleep—
    To the Sloth he's compared by the neighbours ;
His mesmerical trances are deep,
    For at nothing but snoring he labours.
Our youngest's a lad scarcely five,
    But too much of a stoic for talking ;
Though his appetite proves him alive,
    His legs yet have never known walking.

All things, in and out of the house,
    Like statutes, look quiet, marmorean ;
The cat sleeps unheeding the mouse,
    The dog is a true Pythagorean.
The kitten's to lazy too play ;
    The clock is a stopping chronometer ;
The parrot dreams night and by day ;
    Rust hath nailed to " *set-fair* " the barometer.

The door-bell's too lazy to ring :
  The servant's too lazy to clean it ;
The kettle's too hoarse for to sing,
  And the fire's *too low* for to mean it.
No washing is done in our cot !
  The soap is too stubborn for lathering ;
Dirty linen you'd think might be got ?
  No ! the dirt is two lazy for gathering.

The beds I'd send out to be made,
  But Amelia's so oft their possessor ;
On the hearth-rug Maria is laid,
  While young Tom snores aloud on the dresser.
The carpets, like grave-yards, are full
  Of the dry dust of years, if not ages ;
You can't step without kicking a *scull*,
  Though you'll ne'er touch the *bones* of the *sages.*

My horse is an idle old hack ;
  The pigs lie all day in a litter ;
The cows of fine milk needn't lack,
  But they won't chew the cud, 'cause it's bitter.
The hens have agreed *not* to lay ;
  The cock might as lief be a *weather ;*
One summer with *me* makes no hay ;
  Suns and servants are lazy together.

Such a mixture of life and of death,
  Our family circle produces,
That the bellows might furnish us breath,
  But they'll die by our idle abuses.
Some may fancy my sketch overdone,
  And say my production is craziness ;
But as " nothing's new under the sun,"
  There's nothing here *old* in life's laziness.

LIBERTY OF CONSCIENCE IN RELIGION.

As the vast ocean on its bosom beareth
  Fair ships of every size ;
As countless stars the sun's wide splendor shareth,
  And gem the azure skies ;
So diff'rent creeds to *one, grand port* sail on ;
So various faiths keep circling round Truth's sun.

Is *thy* religion, what thou deemest, holy ?
  E'en so, believe, and rest ;
But spurn not *others* with pretentions lowly, -
  For they may be the best.
Doth ceremonial pomp comprise thy creed ?
If so, thy hopes hang on a broken reed !

Hast thou deep charity for *all* opinions *!*
  Dost give *all* hearts their sway ?
Or, dost thou, in Exclusion's cold dominions,
  Chain *all* who leave thy way ?
Believe me, brother, this intol'rant claim
Destroyeth Love, and blurs Religion's name !

The humble valley, in its beauty vernal,
  The sun doth not despise,
But gives that glow, denied to Alps eternal,
  Beneath whose frown it lies.
Thus lowly hearts are blest with Virtue's fires,
While Charity in Pride's chill breast expires.

What ! shall th' unbounded sea of Mercy flowing—
  God's fountain full and free—
Be as a creeping rill in secret going
  To bless alone but *thee ?*
Behold yon rainbow ! in its circling span
It clasps all Nature and embraceth Man !

Oh, tell me not that God the *few* hath chosen,
  And that the *many* die !
The sun, the sea, the earth,—hills fertile—frozen—
  Will all give thee the lie !
God's Mercy, Wisdom, Glory, are unbounded ;—
And thus, vain Man, thy Reason lies confounded !

FACES PASSING IN THE STREET.

THERE's wisdom in the leaf and flower,
  In every bud that blows ;
Each rain-drop of a Summer shower
  A homily bestows.
The stars are eloquent in light ;
  The air with lore's replete ;
And tomes of truth we may indite
  From faces in the street.

Behold yon merry, rosy child,
  Besides the church-gates playing !
His eye is bright, his laugh is wild,
  But ah ! his heart's decaying.
Ere wanes the year a sable crowd
  Upon these steps you'll meet ;
This jocund face will wear a shroud,
  And vanish from the street.

A beauty strikes the stranger's eye, —
  Her voice how rich in sound !
Her cheeks are tinged with healthy dye,
  With love her form is crowned !
The mask hath fallen from her face ;
  There's ruin near her feet ;
A pest-house is her dwelling place ;
  She's loathsome in the street !

Proud man, why dost thou knit thy brow ?
  From Want why turn away ?
Though riches fill thy coffers *now*,
  There comes a reck'ning day !
When scorn shall be repaid with scorn,
  When fortune shall retreat ;
When fawning friends shall from *thee* turn
  Their faces in the street !

Then the poor wretch who craves thy mite,
  To affluence shall rise ;

Oh, man ! had'st thou a prescient sight,
　Thou surely would'st be wise !
Birth, wealth and fame would then appear
　As blessing fickle, fleet—-
Ah ! thou would'st never turn thine ear
　From beggars in the street !

Life's panorama moves along
　With ever-varied view ;
First comes a gay and courtly throng,
　And then a starving crew !
The rolling chariots of the gay,
　Then cold and naked feet ;
Light hearts and forms of deep dismay
　Keep passing in the street.

———

THE HEART'S QUESTIONINGS.

Whither, oh, whither have our friends departed ?
Friends that, like Summer, round our bosoms lingered ;
Shedding their haloes on our days of gladness,
　　　　　Loved and delighting !

Linked are our feelings to their mem'ries honored ;
Sweet the vibration from their choral hymnings ;
Spirits of beauty through the ether wand'ring
　　　　　Calm as the moon-beams.

Faces like angels, from the earth are faded ;
Gone, like meek vi'lets ;—leaf by leaf they wither'd—
Leaving their perfume, as their sweet rememberance,
　　　　　Floating around them.

Where are the young hearts that we loved in childhood—
Creatures that charmed us with the rainbow sunlight ?
Cold are their pulses, marble-like their smiling,
　　　　　Silently slumb'ring !

See yon fond mother tender lilies rearing
Over the dwelling where her fair babe's lying !
Check not her tear-drops watering the pale buds
       Mournfully blooming !

Time dims the eye-glance and the dark lock whitens ;
Wrinkles the forehead, renders forms unlovely ;
Scatt'ring the silver from the hoary temples ;—
       Blighting Life's garlands !

Soon will our dry leaves eddy round our tombstones !
Autumn shall sere them, Winter coldly grasp them ;
Time shall destroy them, but their spirits' fragrance
       Bloometh eternal !

HYMN TO MY MOTHER EARTH.

My Mother, Earth, I hail thee now,
  For thou art green and gay !
Bright streams, like pearly neclaces,
  Around thy bosom play.
Thy waving forests, like the plumes
  Above the conq'ror's brow,
Rise to the heavens in majesty—
  Creation's Queen art Thou !

As lightning wakes the seed to life,
  My soul thy clay possessed ;
Thou gavest to my embryo form
  The pulses of thy breast ;
And then my larva-bonds I burst.
  As nature gave me birth ;
Thy light and perfumed air I breathed—
  Thou art my Mother, Earth !

Within a cradle from thy woods
  My infant head reclined ;
Warm fleeces from thy mountain-flocks,
  My limbs in softness twined.

Mellifluous rills of strength—of life—
    From snowy founts were mine ;
For me thy fields gave varied fruits,
    Thy grapes gushed red with wine.

Beneath thy towering oaks I lay,
    Beside thy floods profound,
And drank inspiring draughts of joy,
    To view thy Spring-time crowned.
Rapture with roseate Summer came,
    And ecstasy had birth, •
To hear the voices of thy groves—
    Thy jubilee, oh Earth !

The glittering pomps that potentates
    And pontiffs proudly claim,
Without thee, Mother, were as dreams,
    Their glories but a name !
Their dazzling crowns, their priceless gems—
    Their equipage—their gold—
Would, like the sun of light bereft,
    Be valueless and cold !

Boundless is thy magnificence,
    Unknown thy precious stores !
Wealth lies in vast but hidden, heaps
    'Neath unsuspected shores.
Mother ! could'st thou at once reveal
    The fulness of thy worth,
Mankind would tremble at thy power,
    And bow to thee, oh Earth !

" Alas ! to Mammon oft they bow ;
    To Moloch's dripping throne !
War-fiends have crimsoned my green breast—
    My peace have overthrown !
Grim Juggernaut hath piled his slaves
    In deluged hills of slain ;
Down-trod my blissful bowers of love,
    And left red Slaughter's stain !"

Yes ! but the sacred holocausts
    Thy hallowed mountains blest !
Deep in thy groaning side, the cross
    Of Calvary was pressed !
Thy rocks were rended as a veil,
    And prophet-shades came forth,
And testified that Jesus died
    To save thy Sons, oh Earth !

Holy art thou, my Mother loved !
    Mankind should hold thee dear ;
Thou did'st Salvation's promised King
    Within thy bosom bear !
The sin-stains, by that Saviour's blood,
    Have vanished from thy brow ;
Resplendent are thy garments fair ;—
    Thou art Heaven's Temple now !

*   *   *   *   *   *

All things in *life* thou hast bestowed,
    For more I cannot crave ;
Yes, my kind Mother, when I'm *dead*,
    Give me a peaceful grave !
And, as thou lov'st thy Minstrel-child,
    Send thy pale flow'rets forth,
To deck the couch where I shall sleep
    With thee, my Mother Earth !

THE GOWAN AND THE DIAL.

A BONNIE gowan, fair an' sweet,
Sprung forth ae morn the day to greet ;
A rainbow hovered 'bune its breast,
Like some gay birdie o'er her nest ;
While butterfly an' hummin' bee,
Enamoured lingered on the lea,
An' stooped to kiss the gowan braw,
For lovelier flower they never saw.

Beside a dial-stane it grew,
On which the sun his shadows threw,
An' wi' Time's pencil marked the hour
That waked to life this infant flower.
No' aft a morn like this was seen,
Sae cloudless, cheerfu' an serene!
Ilk thing o' nature seemed to say,
"My heart wi' pleasure's fu' to-day."

Wi' deeper blush the roses blaw;
The lilies whiten their sweet snaw;
The vi'lets steal a richer hue
Frae the bright lift o' bonnie blue.
The lark sings sweeter on this morn—
Leaves his green couch amang the corn—
Fills the saft air wi' music's power—
Oh! a''things hail the gowan-flower!

The lines o' Time, wi' stealthy pace,
Were creepin' o'er the dial's face,
An' noon in heaven grew hot an' high,
While gloom was wandering o'er the sky.
The thirsty gowan bent its cheek
Amang the grass some dew to seek;
The sun the pearly drink had ta'en,
And for the gowan there was nane!

The Storm-king cam' wi' darkness crowned,
An' flash'd his fiery darts around;
Deep, muttering sounds were distant heard,
And thunder spak his awfu' word.
The hail rushed peltin' in a shower,
An' struck to earth fu' mony a flower;
But still the gowan had nae fear,
The dial's shelt'ring stane was near.

Vain shelter! when the Tempest's wrath
Swept e'en *the dial* frae his path;
Unsparin' the wee, cow'rin' gem,
That sunk wi' crushed and broken stem!

Alas, to slender hopes we cling,
That nought but dark destruction bring ;
And, like the gowan at our feet,
Find promised friendship vain deceit !

Wae's me ! some unexpected power,
Lays our puir bairnies like this flower !
We shield them wi' the tenderest care,
But death flings a' our joys in air !
Nae mair the hand o' Time shall trace
The hours upon that dial's face ;
For now the bonnie gowan's gane,
Where Time nor Shadow there is nane !

GIVE A KISS FOR A BLOW.

THE ruby-lipped roses yield perfume and love,
When the soft-stealing foot of the zephyr goes forth ;
When the gay, gilded butterflies dance through the grove,
And silence is making her couch on the earth.
When a beautiful canopy hangs o'er the sky,
Star-spangled with eyes of the spirits of light ;
When the fulness of love maketh rapture to sigh,
And the moon's filmy rainbow encircles the night.
'Tis a season of sweetness—tranquility—bliss—
While sleep to the eyelids falls soft as a *kiss !*

Now, look on *this* picture ! The roses are dead ;
The tempest of Winter is raging in wrath ;
No longer the butterflies' wings are outspread ;
Desolation and death strew the hurricane's path !
The mist-mantled ghosts of the mountains appear,
And shriek their shrill war-hoop to nature aghast ;
The moon, like the name-plate of crime on a bier,
Gleams hideously pale through the clouds on the blast.
Old Ocean roars madly, like giants in wo,
Or, like whales spouting gore from the harpooners' *blow !*

Come then, ye fair creatures of youth and delight ;
Ye children that bloom like the roses we sing ;
Let our pictures one moment's attention invite,
While Winter we place by your hand-maiden Spring.
Hush, hush ! let us list to the voices that rise !
Zephyr mingles her whisper with tempests that roar ;
Ah ! ye gaze at the love-stars bestudding the skies,
While ye shrink from each billow that lashes the shore !
Thus ye learn, buds of Promise, life's wisdom to show,
By resigning a *kiss*, and restraining a *blow !*

Had the Demon of Discord and Blows ne'er gone forth—
Had War's bloody banners ne'er darkened our plains ;
What millions of spirits had graced this green earth !
What millions of pulses had throbbed in life's veins !
Sneer at Peace, ye grim chiefs ; talk of " National Right !"
Blow loud the hoarse clarions of valor and fame !
Dye your steel in the hearts of your brethren in fight,
That fall for your glory ;—*that conquest is shame !*
He alone wins true glory who tenders his foe
A *kiss* of sweet Mercy instead of a *blow !*

DEATH O' THE WEE PET LAMMIE.

WAKE, rise, my wee lammie, 'tis late i' the morn,
The sun gaily shines on the bonnie ripe corn ;
Round their minnies, the pet things are sporting in glee,
An' lang hae they waited, my lammie, for thee.
Still thine e'en are fast closed—an' thy breath I no' hear ;
Cauld, cauld, is thy brow—Oh, my heart sinks wi' fear !
Look up, wi' ane glint o' thy lauchin' blue e'e,
My winsome, awake, or wi' grief I will dee !

" Pale, pale, as the snaw-drap, an' cauld as the snaw,
Is the cheek o' thy lammie,—its life's now awa' !
Nae mair will its voice send a thrill to thy breast,
For thy lammie is dead ! a' its pains are at rest."

I nursed my dear dautie wi' kindness an' care,
I shielded its delicate form frae the air ;
I nestled an' nursed thee, young charms o' my e'e,
Wae wae to my heart that my lammie should dee !

They hae ta'en my lo'ed lammie, an' laid it to rest,
Wi' the green wavin' grass o'er its bonnie white breast ;
They hae planted sweet flowers by the root o' a tree,
Where the robin mourns sadly, my lammie, for thee.
But I dreamed that my pet to a pasture was gane,
Where the bright rivers rin, an' where winter there's nane ;
To follow THE LAMB, *oh ! an angel to be*—
Then, why should I greet, my blest lammie, for thee ?

THE ROSE'S GRATEFUL ORISON.

As the sun-light, chaste and holy,
  Broke the purpling clouds of day,
A young Rose, with language lowly,
  Oped its ruby lips to pray.

Fragrant was its gentle sighing ;
  Grateful tears stood on its cheek ;
Blushes warm its face were dyeing—
  Nature taught it how to speak.

" Hail to Thee, Life's Source and Beauty !
  From Thy hallowed hands I came,
To perform a pleasing duty,
  To fulfil Thy end and aim !

" Wakened by the balmy fingers
  Of Thy spirits blest, unseen ;
While the matin-star yet lingers
  O'er the pearl-enameled green.

" I behold Thy throne above me,
  Where eternal sweetness dwells ;
View Thy seraph-stars who love me,
  And my sisters Asphodels.

" Thou with perfumed light hast crown'd me !
    Robed me in a lovely dress ;
Gathered fairest creatures round me,
    To behold, admire and bless.

" From the hour when dawning Nature
    Stole upon my opening sight,
To the present, Blest Creator !
    Nought I've known but pure delight !

" Still I cannot bloom for ever ;
    All things on this earth must die !
From the stem my leaves shall sever,
    And my heart shall withered lie.

" By the thorn amid my sweetness,
    Thou hast taught me life is vain ;
Yet I may not blame its fleetness,
    When I hope to bloom again.

" As my soul of fragrance liveth,
    To the heav'ns I may ascend ;
And when Peace her token giveth,
    With her blushing skies I'll blend !"

THE DESPAIRING OUTCAST'S SOLILOQUY.

I'M weary of my miserable life !
The daily round of labour, and the pangs
That lacerate my bosom into madness—
The burden of my life I cannot bear !
Why was I doomed this wretchedness to suffer ?
Come, Death ! I languish for the consummation
Of all life's agonies ! Strike deep the dart !
The churchyard fattens on the *bloated* corse !
My body is a skeleton, and yet
It hath not passed the boundaries of the living ;

Nor hath the marble jaws of dissolution
Swallowed its poverty ! *I* riot not
With charnel-worms as *yet !* I starve ! I starve !
But then, starvation is a common word !
Oh God ! not for myself my wail is raised ;
I have a progeny of pining innocents !
And what shall be *their* fate ?—Oh, die like *me* !
The last, dear wreck of furniture is sold !
My bed ? 'Tis long since any couch I pressed,
Save the mud-floor drenched with the winter rains,
Stenchy and loathsome as the grave I covet !
I have a wife ! Oh, would that she had died,
Ere the gaunt vulture, Poverty, appeared !
I cannot bear her fading form to see ;—
Her deep-sunk, dim-lit eyes that on me gaze,
Like fires within a hollow sepulchre.
Her cheeks are flattened by the ruthless blow
Of heartless Misery ; and her pale lips
Tremble between the hopes and fears of death.
    I look upon my children ; one is young,
Light-locked and joyful.   When the urchin laughs
I feel the poignard of a sharp despair
Chilling my vitals, and my hands I clench,
Demoniacal, to curse the lingering pulse
That keeps my heart alive to wretchedness !
How can I see sweet infancy's delight,
And know that griping want will come anon,
And brand his little, dancing heart with scars—
His merry laugh change to convulsion's pangs ?
He twines his hand in mine ! Forbear, my child !
The big, hot tears roll down my sallow cheeks,
And glisten on his hair.   There is a whisper
In that shining wo ! doth it speak of Hope ?
Away, deceiver ! thou can'st soothe no more !
Thy syren voice hath lost its tunefulness !
Thou sing'st unheeded to the roaring main !
The affluent demigods care not for *me !*
Look on yon pitchy clouds that low'ring hang,
Pregnant with rolling sounds of fatal note,
And think to find in the destructive bolt,
That hurls its vengeance to the trembling earth,

That pity which thy sinking spirit craves !
The thunder still booms on ; the arrowy light
Of its swift sword still slays and desolates.
There is no pity in the earth ! The skies
Look cold and cheerless ! Hope of life there's *none !*
There is no hope, nor help ; yes, fell Despair
Sends a bewildering solace to my brain.
The power that dwells within my dark resolve,
Frenzied to strength by coutumelious wrongs,
Sharpens the dagger and my fate impels ;—
The short and certain passage to the tomb.
What *must* be done I'll *do.*

> The witch of Time,
Perched on the barkless trunk of an old tree,
Croaks the discordant echo to my mind.
I grasp the steel ! Its brightness shows my face,
And tells me that my hair is hoary grown.
Hath age done this ? alas, 'tis icy wo
Hath dried the moisture from the fertile root ;
And my thick locks have blasted into age.
Oh, Life, thou problem, hidden, unresolved !
Made of ingredients as with mysteries !
Thou baff'lest all the chymistry of art ;
No alchemy can show the gold of mind ;
But what have I to do with mind or soul ?
I would that I had neither, and that Fate
Would hasten to complete my mortal misery.
Oh, I could whisper to the world a secret
That soon would find an echo ; for my words
Would open chasms deep in the wreck of Time,
And down their rifted fissures would appear
Thick, rolling, misty streams. Pale ghosts in throngs,
Riding their vapory steeds, and passing still
Huge—haggard—horrible--

> Hush ! hush ! my boy—
Thy mother's dying in thy father's arms !
She's gone, for whom with fate I battled hard !
I have no claim on life—Kiss me, my child !
The Outcast hath fulfilled his doom ! I die ! I die !

THE PEOPLE'S MAJESTY.

SCORN not the lowly men of earth
For lacking wealth and lordly birth;
Nor Labour's fustian robes deride,
For honest hearts beat high inside;
Though coarse the outward garbs may be,
They clothe a nation's majesty!

A nation's wealth by labour grows;
Toil giveth Pomp his meat and clothes;
The miner's pick, the gard'ner's spade,
Nay, *all* the tools of toil and trade,
Work, as wealth's engines, willingly,
And urge the wheels of majesty.

Talent is not to Rank confined;
Toil claims the royalty of Mind.
The forge—the stall—the plough—the loom—
Have taught undying lore to bloom.
In spite of boasting High Degree,
Labour hath immortality.

What are your crowns of gems and gold
But glitt'ring tinsel from earth's mould!
What the rich silks that deck your forms
But shining threads bequeathed by worms?
What is your princely blood to me
Compared with Virtue's ancestry?

What are your collars, garters, stars,
When dimn'd and stained by wicked wars!
Can that blue ribbon near your heart
A conscience calm, and peace impart?
The workman's apron seems to me
A nobler badge of majesty!

Imperial Pride ascends his throne,
As if the world was all his own;

Surrounded by the fawning great,
He deems his power above all fate ;
But what an abject thing is he,
Shorn of his people's majesty !

" *The People*" are two words of might,
The vanguard firm in hottest fight ;
The talisman of mystic power,
That never failed in danger's hour ;
The Pharos in dark Faction's sea,
The dome that shieldeth majesty !

And rulers in the nations vast,
As records prove in seasons past,
Have rued the day, bewailed the time,
When they opposed earth's power sublime ;
For they, as aliens, had to flee
Before the people's majesty.

But, Britons, *we* feel no dismay!
Our Queen we bless—uphold her sway ;
While she, to bind her subjects' hearts
With gentle chains, her love imparts,
That England's Throne may steadfast be,
Based on its people's majesty.

COMPLAINT OF THE DYING NUN.

PALE, on an iron couch, unheeded lying,
  Within a narrow prison, lone and chill,
Behold a Sister of the Order dying ;
Her bosom heaving with its hopeless sighing ;
  A victim to her father's bigot-will ;
A sacrifice of youth and beauty rare,
  Cast, like a broken flower, to wither, there !

Is there no gentle heart, with nature glowing,
  To raise this crushed and broken rose to life ?
Her tears, like some sad brook, must still keep flowing
In secret channels to the world's unknowing,

In drear seclusion with sweet Hope at strife !
Time, that to Guilt himself, doth yield relief,
Mocks her in wo, and spurns her abject grief.

" Why am I here, abandoned and forsaken ?
    Religion will not, *dare* not, claim the deed !
Affection may not say *she* hath partaken
Of this foul work ; for Nature's tones awaken
    Sweet sympathy to see my bosom bleed !
How could'st, thou, Father, doom me to this fate,
And leave thy only daughter desolate ?

" I am thy *only* child !   My mother dying
    Bequeathed my infant bosom to thy care ;
And thou did'st promise to her latest sighing,
Sealing with solemn oath thy words complying,
    That I should never breathe a convent's air !
But hypocrites beset thy will ; behold !
Thy daughter dies, and knaves shall clutch thy gold !

" Did He, the Great Creator, to whose Spirit
    The free-winged lark doth now his matins raise,
Ordain that we, His creatures, should inherit
Monastic gloom to find salvation's merit ;
    Or sing *alone* in convent walls His praise ?
Hark, to the chorussed voices of the sea,
They sing eternal songs of liberty !

" Spreading the vastness of the earth with gladness,
    And giving to each stream its dancing feet ;
Lifting each drooping plant from winter's sadness,
And proving that ingratitude is madness
    In all who choose a soulless, vain retreat,
For the wide space of God's created blessing,
Red'lent of joy, and therefore, worth possessing !

" Do we not change wise Nature's ample measures,
    Pervert her uses and lock up her gems,
When we in cells immure her holy treasures,
Blight all her buds, and mar Affection's pleasures ?
    We tear the clinging tendrils from the stems,
When we incarcerate the young and fair !
Did Heaven make Love to praise Him in despair ?

" Hearts there may be that, blighted and destroyed
    By the world's obloquy, here seek a grave !
Their love-springs are dried up—a desert void—
The bitterness of scorn seems unalloyed ;
    Through time they crawl, like some insensate wave
Of the Dead Sea that labours to the shore
To moan and die,—though it was dead before !

" Father ! thou brok'dst of hearts the truest—best ;
    Robbed me of all that woman cares to hold :—
He, who my love from infancy possessed,
Was driven from thy dwelling like a pest,
    Because he *had* affection but *no* gold !
Thou said'st his *creed* was different from mine own —
And did sweet Jesu die for *me* alone ?

" I dwell in solitude as in the tomb,
    A joyless corse, an animated bust ;
My life is flick'ring like a lamp in gloom ;
I'm buried in a charnel-house of doom ;
    My hopes of happiness on earth are dust !
But why repine ? alas, 'tis now too late—
For Death in kindness comes to arbitrate."

VANITY OF LIFE'S POSSESSIONS.

ONE by one my friends are falling,
    Soon my head with their's shall lie ;
Well ; content—there's nought appalling
    In the knowledge—*all* must die !

Let this care-worn carcase moulder,
    Scarce a meal the worms to feed ;
Can the grave be darker, colder,
    Than this world ! 'Tis not indeed !

Wealth—Possessions—Honor--Pleasure—
    Genius—Beauty—Youth, are found
Filling Life's alloted measure—
    What are all ? Just gaze around !

Wealth ?   A golden cloud of morning,
  Bright'ning in the noon-tide beam ;
With the evening fading, turning
  Grave-like, dark as Lethe's stream.

Vast possessions ? Ruins lonely,
  Crumbling into charnel-clay :
All the rest are grub-hives only,
  Wings they find and flee away.

Honors ? Titles ? Stars and Orders ?
  Hollow crystals blown by air !
Oft the earth's applause for murders—
  Ribbons woven by Despair.

Pleasures ? See yon rockets flying—
  Rushing through the startled gloom !
Now on earth how coldly lying !
  Libertine ! behold thy doom !

Beauty ? Loveliness and Splendor ?
  Will the tomb-worms fear to bite ?
No ! unheeding, *they* shall render
  You, vain gauds, a ghastly sight !

Youth ? Sweet roseate chaplets fading :—
  Rainbows, children of the sun !
Though in lovely vesture 'rayed in ;
  See the hues die, one by one !

Friendship ? Charming in the vision,
  Fatal oft as Eden's tree ;
Falsehood, cowled by dark Derision,
  Bids the promised blessings flee !

Love ?   The hecatomb of mortals,
  Where the burning soul is lost !
Bar yon bright, ethereal portals !
  Lust those regions never crossed.

Where is *Genius?* He whose soaring,
  Like the eagle near the sun,
And the mystic skies exploring,
  Dreamed that Glory might be won?

See him gathering gems, outshining
  All the wealth of earth and main,
Left to starve in mad repining,
  That his *mission* should be vain!

Scorned and jeered by all his neighbors,
  Them for whom his bosom yearned;
Sinking in his spirit's labors
  To be buried, praised, and mourned!

Let us then, since human pleasures,
  Like our bodies, change to clay,
Cling to Virtue's chastened treasures
  That can never know decay.

Treasures yielding Glory—Splendor—
  Youth and Beauty,—Wisdom,—Power—
All that Mercy's hand can tender—
  All that God from Heaven can shower!

SONG OF THE RAIL.

THE lover may chant his serenade,
  And the toper praise his wine;
But, in spite of all that's sung or said,
  There's nought like the railway line!
The eagle may cleave the misty sky,
  And the bounding ship may sail;
But give me the train that can speed amain,
  Like lighting along the rail!

CHORUS.

The rail, the rail! is the song we sing—
  Let the chorus never fail;
As the steam blows out, we will sing and shout,
  Hurrah for the glorious rail!

No more, my boys, with coaches slow,
    We drag along the road;
But swift as the swallow's wing we go,
    For our horses feel no load.
The whip-galled hack, with wearied back,
    Hath no cause to droop his tail;
Like time and tide is the nag we ride,
    And he *steams* it along the rail.

Hurrah for the name of STEPHENSON!
    Hurrah for the HAWTHORNS' tree!
Oh! green be the laurels each hath won,
    By land and the foamy sea.
The panting engine *puffs* their names,
    As it shoots through the distant dale;
Screaming its song as it skims along,
    And laughing, ho, ho! for the rail.

Now, wouldn't our good grandfathers stare
    This mammoth-coach to view,
Sweeping o'er rills, and cutting through hills,
    With a wing like the wild sea-mew?
Their fine old hearts with joy would glow,
    As they gazed on the rapid "mail;"
"Our sons," they would say, "may bless the day,
    For they travel—*to heaven* – by rail!"

The simoom's blast, o'er the desert vast,
    May heap up the scorching sand—
The camel may sink on the fountain's brink;
    But what traveller would pace the land,
When the railway swift, through the burning drift,
    Speeds on like the hurrying gale—
When the tenderest maid is ne'er afraid,
    But trusts every hope to the rail.

In days of old we've heard it told,
    That travellers made their wills—
When to London bound, their friends around
    Deplored their coming ills.

Now off we set without regret—
    At danger what heart need quail?
We fly by chance, to Spain or France,
    On the sweeping wings of the rail.

Oh, *space is lost!* and whats the cost?
    "Cheap trips" is now the word;
Directors wise good things devise,
    And pleasure to *all* afford.
God bless their schemes—may lines, like streams,
    Through every land prevail;
To bring us near to all that's dear—
    Three cheers for the glorious rail!

HOPE IN ALL THINGS.

" Ponet in pulvere os suum, si forte sit spes.'

MORTAL ! who e'er thou art, hope on !
    Let Hope thine anchor be ;
Steadfast to cling amid the wreck
    Of Life's tempestuous sea.
Quail not, though scowling, grim Despair,
Cast his black shadows round thy heart of care.

Hope on ! Behold yon gleaming speck,
    Now dimly, distant viewed,
May, one day, gild the sombre clouds
    Of thy heart's solitude !
That starry eye of Hope is given
To teach thee, man, that God's love lighteth Heaven !

Hope on ! amid the howling waste
    Where Desolation reigns ;
Where Horror, like an incubus,
    Broods o'er the dreary plains ;
Hope on ; faint not ; thy steps shall bring
Thy thirsty spirit to the gushing spring !

Hope on !—in all thy wretchedness—
    When Famine gnaws thy heart ;
When starving children die for bread,
    And thou can'st none impart ;
Let not their cries thy hope appal,
Use thy best means, and God will succour all !

Hope ye, *in all things*, cheerfully !
    There's balm in Hope's sweet breath ;
'Tis as the dew of fading flowers,
    The buckler unto death.
'Tis as the rainbow to our tears,
The seraph's voice to lull our bosom-fears.

Hope on—e'en though a sinner vile ;
    The spark of grace divine,
Shall make the dungeon of thy heart
    A bright, celestial shrine ;
Thy hope, like Magdalene's, shall rest,
Eternal in the regions of the blest !

OH, WAD MY GRAY LOCKS BUT TURN.

Oh, wad my gray locks but turn
    To the jet o' the raven's plume !
An' wad my dim e'en but burn,
    An' their sparkles o' youth resume !
Oh, Lizzy, that I were young ;
    Ye wadna hae love like me ;
Wi' my arms around ye flung,
    Right happy, my lass, we'd be.

Oh, Lizzy, but ye are braw !
    Like the stars i' the lift your e'en ;
Your feet an' your waist sae sma',—
    Dark locks, like the silken sheen.
Your lips, like the clefted rose ;
    Your teeth, like the ocean-pearl ;
Your bonnie white forehead an' nose ;
    Oh, Lizz, you're a charmin' girl !

As you sail on the sea in your boat,
   Wi' your jacket o' hollan' sae white,
You seem, like some birdie, afloat,
   Or a cloud in the calm moon-light.
I gaze on thy form wi' tears,--
   But its daft in a fule like me ;
For I double the count o' thine years,
   An' my wife, Lizz, thou never may'st be.

Now sin' I am auld an' gray,
   An' canno' ca' thee, my ain ;
For a blessin' on thee I'll pray
   That thy breast nae grief may ken.
For this warld's like the changefu' sea,
   An' *maun* hae its tantrums o' strife ;
But I trust that thy God will be
   Thy anchor in storms o' life !

THE PUIR AULD MAN'S DITTY.

Fu' dowie an' drear is the tale frae the auld ;—
'Tis the wail o' the nicht when the winds russle bauld ;
'Tis the grane that is heard through green willows to creep,
As they bend o'er the sod where our lost bairnies sleep.
Will ye heed an auld man ?   Ninety winters are gane,
Syne my mither, wi' joy, ca'd her Robin, her ain ;
Syne the morn when my father knelt down by his chair,
An' prayed that his Maker wad guide me wi' care.

Ninety years ! I look back to a land far awa',
That I seem to hae travelled in nae space ava' ;
An' I won'er to think how the rocks, hills and streams,
Could hae slipp'd frae my feet ;—hae I wandered in dreams ?
Wae's me ! ilka step comes like bells on the wind,
Oh ! I hear a' the voices, that ance spak' me kind ?
I see the wee gowans, still bonnie in bloom,
Ah ! sune will they grow by the side o' my tomb.

The hame o' my childhood nae langer is seen ;
The cottage is gane, where aft happy I've been !
The loch at my feet, where the siller trout play'd,
Seems to sab at the changes that Ruin hath made !
They levelled the brae, an' they felled the auld tree,
Where the names of my Jean an' her Rab's used to be ;
Like that tree I maun fa', an' they'll fill up the brae
Wi' the mools o' the kirk where I'll sleep to decay.

When I was a callant, young, feckless an' braw,
Unheedin' what breeze frae the welkin might blaw,
I felt as if sorrow were naething to thole,
For it never had bound my glad heart in control.
My sheep wandered happy ; I whistled, an' sang
The bonnie Scots ballants, the simmer-day lang ;
At nicht, a snug corner, wi' Jean by my side,
Was a' that I heeded—nought else was my pride !

A spunk frae the peat-low may burn a hale toon,
Sae a light frae her e'en-giance enkindled luve sune ;
I gazed, an' I sighed, till my heart throbbed wi' pain ;
Yet I lo'ed what distressed me, for Jean was my ain !
On a fine simmer-morn, to the kirk we repaired,
To auld Simon Elder our plight we declared ;
We link'd twa fond hearts in Fate's destinies twa,
Determined thegether to rise or to fa'!

I canno' forget ! why, it seems like yestreen—
When I led to our cottage my bonnie bride, Jean !
How my puir mither kissed her wi' tears in her e'e,
An' I laugh'd, till I wept, the fond couple to see.
Then I thought that this warld was an Eden o' bliss,
For I shared in love's joys—in my Jean's honied kiss—
Wae's me ! but the Simmer o' life disna' last,
The Winter *will* come when the Autumn's gane past !

My bairns, we had five—*were a' lost in a week !*
Disease cam' an' blighted the rose on ilk cheek ;
An' my Jean waned awa', like a cloud-covered licht,
An' sunk in my arms on a Sabbath's still nicht.

Heart-broken, an' madden'd by a' that I saw,
I fled frae the cottage on Ruin to ca'!
Nae hope in my bosom, my head in a flame,
I sought wi' the base what I fand no' at hame !

To droon the remembrance o' days that had been ;
To banish the memories o' luve an' my Jean ;
To shut out the ghaists that aft rose to upbraid,
Ilk nicht was a scene o' wild riotin' made !
But my cash was sune spent, an' my credit a' gane ;
The *friends* I had feasted then left me alane !
Noo a beggar I wander to market au' fair,
Wi' my wallet aft toom, an' my heart fu' o' care.

I'm a feeble auld man, wi' the grave at my feet,
The only true refuge frae want an' deceit !
The worm my companion in darkness will be,
But my saul shall arise wi' the blest an' the free !
They tell me, my spirit's no fit for the change,
That in dreary Eternity sune it maun range ;—
Weel, weel, my puir saul, *is the wark o' a God*,
An' He will tak' tent o't, when Rab's 'neath the sod !

———

SANG TO MY WEE WEE WIFIE.

I LO'E my wee, wee wifie
    In spite o' strappin', glow'rin' queens ;
She is sae jimp an' handy,
    She looks a lassie in her teens.
Her step's sae light—she springs sae smart—
    Her goon she kilts wi' sic a grace,
That her wee foot may win the heart—
    But oh ! he's slain that sees her face !

I lo'e my wee, wee wifie,
    For weel I ken she loe's me mair
Than laird, or gallant pawkie,
    That fain wauld lo'e my wifie fair.

She tholes my slight when I forget
  The kindness that should be her ain ;
She never glumps, nor tak's the pet,
  For weel she kens that flytin's vain.

I lo'e my wee, wee wifie ;—
  Though ither e'en may on me glint,
She ne'er looks sour, nor jealous,—
  She scorns to tak' an evil hint.
I dinna swear, we *canna' flyte*,
  An' turn our backs wi' hasty fling ;
But wow ! before we sleep at nicht,
  Our arms around ilk ither cling !

I lo'e my wee, wee wifie !
  I've lo'ed her weel these mony years ;
We had our simmer-pleasures ance,
  Now we maun chance the winter's tears.
But till the day I'm failed an' auld,
  If sic a time I'm born to see—
I'll shield her frae the storm an' cauld,
  And lo'e her till the day I dee !

———

LET US HELP ONE ANOTHER.

LET us help one another wherever we be,
And cherish kind feelings for bondmen and free ;
For we know not how soon we may need a friend's aid,
To restore us to light as we mourn in the shade !
Should the sceptre of rule to our hands be consign'd,
Let us govern with justice, in mercy be kind ;
And, like oaks of the forest, our royalty show,
By protecting the primrose that nestles below.

Let us help one another, though wealthy and great,
The gifts we confer will increase our estate ;
Like the seeds cast to earth, they will gratefully rise,
And build us a bower of bliss in the skies.

For riches, like rain-bows, acknowledge their birth,
From clouds of bright promise, and span the wide earth;
And the bountiful Giver exalted shall shine,
Converting sad rain to soul-glories divine.

Let us help one another, though lowly we stand,
Our Maker accepts e'en a *mite* from our hand;
For, as moments are threads in the vast web of time;
As a drop forms a portion of ocean sublime;
So a *wish*, from the heart, human ills to remove,
Is a spark from God's planets of Mercy and Love :—
And though dense seem the clouds that our efforts oppose,
Let us strive to dispel the dark gloom of man's woes.

Let us help one another, and work to reclaim
Poor wretches polluted with sin and with shame;
But ne'er let us banish the sinner with scorn,
Lest in plucking the *tares* we should root up the *corn!*
Remember the rose-bud we found in our walk,
With its leaves crushed and soiled, and its down-trodden stalk;
Soon its beauty returning rewarded our care,
Blushing forth grateful thanks—breathing incense of prayer!

Let us help one another, whate'er be the need;
Unmindful of nation, complexion, or creed;
Let no bigot-born scruples, fastidious and vain,
Bind our hearts, or our hands, when our neighbours complain.
Let our aid spring spontaneous, like wild flowers from earth,
That the poor and the hungry relieved may go forth;
That life's wounds may be healed, that life's wearied may rest,
And that man, blessing man, by his God may be blest!

———

THE LAY OF THE REGISTRAR.

This is the Lay of a Registrar,
    As his pen o'er the paper flies :
"Creatures of Earth, I await your *birth*,
    To your *weddings* I go, and, with face of wo,
        Groan when the lov'd one dies!

Full is my book, like a church-yard nook,
  With the records of young and old ;
Flowers of life on my pages are rife,
That soon must fade, and withered be laid
  Deep in the charnel-mould.

Many come *gay* to the Registrar,
  Flutt'ring, like Hope on the wing !
Beauteous and young, with faltering tongue,
That change their nooks in Mortality's books,—
  Dying, like days in Spring !

Many come *sad* to the Registrar,
  Hiding their error and shame ;
Content to dwell with those they love well ;
And clouds now spread o'er the bridal bed,
  Brighten, like noon-day's flame.

Mine is the volume of joy and wo,
  Gilding, or shadowing all ;
Blushing in bloom, or wasting in gloom ;
Gay as the lark, or as night-birds dark ;
  Covered with pomp or pall ;

Buds of life's beauty spring for aye,
  Daisies 'mid pampered flowers ;
Primroses meek with the tulips sleek ;
The dahlia proud, with the violet bowed,
  Filling my papyrus bowers.

Look on the scroll of the Registrar ;
  Many blossoms have passed away !
Where scull and bone, and the cold, white stone ;
Where yew-trees bend over foe and friend ;—
  Flowers are changed to clay !

Sad are the tears of human woes ;
  Hidden the lives I write ;
In every birth of a child of earth,
Sunshine, or gloom, must be its doom—
  Oft'ner clouds than light !

Rich may the blood of the baby be,
　　Gems on its brow may glow ;
The pestilent wing of the spoiler-king
Darkens its face, and its regal grace
　　Lies, as a pauper, low!

Life is a vast and changeful sea,
　　Billows run seeking their goal ;
Kissing the sand, or lashing the strand ;
Not two that strike are ever alike,
　　Constant as time they roll !

Varied the scenes that meet mine eyes ;
　　Riches and poverty blent !
A mingled web of the quick and the dead ;
Of Hope new-born and Despair forlorn—
　　For bridal or burial meant.

Never you sneer at the Registrar,
　　For great is my power and sway !
I link the chain of pleasure and pain ;
And order a bed for the silent dead !
　　I'm king of the crib and the clay !

Mortal am I, *though a Registrar*—
　　To dust, like my friends, I'll turn !
Mingled among the mouldering throng,
My bones shall lie, and my deeds shall fly
　　Scattered, like mists of morn !

THEY'RE A' COME WOOIN'.

THEY'RE a' come a-wooin' to me, guid lack !
There's the laird o' 'Glentilt, but he has no'a plack ;
Tam Simpson, the writer, an' Donald Macfa',
An' a fouth o' young spunkies come booin' fu' law.

There's high-showthered Davie, an' Sawney MacDuff,
An' Jabson, the schuilmaister chiel'—the auld coof!
Wi' his lang bummin' drone o' his Latin an' Greek,
An' his crambo an' clinkum that last for a week.

Fat Duncan cam' *ben* wi' his poke fu' o' meal,
An' spiered wi' a laugh, if the leddy was weel ;
But the *leddy* can tell him—the hopper-back'd fule—
That nae miller she'll marry her spirits to snool !

The laird's ta'en a frisk *me* "his dawtie to ca',"
An' vows that my forehead is whiter than snaw ;
But it is no' my *beauty* that wins me sic fame,
'Tis my *gowd* that has kindled his flatterin' flame.

The Dominie, too, when a lass at his schule,
Ca'd me glaiket an' daft, an' neist door to a fule ;
Now he bobs an' he bends, an' writes sangs to " Miss Deans"—
Fause fa' the auld skelper ! I ken what he means !

Hech, mither ! the gallants gang gicht in their praise !
They powther their tappins an' don their braw claes ;
They buy me fine goons, an' they bring me rich lace ;
Faith, I'll tak' a' their presents to prove I hae grace.

The minister's aft wi' his sermon perplex'd,
He glints to my pew, an' gangs clean aff his text !
As to singin', puir bodie ! his tune twists aglee,
Nae wonner he's thinkin' o' money an' me !

My puir doited granny ne'er fancied her gowd
Wad hae broucht to her Jenuy o' luves sic a crowd ;
For scant were my friends when my pocket was toom,
An' tongues 'bout my beauty were *silently* dumb.

But I care no' for a' the braw wooers on earth,
For their lands an' their gear ; for their bluid an' their birth !
O' their blether an' courtin' I winno' tak' tent,
Weel I ken a' their luve for my tocher is meant.

Now Robin was constant when poortith was mine,
Syne gowd is my ain to my Rab I'll incline ;
Though, wow ! the puir lad thinks his chance is but sma'—
But Robin I'll marry in spite o' them a'!

THE MAJESTY OF VIRTUE.

To please the world and all therein,
    To minister to Pride ;
To bow to Arrogrance supreme,
    And keep to Virtue's side,
Is such a task for mortal man,
    Upsetting reason quite !
Still we must strive, in all our ways,
    To do what's just and right.

Contending creeds have ever *been*,
    Methinks, will ever *be ;*
They rise like rippling waves, but grow
    To billows of the sea !
But when the boist'rous storm is o'er,
    Truth flows in liquid light ;
For potent Truth shall e'er prevail,
    And prove his dogmas right.

To hold our high positions firm,
    And win the world's applause,
'Tis not enough our friends to love,
    And keep our nat'ral laws ;
External looks are hypocrites—
    Though vicious folks we slight,
Unless we good example show,
    We only mock the right !

It matters not what *rank* we hold,
    The mighty, or the mean,
Begging our crust from door to door,
    Or dwelling with the Queen :

In simple phrase our lot is cast,
  In Heaven's omniscient sight :—
And, rich or poor, each man is bound
  To follow what is right !

Our epitaphs are lies on stones,
  That mock the dead below ;
Let Virtue's actions be our pride,
  And Truth's bright pen shall show,
That marble moulders into dust ;
  That Time must cease his flight ;
But never can Death's shadows dim
  The glories of the right !

MERCY'S VISITATION TO THE SICK.

The Angel of Mercy beheld with a sigh,
The sick and the lame in an Hospital lie ;
Not a nook in the building but held the low bed,
Where suffering and sickness together were laid.
Still comfort and cleanliness soothed them in grief,
And lent a repose near akin to relief ;
Their moanings were mingled with Gratitude's breath.
And they blest the benev'lent when sinking in death.

The Angel of Mercy passed on with a tear,
And came to a close-crowded lodging-house near ;
Oh, Wretchedness, Squalor and Crime in that place,
Had poisoned each heart while they pinched every face.
There mothers lay dying, *there* husbands were seen,
Ragg'd, drunken and fevered, unholy, unclean !
The children, half-naked, with leperous skin,
Contagious without, and polluted within.

A hoary blasphemer sat nursing a child,
And teaching it oaths which it uttered and smiled ;
While a prostitute, worn by disease to the bone,
Lay sobbing, unheeded, forsaken, alone !

Lame mockers and blind—maid and matron were there,
The child of misfortune, the wretch in despair ;
The fetid and foul, with the healthy and hale,
Youths, old in their vices, girls, vicious and pale !

" Holy God !" sighed the spirit, " these creatures behold !
Here are mingled the wolves with the sheep of Thy fold !
Is there no House of Refuge these sick to contain,
To separate crime from misfortune and pain ?
Shall sin league with suffering ? must pestilence spread ?
Doth Benevolence slumber ? Is Charity dead ?
To the ears of the gen'rous my plaint shall arise,
For my mission is Mercy from Love in the skies !"

The angel flew onwards, 'mid silence and night,
On a moon-beam that silvered a castle's proud height,
Swiftly gliding, arrived where the Baron then slept,
On the sleeper she gazed, and, low kneeling, she wept,
For his features were noble, frank, manly and brave—
With courage to conquer, with pity to save ;
Generosity shone, like a star, on his brow,
" Praise, Praise !" cried the spirit, " Heaven prospers me now !"

Then gently outstretching her wings o'er the bed,
With incense of Prayer a gold censer she fed ;
And while wreathing Devotion in fragrance arose,
The Lord of the castle awoke from repose.
Sore troubled he seemed with the visions of night ;
He knew not why tears were dew-dimming his sight,
But dreams, full of sadness, had caused him unrest,
And now lay, like an incubus, cold on his breast.

Through the gates of the castle the noble hath gone,
To the Hall of the Hospital speedeth he on ;
Ah, soon his dark dreams are interpreted clear,
For the low moans of sickness fall sad on his ear !
He learns what the house and its patients require,
And his bosom enkindles with generous fire ;
Rich in bounty and purse, his warm heart overflows,
And one thousand bright pieces of gold he bestows !

The fountain once opened, increased are its streams—
Like a di'mond in sunlight, Benevolence beams !
New jets soon arise, and prismatic they shine,
While Charity spreadeth her sources divine.
Thus, as lands, parched with drought, in dumb sorrow complain;
As flow'rs, corn and herbage rejoice in the rain ;
So the wail of life's suff'rings have drawn from the sky
An angel of Mercy, Love's rain to supply !

THE PHILOSOPHY OF POVERTY.

WHEN the poor by their grumbling can better their state,
   'Twere wise to be groaners together ;
But as murmurs remove not the shadows of fate,
   'Tis like weeping away the wet weather.
Though no houses we own, no one craves us for rent ;
   We dread neither tax nor distraining ;
Though straw be our pillows we'll slumber content,
   If, like birds, we but roost uncomplaining.

As wealth never burdens our pockets or brains,
   No thieves of our cash can divest as ;
The Stocks' fluctuations ne'er alter our gains,
   Nor courts of Exchequer molest us.
Though shabby our coats, we possess a good skin,
   And we challenge the tailors to dun us ;
Our hearts beat as merry torn vestments within,
   As Fashion's proud creatures who shun us.

On game and ragouts, by good luck, we ne'er fared ;
   No *sole* can accuse us of murder ;
Our stomachs with stuffing were never impaired,
   Thus our appetites keep in prime order.
Malthusians may blame us for wedding our mates,
   Without ample funds to support them ;
We gave them true hearts as the best of estates,
   And they know that no envy can hurt them.

Temptations environ the wealth of the proud ;
　Like a lamp in a sepulchre burning,
It attracts the foul things of corruption to crowd,
　Where decay lies to ashes fast turning.
Change the lot of the poor to the grandeur of earth ;
　Let their foreheads with gems be surrounded ;
May they not, as oppressors, destroy human worth,
　And with obloquy vile be confounded ?

We sigh not for gold that with life will elope,
　But we gather that glorious treasure
Which shall yield cent. per cent. in the Bank of Good Hope,
　And endow us with funds beyond measure.
For a heavenly world is not purchased like this,
　Else few of the lowly could enter ;
But the poor, thanks to God ! are not aliens to bliss,
　So to pass the bright portals we'll venture.

THE POET'S CHOICE OF A GRAVE.

> "I wish I were where Ellen lies,
> 　For day and night on me she cries,
> 　And, like an angel from the skies,
> 　　She seems to beckon me."—MAYNE.

THE day will come, when pale and cold,
　Thy once-loved Bard shall sleep ;
When every lay his humble muse hath sung,
　In cadence sad, or jocund vein,
　A memoried nook shall keep,
And linger in the accents of thy tongue.

Oh, let me rest in some green mound
　Where fragrance breathes around ;
Where smooth-leaved trees droop mourning o'er my tomb ;
　Where friends may wander forth at eve,
　To ruminate, and grieve
That love should die, or friendship fade in gloom.

But ah ! let not my form be cast
  Amid the throngs that lie
In town grave-yards, where yellow sculls aghast
  Glare on relations wandering by ;
  Where mouldering bones are seen
Strewing, with horrid waste, the festering green !

No monumental bust I crave,
  To mark my lowly grave,
I would, that, in some grassy nook, alone—
  Where the wild flowers delight to grow,
  Were placed a simple stone
To tell my name, and my last refuge show.

Oh, I could leave my life in air
  To be reposing there !
There the small birds my *requiem* sweetly singing,
  Mingled with tones of church-bells ringing,
  There perfumed gales might wander lone,
And kiss the dew-filled flowers beside me strown !

Silence around the dead should dwell ;
  Their tombs remote should be
From giddy throngs, from laughter rude and yell,
  From words profane and ribbaldry !
  Not that the dead can *hear*—
But from respect of spirits hovering near.

Fragrance should float around the dead ;
  The incense of sweet air,
Should, as a halo, guard the narrow bed,
  And brightly, fondly, linger there !
  Then Memory's balmy breath
Would keep from dull decay the loved in death.

And when the silvery moon-beams rest
  Upon thy poet's breast ;
When half the world lies buried in repose ;
  His grateful spirit may arise,
  To guard thy slumbering eyes,
And give a glimpse of heaven to calm thy woes.

THE LEGENDE OF ST. GOODRICKE THE HERMITTE.

Oh, a goodlie man is the hermitte olde;
    He ceaseth not to pray;
The devill's sore wrothe to him behold;
    For hee kneeleth nyghte and day.

Now Goodricke hath stripped his garments olde,
    And, for his passion's sinne,
Through long winter's nyghtes, in water colde,
    He prayeth upe to the chinne.

The devil wold steale the garmentes olde,
    As on Weere's bankes they be;
But the hermitte *Pater* and *Ave* hath tolde,
    And the fiende is forced to flee.

"And why," saide the fiende, "wear coates of mail?
    And why tormente thy skinne?
And why dost stande in Phincanhale,*
    In water upe to the chinne?

"And why dost reste uppon a stone,
    When feathers thy pillowe mighte bee?
And why dost slumbere all alone,
    When a wife mighte comforte thee?

"Why mingle with meale the ashene blackie,
    When the meale is goode withoute?
Come, strippe that jerkyne from thy backe,
    And turne to the worlde about!"

Now Goodricke he telleth his beades faste;
    His prayers a tome would fille;
O'er his little crooked finger the stringe is cast;
    But the fiende keepeth tempting stille.

* Finchale was anciently written *Pincahcal, Wincanhale, Phincanhale*, and *Fincley.* The latter name is generally adopted by persons residing in the locality of the ruins.

Faire damoiselles come, with beck'ning dumbe,
    And sorely his sighte assaile ;
Their scanty dresses his heart distresses,
    And he groans in his spirit pale.

And more and more they vex him sore ;
    He rolls mid the thorns and briars ;
Till worn and torn, with breast forlorn,
    He hath quenched unholy fires.

The wounds of his fleshe hee keepeth freshe,
    By pouring white salte withinne ;
Oh, never did man of a mortal spanne
    Soe punish his wounded skinne.

The fiende is enraged the saint to see,
    And blackens in hellish frowne ;
And quicke draweth near, smites Goodricke's eare,
    And hurls the hermitte down.

But Goodricke hath signed the holy cross,
    And the fiende is putte to flighte ;
And never agayne could he worke such payne,
    As he did withe his blow of spyghte.

*   *   *   *   *

St. Goodricke hath dreamed a blessed dreame,
    And he saw St. Cuthbert stande ;
Who tolde him to crosse the ocean's streame,
    And wende him to Holy Lande.

Away and away the pilgrim went—
    Away over sea and lande ;
He kneels him downe, and leaves his shoone
    By the waves on the Jordan's strande.

And agayne he hath came barefooted here,
    And builded a thatched celle,
By Phincanhale, on the bankes of Weere,
    A hermitte for lyfe to dwelle.

Then bend ye downe, ye monarche and clowne,
    And ladye with silken veste ;
And pray to the sainte to heare your plainte,
    To grant your poore sowles sweet reste.

THE REPENTING PRODIGAL.

Oh, a sinner am I, undeserving of love !
Fool ! why did I madly from virtue remove ?
I have broken the laws of my Father and God,
And I bow to the stroke of His merciful rod !

What a sinner am I ! how ungrateful and base,
To despise His best love, and His goodness disgrace—
To break from His tender embraces with scorn —
Oh, Father, too long with my crimes thou hast borne !

My substance I squandered with reprobates vile ;
They plundered my gold while I basked in their smile ;
They stripped off my robes, and then hurried me forth,
To a desolate couch on the rocks of the earth !

The rags of the beggar scarce cover my skin,
I am starving, yet cannot to labour begin ;
To beg is most hateful ; what mis'ry is mine,
For by want I am forced to steal husks from the swine.

The meanest of serfs on my Father's estate,
Compared to my station, are noble and great ;
Nay, the dogs in their kennels would shun my repast,
And die ere they'd break on my garbage their fast.

I will rise from my wretchedness, leave this deep wo,
To the arms of my pitying Parent I'll go ;
On His neck I will weep, I will hang on His breast,
He will pardon my sins, and my soul shall find rest !

THE STRICKEN HEART!

Oh, dinna spier why I am greetin', ;
  When pleasure's tear- drop shines !
Wi' Jean I've had a happy meetin',
  To-morrow she'll be mine !
I'm sure I canno' sleep a wink—
I'll lie and on my lassie think,
Till mornin' comes to tie the link
  That binds my luve to me.

Oh, dinna spier why I am greetin',
  My heart wi' fear's oppressed ;
Wae's me ! the morning's hoped-for meetin',
  Has filled wi' grief my breast.
I met her mother at the yett,
Her cheek was wan, her e'e was wet,
Her words I never can forget—
  " I fear puir Jean will dee !"

Ye needna spier why I am sabbin',
  My heart wi' wae maun break !
The fairest flower hath death been robbin',—
  The weeds he scorns to seek.
They've ta'en my winsome flower a'wa',
They've laid her 'mang the drifted snaw ;
But near thee, Jean, I'll slumber law,
  An' on thy grave I'll dee !

THE INCREDULOUS REPROVED.

Away, vain unbeliever ! Dost presume
  With breathing blasphemy,
Like some hot, desolating, dire simoom,
  To cloud the blessed light of christian joy,
  And God-stamp'd images of life destroy—
And blast our hopes of immortality ?

Away! The sire that gave thy pride its birth
Hath found a child in thee!
He dared a war to wage with Heaven's Supreme,
And when he failed th' Eternal arm to foil,
Raked up the reptiles of this nether soil
His sycophantic, servile slaves to be!

Go, herd with foul hyenas of the waste,
And, in some Memphian crypt,
On mummied bodies satiate thy taste;
Or lap warm blood with wolves, if thou'rt inclined
'Mongst *soulless animals* to choose thy kind!
For such thou'lt be of God's bright spirit stripped!

All near approaches to thy outward shape
And carriage, firm—erect—
Are but the brutes, the baboon, or the ape,
Of reason, intellect, and soul devoid—
Of speech divested, by thee, Man, employed
To lie, blaspheme, who should Heaven's gifts protect!

Thou hast a deathless soul that *cannot* die!
Forever and forever
Thy spirit, or in wo, or bliss, shall fly
Amid the realms eternal, when Earth's space
To a wide blank of nothing shall give place;
When Time lies buired with his empty quiver!

Exulting thought! to triumph over death,
And with us bear that spirit,
That entered with our first inspiring breath!
The secret perfume and the hidden ray,
That shines, and breathes, and purifies our clay;
That shall through endless ages life inherit!

Say, unbeliever, can'st thou still degrade
Thy Maker and thy kind?
Thou hast against God's attributes inveighed,
While, like the electric language from the wire,
Thou bear'st the urn of intellectual fire,
That glows in look and tone, in heart and mind!

When the red lighting writes Jehovah's name
  On the dark scrolls of Heaven ;
When sky-clad mountains wreathe their peaks in flame,
  And the majestic thunders bound along,
  Like giants rolling through a battle-throng,
When ocean shudders and the welkin's riven ;

Then calmly ask thy heart, "Have I a soul,
  That must not, *cannot* die ?
" *Thou hast !*" shall echo loud from pole to pole !
  " *Thou hast !*" the ocean from his depths shall cry !
  " *Thou hast !*" the rocks and mountains shall reply ;
"*Thou hast !*" shall peal the thunders o'er the sky !

FATE OF THE SHIELDS PILOTS.

Sad by the brink of the rolling deep,
'Neath the old Castle wall, let us muse and weep ;
Let our tears fall fast in the briny flood,
As we mourn for the Pilots—the brave and the good.
When the storm lashed white the billowy way,
No sailor-crew were so bold as they ;
" Pull a-head, brave boys !" was the Pilots' cry,
" We but *once* can *die !* We but once can die !"

Struggling with fate and the tempest's might,
A ship on the " Herd" met the Pilots' sight ;
The Life-boat, manned with her fearless crew,
Like a swift-wing'd bird, o'er the ocean flew.
And high were their hopes the seamen to save,
And bear from the wreck the true sons of the wave !
" Pull a-head, brave hearts !" was the Pilots, cry
" We'll save them, or die ! We'll save them, or die !"

Mounting the surge, like a steed well trained,
The boat with her crew hath the vessel gained ;
Captain and sailors now crowd to the deck,
Oh, eager to 'scape from the stranded wreck !

But the Storm-fiend laughs and waves his wing,
And grasps the cold hand of the skeleton king !
The Life-Boat turns 'mid Despair's wild cry !
Twenty Pilots die !   Twenty Pilots die !

Wailing and grief rend the murky skies,
The widows shriek loud 'mid their children's cries ;
Their husbands and sires were engulphed in the wave,
Near their own happy homes sunk the Pilots brave.
Oh, come then, ye gen'rous, from hut, house and hall ;
Queen, peer and peasant, with *help come all !*
Give your gold, give your pence, relief to buy ;
For " Good deeds never die ! Good deeds never die !"

THE TWIN MITHERLESS LAMMIES.

Twin bonnie, wee lammies were bleatin' sae sair,
That the rest o' the flock wandered saddened wi' care ;
An' joined wi' a wail an' lamentin' sae loud,
That ilk dam sought her ain frae the sorrowfu' crowd.
Ah, weel might the lammie-twins bleat then an' cry ;
For the teats o' their mither were milkless an' dry ;
An' weel might the creatures wail sad in their mane,
For their mither lay dead, an' as cauld as the stane.

Twa cannie young lasses that mornin' were seen,
Kneelin' low wi' the lammies, wi' tears in their e'en ;
They fed them wi' milk an' wi' bannocks the best,
An' tenderly laid them to sleep on ilk breast.
But oh ! there's nae fountain like nature's ain stream !
An' ane o' the lammies ne'er waked frae its dream ;
Wi' a sigh frae its heart, an' ae cringe, it was gane,
An' left its wee sister in sadness alane.

But the mitherless weanie was tended wi' care,
Day an' nicht its kind nurse soothed its cries evermair ;
She pried its sweet mou', and she wiped its blue e'e,
Sayin', " Bonnie, wee lamb, I'll be mither to thee !"

Then the lammie grew cantie, the wee thing looked smart,
An' Hope set her bow in the nurse's warm heart ;
She watched it wi' joy thrivin' bonnie an' braw,
For she lo'ed the puir twinnie the best o' them a' !

But when roses are severed that twin-buds hae grown,
Sune the pale, withered leaves on the earth will be strown ;
Sae the lammie fell sick, an' it pined ilka hour,
Till death plucked its life, as a bairn may a flower.
Sair, sair was the breast o' the nurse, as aloud
Rose the wail o' affection ; tears fell in a crowd !
She pried its cauld mou', an' she closed its dim e'e,
Sabbin' " Bonnie, wee lamb, my heart's waesome for thee !"

———

GOD PRESERVE THEE, QUEEN VICTORIA !

This Poem was written in the days of "ALBERT THE GOOD."

God preserve thee, Queen Victoria !
    Virtue guard thy earthly throne ;
May thy reign be famed in story,
    Crowned *by peaceful deeds* alone.

Far from thee be scenes of slaughter !
    Let thy *moral armies* prove
That old England's Queen and daughter
    Conquers by the powers of *love!*

Grant thee courage in all perils ;
    Mercy on thy judgment-seat ;
Grace to stay Religion's quarrels ;
    Wisdom when thy councils meet.

May'st thou view all creeds uniting ;
    Sects composing one grand chain ;
Lifting up one voice, delighting
    Angels by one glorious strain !

Then shall Jew the Christian pride in ;
Covenants shall be exchanged ;
Love, in mingled currents, gliding
Round the hearts too long estranged.

Crosses then on Mosques shall glitter ;
Bigotry shall prostrate fall ;
Ancient feuds, like webs, shall fritter ;
Charity shall govern all !

God preserve thee, Queen Victoria !
Grant thy Consort life and health,
To advance thy nation's glory,
And increase industrial wealth.

May he foster Art and Science ;
Lend to Genius wings of fame ;
Give Invention Truth's reliance,
And the poor man's deeds proclaim!

Then *his* name, with *thine* in glory
Shall in every land be known ;
Stranger-tongues shall shout " Victoria !"
Hail Prince Albert as their own !.

God preserve thee ! May his blessing,
Like the dew of heaven, descend,
Thy fair children's hearts possessing
With that peace which cannot end !

Peace ! oh, lovely spirit, hover
O'er this line of future kings !
As meek doves their nestlings cover,
Shield them with thy halcyon wings !

Sword and bay'net-steel, transmuted,
Shall have *wiser* purpose *then ;*
Glittering where good grain is rooted,
Cutting *corn* instead of *men !*

Colleges and Schools shall flourish ;
Industry shall reap renown ;

    Gaols and gallows-trees shall perish ;
      Hangmen then shall be unknown !

    Albion ! thou, with jubilation,
      Shalt Victoria's children see,
    Monarchs of thy throne and nation,
      Rulers of the blest and free !

    God preserve thee, Queen Victoria !
      Virtue guard thy earthly throne ;
    May thy reign be famed in story,
    Crowned by *deeds of peace* alone !

THE PROTECTED FEMALE.

KIND SIRS, I'm very nervous, oh, to my story list !
I hope each gent will prove himself a true *protectionist.*
Though long time unprotected, a female full of wo,
But now I've got a lover I care not were I go.

We now go out a-shopping, the young man at my side,
I sport the orange blossoms—folks take me for a bride ;
And should the foppish fellows e'er dare to laugh or stare,
My young man looks *so* savage, aye, *he* defends the fair.

Last night from work I hurried, the clock was striking ten,
I always am *so* frightened—I'm terrified of men !
Just round a corner turning a blackguard caught me tight,
But up came John, my lover, and hit him left and right.

At church our pew's so handy—a place just nice for two—
We find each other's lessons, and all things else eschew.
Last Sunday, quite astonished, a stranger I espied,
And as *my* John was absent, why *he* sat by my side.

'T was while the boys were chanting—of course I sung the psalm—
"My love ! my own sweet singer !"—the stranger said, so calm—
But John came close behind him—he's as cunning as a fox,
"Amen !" the boys responded—John gave his ears a box !

A girl there's with me working, she steals without remorse ;
The master *me* suspected—the police came, of course ;
They searched my bag and basket—what think you of this jade ?
She'd placed among *my* cuttings, ten yards of rich brocade ;—

They spoke about the station—and there I'd gone I know,
But John came to the rescue, and eased me of my wo !
This roguish lady's sweetheart to John had told her crime,
So I obtained my freedom, and Jane was nabb'd in time !

But now I am determined that married I will be,
And John shall *still* protect me, and take his chance with me ;
And *when* babes unprotected upon their mother call,
Why *I* must then protect them, as John did *me*—that's all.

DEATH OF THE EMIGRANT.

WITH a tear-dimn'd eye, but a hopeful breast,
    From the land of his birth he departed ;
Tho' few were his words, his accents blessed
    The feelings of friends true-hearted !

'T were a mournful sight for a gen'rous eye,
    To have marked his soul's emotion ;
For his voice came thick with a last " Good bye !"
    As he thought of the billowy ocean.

Remembrance brought back the happy times,
    When Friendship and Mirth were around him ;
When his song arose, like the heart's loved chimes,
    And the hail of Gladness crown'd him.

He thought of the days on the banks of Tyne,
    And his lip was observed to quiver,
And a tear from the heart was seen to shine,
    As he sighed " we must part forever !"

The ship sails on o'er the deep, blue wave,
　And the night-breeze moans in sorrow ;
And sharks follow fast with a hungry crave,
　For a feast they shall have to-morrow.

Yea, Death broods there, with his Upas blight,
　The sick, as in sheep-pens, are lying ;
The once gay hearts bid the world " Good night !"
　Oh, how sad were these emigrants' dying !

The vessel hath gain'd the wished-for land---
　But where is our friend that we cherished ?
Doth he live to inhale the breezes bland ?
　Or, hath he with fever perish'd ?

He lives ! but his life is a fading ray,
　For the simoom-cloud is o'er him ;
Though bright is his eye—still dull decay,
　And death stand grim before him.

Three days on a stranger's bed he lies—
　Like a bird with an arrow wounded ;
Earth's hopes depart, but the opening skies
　Give promise of bliss unbounded !

———

IN MEMORIAM.—REV. JAMES STANDEN, M.A.,

Who died of Fever caught in the discharge of his sacred duties,
October 11th, 1847, aged 41 Years.

THOU art gone, faithful Priest ! still thou seem'st to be near us—
　Thy grace and thy gentleness never can die ;
Thy form, like a rainbow, still lingers to cheer us,
　To gild sorrow's clouds that yet darken our eye.

Thy mission, dear Standen, was peace to poor mortals ;
　Thy words fell like dew on the perishing flowers ;
We were led to behold at the heavenly portals,
　Redemption's bright crown, that, through Jesus, is ours.

At the fountain baptismal thy mien was inviting ;
   The babe to thy bosom was tenderly pressed ;
Thy count'nance all radiance, as Satan's hopes blighting ;
   For that spirit was rendered as pure as the blest.

When the sinner, repentant, sought mercy from Heaven,
   Thy tears were oft mingled with those that he shed ;
By the Saviour's command, absolution was given ;
   With the food of the Angels a mortal was fed.

Thy smile beamed in darkness, in fever-fraught horrors ;
   Thy mellow-toned voice soothed the dying one's breast ;
'Mid the mis'ry and squalor of poverty's sorrows,
   Pouring balm to the wounds of the sick and distressed.

At the altar devotion thy forehead encircled ;
   The flame of chaste love shone, like bloom, on thy cheek ;
Thy eyes with the beams of mild charity sparkled,
   Like light fell thy blessing, soul-cheering and meek.

With action majestic, benignant and lowly,
   Thy image before us we seem to behold ;
Hushed silence hangs list'ning thy eloquence holy,
   Each accent a pearl, every sentence like gold.

Thou hast left us to mourn : can we cease to deplore thee !
   Yet our love, noble Pastor, is faithfully shown ;
If a sigh, or a tear, to this earth could restore thee,
   All semblance of sorrow should never be known.

Oh ! grant that no accent, unthinkingly spoken,
   Or venial ommission, thy crown may withold ;
This prayer, dearest Father, our love's truest token,
   Shall be breathed till we slumber heart-broken and cold.

Thou hast gone to the mansions of glory supernal ;
   " Thou hast fought the good fight," and the conquest is thine ;
Thou hast changed this dark vale for a kingdom eternal.
   Through ages unnumbered an angel to shine !

SHOW ME THY HEART.

Show me thy heart ; thy tongue speaks fair—
  Thine eyes are eloquent with love ;
But all may be as empty air
  That stirs the silent grove.
And oh, love's secret mine
  For *me* may hold no part ;
  If thou dost truth combine,
    Show me thy heart.

Show me thy heart ; I will believe
  Thy tongue and eyes are kind ;
Yet *both* can love deceive,
  For words are only wind ;
  And eyes, like meteors, glow,
  When they delusive dart,
  Portending death and wo !—
    Show me thy heart !

FROM THE CRADLE TO THE GRAVE.

Suggested by an Act Drop painted by Mr. Stuart H. Bell, of the Royal
Wear Music Hall Sunderland.

Now the last link that binds the bold ship to the land
  Hath been severed, and off goes she,
While the red wine flows o'er her beautiful bows,
  As she's launched in the deep blue sea.
What a glorious sight to behold in her might
  This vessel of beauty and grace,
Produced at the will of famed builders of skill,
  On the main, like a queen take her place.

    Chorus—Then hurrah for the bark, the gallant bark,
        As she glides on her path to the wave,
        Like a creature of life, she begins the strife,
        From her cradle e'en to the grave.

Hurrah ! now she glides with the breeze and the tide,
   O'er the billow's sparkling foam !
With a graceful swell she bids farewell
   To the shores of her native home.
Thro' the crowded piers, mid rejoicing cheers,
   And the voices that cry—" *God speed !*"
With heaven's clear light, on her canvas white,
   She bounds like a well-trained steed.
               CHORUS—Then hurrah, &c.

Now struggling for life 'mid the hurricane's strife,
   And the billows like mountains rolled ;
The doom of that bark, in the tempest dark—
   By the storm-fiend's shriek is told.
Her glory and pride are scattered wide,
   For the skill of her captain proves vain,
And alas ! for her crew, the noble and true,
   They have sunk ne'er to rise again.

   CHORUS—Then mourn for the bark, in the tempest dark,
             And the crew that were lost in the wave,
               For the ocean of life hath its calm and its strife
               From the cradle e'en to the grave.

Behold her a *wreck*—from her keel to her deck !
   Like a tower of strength o'erthrown,
She will glad no more the crowds on the shore,
   For the reign of her splendour's gone.
She sailed away—*strong, proud,* and *gay*—
   From her home in life's young morn,
Now the waves have roll'd thro' her cabin and hold,
   And she lies like a log forlorn.
               CHORUS—Then mourn for the bark, &c.

THE WITHERED BLOSSOM.

I SAW a young and gentle flower,
   Transplanted from its loved parterre,
Blooming within a lowly bower,
   Beside the willow-leaves of Care.

Her fostering breath Affection gave,
　And Pity's dews upon it shed ;
Sweet Love did all she—could to save—
　Alas ! this blossom withered.

I saw that young and gentle flower,
　Its perfume wasted—beauty gone ;
I saw it in the spoiler's bower,
　And wept to see the blighted one.
There was a manly form that stood,
　With round drops swimming in his eye ;
His heart shed then its tears of blood ;
　This blossom was his dearest prize.

I saw the big, bright tears descend ;
　I heard the heavy sobs of grief,
With meek Affection's murmurs blend,
　For this lost bud of beauty brief.
A seraph, sped on wings of gold,
　Beheld this blossom fade and die ;
Raised it, from slumber pale and cold,
　And bore its fragrance to the sky !

———

MY GRANDFATHER'S PORTRAIT.

Here, on the tablet of my gratitude,
My more than parent's honoured name I write:
Failing to leave my humble tribute now,
Let Obloquy, with burning brand, appear,
And stamp my muse with shame !

I GAZE upon thy face till my vision, through my tears,
Grows dim as rainy clouds, at the thoughts of other years.
I gaze upon thy face, and my heart is like to break ;
Vain, limner, is thy skill ! this cold painting fails to speak.
I still must look and love ; what a father I behold !
Oh ! that such love as his should ever slumber cold.
Prometheus' flames I need, yet my heart's a living fire;
Oh ! what are burning breasts to thy ashes, hoary sire ?

A tiny boy was I when first he met my view ;
Hair like the driven snow, Care's wrinkles not a few:—
He took me on his knee, as inviting words he said ;
He " hoped that I was good, and my father's words obeyed."
He spoke not of my mother—the reason may be guessed—
Deep in the clay she slept, with the flowers upon her breast.
An only son had he : my grandsire loved him well ;
But what we love must die, and thus my father fell.
Oh ! oft I sadly muse on that night of woe and dread,
When burst my grandsire's grief ! his only son was dead !
There is a plaintive sadness in the melancholy rill,
As it purls, and sighs, and languishes, and weeps beneath the hill ;
As it whispers to the breezes a love-forsaken tale,
Till, meeting other streams that mourn along the vale,
Together slow they wander, increasing in their wo,
Till rivers join their doleful dirge, as to the main they go ;
Then hoary are the billows' heads, and briny are their tears ;
For there the ocean heaves and moans for everlasting years.
A broken spirit who can heal, or nature's feelings bind ?
The eye may seem by grief undimmed, the brow appear resigned ;
But open thou the stricken heart, what anguish shalt thou find !
Fresh wounds still bleeding, burning thoughts, like caustic in
      the core ;
Affection brooding o'er lost hopes ; love weeping evermore.
I was a tiny boy, of parents dear bereft ;
A rainbow-tinted, straggling cloud, in the horizon left.
The dull, wide waste of life to tread without a friendly hand ;
An exile from a parent's hearth, an orphan on the strand.
No—no, we were not friendless left ; thy more than father's care,
Four orphans sheltered in thy home, thy welcome board to share.
God rest thy gen'rous soul in peace ; thy body now is dust ;
But Charity, like thine, hath heard the sentence of the just.
Now, as I fix my eyes on thee, a smile thy mouth illumes ;
The rigidness of painted forms a life-like warmth assumes :
A consciousness that soul is near ; a halo round the dead ;
A noiseless stirring of the air, a breathing perfume shed ;
A mingling of delicious tints to paint a sleeping cloud ;
A silent motion, as when spirits vest them in a shroud.
Thy lips e'en glow with eloquence ; thy well-known voice I
      hear ;
Words that awake not Solitude, yet seem to reach her ear

Sounds, such as breathe in infants' dreams, the spirit of our
    speech ;
Which mortal hearing seldom knows, which Fancy's oft may reach.

" Well pleased am I, my grandson Bard, this tribute from thy
    muse
Falls kindly on my grass-grown grave, in memory's holiest dews·
No sculptured stone points out my tomb, but thou hast raised it
    where
At morning, noon, and eventide, may offered be thy prayer.
The marble mockery of the proud my spirit heedeth not ;
I live, my grandson, in thy heart, there ne'er can be forgot !
'T was I, alas ! first nursed thy muse—my own neglected, died ;—
Upon thy youthful minstrelsy I looked with grief and pride !
The scornful world, the heartless crowd, that mock the poet's
    strain,
Oft made me curb her buoyant step—to curb thy muse was vain.
Ere my white head had sunk to rest thy fame was not unknown ;
I joyed to learn thy song had fared much better than my own.
But heed thee ! dang'rous is the path by Flatt'ry's lines beset ;
Walk on the road to Virtue's goal, and never God forget !
The giddy height Ambition loves thy heart must strive to shun,
And, though thy Muse an eagle prove, soar not too near the sun :
Be humble, and the just shall love ; thy genius shall be great,
If thou with good and honest men establish thy estate !"

TO A YOUNG LADY.

" Know then this truth, enough for thee to know,
    Virtue alone is happiness below."
                                        POPE.

THE rosy morn, the moonlit sky,
    And wand'ring stars with spangled feet,
Delight the heavenward lifted eye,
    And yield the bosom pleasure sweet.
Yet these are nature's *outward* forms ;
The brightened clouds of secret storms ;
The smiling depths where Ruin lies ;
The thunder-dreams of moody skies,

Ere lightning's lance-like arrows streak,
With flaming gash, the tempest's cheek

Fair Girl! the beauty of the mind
Leaves all such transient gleams behind :
For what is youth's health-glowing face,
But green decay and fading grace ?
What the swift flashings of her eye,
But meteors darting through the sky,
In thickest gloom to pass and die ?
Nay, what are *all* the spells that hold,
By passion's chain, this breathing mould—
What are they *all* ? Young morning-clouds
Gath'ring their charms for darkling shrouds ;
Soon lustre-wasted, cold, to sleep,
As silent shadows, on the deep.

To gaze on Sculpture, when the art
Can only marble grace impart ;
To look on Painting's life-like skill,
Is only *mimic* beauty still !
But when the eyes, admiring, roll,
And trace the loveliness of soul ;
When in soft Nature's charms we find
The face a halo of the mind ;
Behold the spirit's flames unite,
And glow with living, holy light :
'T is then, oh ! *then* we raptured feel—
'T is then we cannot love conceal ;
The air teems with delights untold,
And gladness beams like liquid gold.
For what a sea of pleasure rolls
Through chaste, unstained, and sinless souls !
How unconceived, how unconfined,
The aspirings of a sainted *mind !*
A flame, God-lighted, rising still ;
A fire that Envy cannot chill ;
That slander, with his poisoned breath,
Fails to extinguish into death ;
Though seen, perchance, to faint and quiver,
Flashes to life and burns forever !

Thrice blessed Virtue! did the vain
And worldly fools, who thee disdain,
Know thy angelic, deathless charms,
The wanton Vice, with palsied arms
And withered cheek, would, as a dream,
Flit at thy coming, beauteous Beam!
Such, my young Rosebud, be thy aim
And consolation, and thy name,
In the just record of the skies,
Shall flourish, when creation dies.
Virtue, the loveliest of the rare;
Her breathing sighs a balmy prayer;
Her eyes rest on the skies alone;
Her heart beats music's sweetest tone;
Her hand the wounded heals, and lends
The union crown to fallen friends.
Oh! she is lovely! see she smiles,
And Heaven unfolds her countless isles.
Behold her! are their charms on earth
Like hers—so full of priceless worth?
Salute her! she is "full of grace;"
Peace is reflected in her face!
Bless her! and she will love bestow
To light this wilderness below:
Love her; and emulate her love;
Mount, on her wings, to bliss above!

TO ELIZA COOK,

The celebrated Poetess.

AMID the sangs an' cordial cheer
That usher in this guid New Year,
It wad, I think, seem verra queer,
                 An' unco dree,
If I forget my "sister" dear,
                 Or "sister" me.

The yule-sparks vanished ane by ane ;
The mistletoe awa' is gane ;
The guse is polished to the bane,
   The cogie's toom,
An' memory's stars are left alane
    To pierce the gloom.

When Christmas brought thy lyre o' fame,
I could not rest an hour at hame,
Till I had twined, wi' verse, thy name,
   And strung my rhyme
Wi' fond Affection's holy flame,
    Unfeigned this time.

I canno' help it, if I 'm daft,
Aiblins I 'm like the "gentle craft ;"
I ken I 'm just a pickle saft
   In heart an' heed ;
Wi' friendship never ance abaft
    In time o' need.

And maist folk, o' this side o' earth,
Whate'er their station or their worth—
Blazoned in arms, or mean in birth—
   Some help require ;
I wish, for sense, to usher forth
    My modest lyre.

I gi'e them a' I can, nae mair,
Though poor the offering is, they swear ;
But thou, Eliza, hast a share
   O' the Muses' wealth ;
Heaven grant thou may'st preserve it fair,
    Wi' peace an' health.

The Leap-year is the ladies' chance ;
'T is then the dawties may advance,
An' steek puir sauls wi' Cupid's lance,
   That twa-edged blade ;
Nae revolution dune in France
    Sic war e'er made.

I wonner aft if *ane* I ken
Cares aught about the gawky men ;
Or if she hings her haffits, when
             They speak o' Cupid !
Aiblins she values mair her pen
             Than coofs sae stupid.

In this braw month we dedicate,
Ae day to Poetry an' Fate ;
The Twenty-fifth, an epoch date
             Frae Scotia's page ;
Rob Burns's birth we celebrate
             On Friendship's stage.

"The bluid-red rose at yule may blaw,"
And tender lilies bloom in snaw,
But Robin's name, whate'er befa',
             Shall honoured be ;
That he was king amang us a'
             Thou wilt agree.

What joy, if we could see him hear,
Toomin' his cogie o' brown beer ;
Singin his rantin' carols clear
             Amang his friends !
But no ! he keeps the guid New Year
             That never ends.

The New Year's come—but is na' gane :
Could we but see the grief and pain,
The wishes an' the struggles vain ;
             Hopes lost for aye—
Withered beneath the world's disdain,
             We'd curse the day.

But Fortune wisely veils her face ;
Ye may not coming evils trace ;
Yet night hath morning in her race,
             And morn shall shine
Resplendently with God's own grace,
             His light divine.

Young Hope was aye the poet's dower ;
Eliza, may'st thou feel her power,
When Sickness and the parting hour,
                        On thee descend !
Oh ! may she come—a gowden shower,
                        With bliss to blend.

IN MEMORIAM.—CHARLES MILLER,

Musician, of Newcastle-upon-Tyne.

THE minstrel Miller is no more,
    Mute is his tuneful lyre ;
Now quenched in night, forever lies
    Its Promethean fire.
Oh ! where are now the thrilling tones
    That woke the trembling strings ?
Where are the radiant streams that gushed
    From Music's magic springs ?

The rapture-raising cadences,
    The undulating strains,
Wand'ring the maze of harmony,
    Like stars o'er heavenly plains !
Where are they now ? the balmy gale
    That bore their sweetest tone,
Hovers around his tomb, distressed,
    And murmurs "they are gone."

Gone, like the smile of dying day
    That lingered on his doom ;
Gone, like the meteor-spark of joy,
    To Sorrow's dreary gloom ;
Gone, like the di'mond that is seen
    A moment on the wave ;
Gone—sunk—in ocean lost—
    The ocean of the grave !

The Grave ! and do the loathsome things
   That crawl the bones among
Mingle and dare contaminate
   The breast of holy song ?
And can the angel Melody
   Find not a fitter bed,
But fold her iris-plumes and sleep
   Companion with the dead ?

Oh ! ye who drank his nectared cup,
   And caught th' inspiring lay,
Ye will not let his memory sleep,
   And, like his form, decay ?
Ye will not let the cold, dull tomb
   The minstrel's fame enshroud ?
No ! place it, with its kindred lights,
   High on a golden cloud !

TO THE "BROTHERS OF ST. VINCENT OF PAUL."

" ' Had you been of the order of MERCY instead of the order of *St. Francis*,
poor as I am,' said I, pointing at my portmanteau, ' full cheerfully should
it have been opened to you, for the ransom of the unfortunate,' "

STERNE.

'Tis Evening ; and the majesty of Day
Sleeps, on his purpled couch, and dreams away.
The vale, erewhile so beautiful, becomes
A misty picture indistinct by glooms :
Thick clouds are gath'ring o'er the the starless sky,
And, one by one, Earth's fair creations die.
Where is the gorgeous pomp of Nature now—
The glitt'ring streamlets and the hill's green brow ?
Where the magnificence of gilded waves ?
Black plumes they heave above chaotic graves.
Where is the rainbow-crested, foaming fall,
The pillared temple, and the rocky hall ?
Darkness, like death, envelopes—buries all !
Type of Cimmerian ignorance that rests
In tenfold gloom, in men's untutored breasts ;

Where God-like Virtue lies, a pearl unknown,
A gem of glory mortals fear to own !
Benighted souls where Wisdom fain would 'bide ;
Which Vice hath veiled, abandoned and destroyed.
Eyes that were lighted heavenly orbs to shine,
Clouded by woe and drenched in boiling brine ;
Tongues that were formed to rapture and inspire,
Darting the baleful curse of lawless ire ;
Hearts, round whose fibres Envy's snakes are curled,
Made by His hand that balances the world :
Yea, the whole structure of man's noble frame,
Once Eden's glory, now the hell of shame !
Oh ! this dread picture of dismay remove ;
Let me behold a glimpse of light and love ?
'Tis dawning Morn !   The lark now carols loud,
And breathes sweet welcome to the bright'ning cloud ;
Their regal heads the waves of ocean raise ;
The mountain-forests bend in awful praise ;
The leaping waters, waking into joy,
Their foam-gemmed incense scatter to the sky.
The world awakes ! the sombre veil is past ;
The Sun ! the glorious Sun ! behold, at last.
Hail, thou effulgent image of the mind,
Rising divinity of day, enshrined
By countless myriads of di'monds rare—
Like thy Creator, walking on the air :
Emblem of Charity ! the fairest, best,
The purest seraph of th' unnumbered blest :
The spirit's *El Dorado*, where the mine,
Rich, unexhausted, proves the soil divine ;
Where Virtue revels in eternal bloom,
Feasts on ambrosia, fearless of the tomb.

Give then, ye Brothers of St. Vincent, give
Your souls to Charity, and they shall live ;
Gird on the armour that the world defies ;
" Fight the good fight ;" receive the glorious prize.
Take not alone the *outward forms* of Love,
But let your actions *inward* graces prove.
High is your station, your vocation great—
Let not *mere pomp* determine your estate :

Allegiance to the " Holy Rood " ye owe—
Fear not to strike, but never wound a foe.
Let Crime and Wretchedness awake your care,
Snatch the deluded victims from the snare.
Be gentle, kind, forgiving ! do not blame,
With a harsh word—ye carry Mercy's name.
Teach the poor sinner for the sake of Him
Who, on a cross, out stretched each nail-pierced limb.
Fear not to mingle with the thief depraved ;
Such Jesus sought, and such, repentant, saved.
Turn not away the vicious and the lewd ;
The adultress-heart, by Jesus, was subdued.
" Go thou and sin no more !" Oh ! mild command !
What heart of iron could these words withstand?
No shower of rocky fragments e'er could move
A sinner's breast like Mercy's words of love.
Go, then, ye brothers of St. Vincent, go,
Soothe the afflicted, meliorate their woe ;
Poor the cool balsam to their burning breast ;
Pray for the the wretched ; bless, and ye are blest.
Through filthy alleys to the fevered bed
Where aching Anguish rolls his restless head,
Where foul disease pestiferous dew exhales ;
Where Vice, in all her wretchedness, prevails.
Go, welcome messengers of peace and love,
And ye shall shine, as stars, in skies above !
Where is the mind untaught ? there Wisdom lend :
Where is the doubtful ? Truth with Mercy blend :
Where are thy foes ? their deepest wrongs forgive,
And let thy charity their faults outlive !
And, when their bodies cold and mould'ring lie,
Pray that their souls may pardon find on high.
And thou, dear Standen, for this work decreed,
Firm in thy nobleness of soul, proceed ;
Exhort, inspirit, cherish, and refine
These young aspirants to a fame divine :
Cheer them with smiles approving, warm each heart ;
Teach them to bear a self-denying part ;
Guide them to Virtue's amaranthine bowers,
Where sainted Piety employs her hours :
Be thou their faithful shepherd, to uphold

Their feeble steps, and lead them to thy fold.
Oh ! watch them ; for, like Peter, *one* may fall,
But he, soul-strengthened, may confirm them all.

ON THE DEATH OF MY ONLY DAUGHTER ;

Who died Dec. 12th, 1846, aged 16 Years.

WHEN Ellen, our dear, darling girl was born,
   Joy like a cloudless sun, beamed brightly o'er us ;
With jocund hearts, we hailed the happy morn,
   Nor saw the gathering destiny before us.

Hope winged our thoughts to future days of bliss ;
   The many-tinted Fancy bent delighting ;
Anticipation saw no world but this ;
   The skies were lovely and the view inviting !

First-born of youthful love ! with anxious care
   Thy tender mother reared her infant blossom ;
And, lest its leaves might feel the chilling air,
   She warmed them, lovingly, within her bosom.

Oh, retrospection vain ! The days are fled—
   Passed to the gulf where Time no days can number ;
Ellen, thy much-loved parents mourn thee dead,
   But sighs and tears can ne'er disturb thy slumber.

Thy childhood, Ellen, let me once recal—
   Thy young, fond, mother patient in her sorrow ;
Whate'er misfortunes might her hopes befal,
   She looked for brighter prospects on the morrow.

Thy youth—ah, now the flowers of Fate must bloom ;
   The poison-seeds are in thy glad heart lying ;
Flushed is thy cheek with beacons of the tomb ;
   With crimson clouds that come when day is dying.

Oh, what are all our painted dreams of joy,
  Our sanguine fancies, and our wrapt emotions?
Webs, that a breath of Sickness can destroy—
  Straws, that are lost in Ruin's gulping oceans.

    *   *   *   *   *

The dark-robed tempest rides the wintry sky;
  The cat'ract's foam in sheeted ice hangs chill;
Thick, driving clouds of blinding hailstones fly;
  The Storm-fiend thunders from his snow-crowned hill.

And dreadful is the scene. The night descends—
  Oh, dismal night! Without, the blast is raging;
Within —surrounded by her weeping friends,—
  My dying daughter struggles—death engaging.

Hope's meteor-stars in her bright eyes are glowing;
  Her smiles, how lovely, and her words, how tender!
She knoweth well, that to the grave she's going;
  She also knoweth, God can still defend her!

We saw thee not, loved daughter, till thy form
  Was stricken into marble, mute and dead :
We sought to yield our last embraces warm;
  Upon thy clay-cold cheek our tears were shed!

But thou art happy, Ellen. At the throne,
  Where Mercy's wings forever shine extended,
Make our unworthy plaints, lost girl, thine own;
  And blessings shall with all our woes be blended.

———

THOUGHTS ON THE PRECEDING.

Oh! that I could regenerate
  My daughter's clay! her heart should beat forever,
And flow, defying change and fate,
  With purple life, like an eternal river;

Still running, but ne'er run ;
Rejoicing, like the sun,
    Without the clouds of Time ;
A flower without decay—
A never-setting day—
    An unexhausted prime.

I weep ! and some my woe offendeth ;
    Firm is my faith, and yet I sit repining :
The gleam that Hope to Sorrow lendeth,
    Flickers and faints, and ceases in its shining.
        Still there are lips that jeer ;
        Aye, mock the falling tear,
            As womanish and weak ;
        My heart is not of steel ;
        Affection's throbs I feel,
            And tears still blanch my cheek.

I strive—but cannot curb my grief ;
    The pale horse leads me to my darling's grave ;
In tears alone I find relief,
    For mem'ry rushes on me like a wave.
        I see her in my mind ;
        Her smile, so blandly kind,
            Still on her father beaming.
        Oh ! could she wake to life,
        I'd guard her from all strife—
            Nay, e'en from danger's seeming.

I loved her, and must ever love,
    Till I am lost in Lethe's silent slumber ;
Now she is gone to skies above,
    My spirit yearns to join the happy number.
        To hymn th' Eternal Cause
        Of Nature and her laws ;
            To love without alloy :
        What thought can equal this ?
        To share my Ellen's bliss,
            In everlasting joy !

THE SPIRIT'S CONSOLATION.

Lines on the Death of the Prince Consort, Humbly inscribed to Her Most
Gracious Majesty.

VICTORIA, my beloved Queen ! my own sweet, faithful wife,
Thou art to me—now spirit-robed, e'en dearer than in life ;
Then all thy cares mine own were made—for cares all states
    beset—
Thou wast the sunshine of my heart ; my spirit's star thou'rt yet.

A nation's tears, blent with thy grief, are shining on my tomb ;
Lit by thine hand, the lamp of love, death's darkness doth illume.
Mourn not, Victoria, that my seat stands vacant and alone ;
My spirit hovers always near thy Councils and thy Throne.

In death I saw thee cling to me, as moonbeams to a cloud ;
Thy wail of widowed woe I heard, beheld thee anguish-bowed ;
My children's sobs of sorrow fell upon my spirit's ear,
When, dead to sighs and words of grief, my form slept on its bier.

O thou, my eldest-born of love, my earliest pledge of bliss,
Thou wast not near thy father's bed to take his last, fond kiss !
But thou and thy sweet royal babes, and he of Prussia's line,
Have with the tears of holiest love adorned devotion's shrine.

My Alice ! Oh how beautiful is sweet affection's flower,
When all its fragrance it exhales in sorrow's darkest hour ;
In thy chaste soul love's blossoms blow ; may God's eternal
    spring   [wing !
Keep them from tinge or taint of earth, beneath His shelt'ring

My Albert ! son and heir of all that kings may splendour deem,
O gather from my early doom the moral of life's dream !
Tread thou the paths that good men walk in majesty sublime,
And from the seat of regal pomp to thrones celestial climb.

Solace thy mother in her woe, for she shall surely mourn
The absence of thy father lost, shoud'st thou not light love's
    urn ;—

Be to her heart and to her throne all that my son should be,
And thou shalt live in Briton's love the Father of the Free !

My sailor boy! my Alfred brave! and Leopold, my child!—
Thou who so lately kiss'd my lips and on thy father smiled—
Ye both were spared the mournful scenes of death and sad
 dismay :
Thou, Alfred, o'er the surging main—thou, Leopold at play.

  * * * * * *

O, my Victoria ! could earth's grief on spirit-beings rest,
The thought of thine unhappiness would shroud in woe my breast ;
But sighs and tears can have no place where joys eternal reign,
There is no sorrow in those realms—the angels know not pain.

The wreath thy gentle fingers twined were lilies woven well,
And every tear was love's own gem that on the chaplet fell.
Pure, as the lilies white, thy heart, as sweet thy perfumed
 breath,
Though paler were thy cheeks of woe when I lay cold in death!

Thy fadeless chaplet binds my brow, thy tears shine star-like
 there,
For angels wove them in the crown they bade thine Albert
 wear.
Such holy off'rings could not be time-withered in my tomb,
Love's seraph bore them in her breast, 'mid bowers of bliss to
 bloom !

SUNBEAMS ON THE HEARTH.

LAUGHING and leaping gay ! where is the child like mine ?
His cheeks are soft as silk, with a rosy tint like wine.
I lookt in his dark blue eyes, as stars gaze on a stream,
Twin babies I saw therein, laughing, as in a dream.

My babe's red lips clung close to my breast ; I held him there ;
Like sunbeams—lines of gold—were the threads of his wavy hair.
I felt, as my infant lay with his lips so close to my heart,
That the love for my child was more than fate could dare to part.

The bells of his coral rang with a distant, fairy tone ;
They were angel-bells of joy that this child was all my own.
He slept, but my heart beat so with the bounding throbs of bliss,
That I wak'd my fair, young boy, with a close, endearing kiss.

He open'd his dark blue eyes, and lookt on my face, like a
    flower,—
Then down, down, down the lids dropt, with a dreamy power ;
Soon fast asleep he fell ; to his lips a smile arose,
Like light on twin cherries ripe, kissing them in repose.

This is my first-born boy ! O kisses ! my boy is asleep !
To wake him from his soft dream might cause my child to weep.
But his eyes no sorrows may shed ; my heart would surely break,
Were a tear his eyes to dim, or stain his beautiful cheek.

Oh, sorrow's for loveless Age, and grief's for Misery's forms ;
The little, blue cloud rains not ; 'tis the black gloom sendeth
    storms ;
And, who would not weep to see his blue orbs bathed'in woe ?
Then, what hath *he* done to grieve ? no angel's more pure, I
    know.

Ah, see his tremulous lips ! and his quivering eyelids view !
He lifteth his looks in sleep so high that you lose the blue.
Ah, smiling again, my child ! I wonder what gladdens his eyes ?
Oh, he follows the gilded wings of angels that heavenward rise !

Happy am I, O God ! with this lovely babe at my breast,
There is joy in my soul and peace ! indeed, indeed, I'm blest !
My husband is faithful and kind ; what woman desireth more ?
If this be a dream of bliss, oh, ne'er let the dream be o'er !

———

SHADOWS ON THE FLOWER.

STEALING are thoughts of fear, like mists around the moon ;
Or a jarring discord slight in a loved, melodious tune.
Love's wings dim shadows cast o'er the curtains, white as wool,
As faint, low sighs are breath'd o'er her baby beautiful.

The shades of sickness fell o'er the brow of her sleeping boy ;
His feverish breath bedimm'd Life's silverd glass of joy ;
Startings and tremors strange awoke on his mouth and breast,
As if in dreams he saw dark forms of things unblest.

Startings and tremulous thrills, as when weak lilies fair,
Feel on their fluttering leaves the winter's icy air ;
Or the sunset-gilded lake that slumbers, like glittering glass,
Seems shiver'd to fragments bright, as wintry breezes pass.

Quicker the mother's heart is beating in doubt and fear,
Like a bird with a serpent's gaze fixed on the flutterer near ;
Quicker the mother's heart now throbs by her moaning child,
Like a butterfly's quivering wings when the night-breeze
    gambols wild.

Blue lines are under his eyes, and his mouth its smile hath lost ;
The sunny head and the little hands, like flowers on waves, are
    tost ;
The quivering eye-lids ope, and the brow strange wrinkles show,
And the rose on his cheek grows pale as the tainted, sickly snow.

There's a stir of the curtains white where the mournful moon
    looks in,
Is it Fancy's eyes that mark a face with a dull and gloomy grin !
From the fire a coffin leaps out ; there's a sound of retiring
    wings ;
And the knoll of the passing-bell o'er the night's still bosom
    rings.

Mother ! thou lovest thy child with a love too deep and strong !
God thou hast nigh forgot, and this love for the earth is wrong !
Thine idol shall broken be, and the dust shall cover thy boy,
That thy heart's best love may be turn'd to heaven and endless joy.

Rent is thy robe of hope, and the cup of its bliss destroyed !
Kneel mid the ashes of woe ! let prayers be now employed !
Prayer and praise to Him, who giveth and taketh away ;---
For the end of earthlg love is a coffin, a shroud—and clay !

THE STORM, THE WIND, AND THE RAIN.

DARK was the night, and a surging sea—
As a mother look'd forth with a tear in her e'e,—
  O, the storm, the wind and the rain !
Her dear boy then was clinging fast,
With hands benumb'd, to the rolling mast ;
He was shrieking loud, as he sunk at last,
  Lost 'mid the storm, the wind, and the rain.

Huddled 'mid rags, in a garret lone,
Lay a female form of skin and bone ;
  O, the storm, the wind, and the rain !
Twin babes on her thin bosom lay,
Dead as stone, and as cold as clay ;—
While their mother gasped her life away,—
  O, the storm, the wind, and the rain !

Shivering, a beggar-man wandered on,
Shelter or help he findeth none ;
  O, the storm, the wind, and the rain !
Many friends had he when Fortune smiled,
Now he in anguish weepeth wild,
Driven to the door by his only child,—
  O, the storm, the wind, and the rain !

Bowed, as in prayer, a miser old,
Counts his bright heaps of yellow gold ;
  O, the storm, the wind, and the rain !
One shining piece that glittered there
Had blest the dying widow's pray'r,
And calm'd the beggar's deep despair,—
  O, the storm, the wind, and the rain !

See, a white figure glideth past,—
Stands, by the darkling deeps, aghast—
  O, the storm, the wind, and the rain !
With madden'd heart and eyes of flame,
She thinks on home—lost Virtue's fame ;
Plunges to death and endless shame !
  O, the storm, the wind, and the rain !

Rolling in wealth, see Pomp and Pride,
Shutting their ears to those who cried,
"Help!" in the storm, the wind, and the rain!
On to the levèe, rout, and ball,—
To gilded roofs and festival—
Heedless of crowds that starve and fall,—
O, the storm the wind, and the rain!

But see, yon noble Christian hies
Sad hearts to cheer, wipe sorrow's eyes,
Calm in the storm, the wind, and the rain!
Around his path Heaven's blessing flows;
Good angels guard him as he goes;
God grant such hearts for human woes!
O, Life's storm, the wind, and the rain!

THE DAHLIA AND THE ROSE.

A DAHLIA, 'neath the summer air,
To full-fed, haughty pride had grown,
Deeming her looks more bright and fair,
Than all the gems by Flora known.
She scorn'd to breathe a perfumed prayer
Before imperial Nature's throne:
And thus, like silly sons of clay,
She trifled golden time away.

Beside her, modest, pure and sweet,
A Rose blushed beauteous to the day;
Like Virtue in her heart's retreat,
Breathing to heaven her constant lay.
This Rose's lips were places meet
For butterfly and bee to stray;
And every breeze that whispered there,
Lingered to join Love's balmy prayer.

Bright angels at the ev'ning-hour
Would hover round the Rose's breast,
And list'ning to the prayerful flower,
Would waft to heaven each breathing blest.
There is such meekness and such power
In silent thanks by love expressed, —
That e'en the sinless spirits sighed
To mark the pray'rless Dahlia's pride.

The sweet Rose faded when the sun
Of golden summer pass'd away:
The Dahlia gladly looking on
The Rose's calm and meek decay.
" My rival's reign of beauty done,
Of praise I now shall hold the sway ;"
But winter's snow was seen to fall,
And Pride lay buried 'neath its pall.

Soon was the haughty Flow'r forgot,
Her scentless leaves were trodden low ;
While sweetness mark'd the fragrant spot
Where late the Rose was seen to blow :
For pride in memory bloometh not ;—
She holds no seat on God's bright bow ;—
But Virtue's hallowed hymns arise
In greatful perfume to the skies.

THE LABOURER'S DREAM.

A LAB'RING MAN, his day toil-done,
  Slept soundly on his humble bed,
Ready to meet the rising sun,
  To win his hard-earn'd daily bread,
Dream'd of a high and golden throne,
Where he was king, and ruled alone.

Gorgeous his robe and gemm'd his crown,
  Around him throng'd the proud and great ;
His word could hurl the haughty down,
  Or lift the poor to wealth's estate.
Bright stars of beauty near him shone,
While rank bent suppliant at his throne.

Sumptuous his banquets, serv'd in gold,
  Rich wines danc'd o'er his goblet's brim ;
Still fear ran through his bosom cold,
  Lest poison might his glories dim ;
For treason's hands had chang'd to stone
Past rulers of that dazzling throne.

His couch was of the softest down
  That plum'd the cygnet's silken breast,
But oh ! night shades, like demons, frown,
  And chase away all thoughts of rest.
From dark till dawn, with sigh and groan,
He toss'd—though he was king alone.

Sudden, a loud and mocking yell,
  Rose wildly on the startled gloom ;
The monarch heard a clanging bell,
  And leaping up, as from a tomb,
Glared round ! The workman's dream hath flown ;
Where now the crown and golden throne ?

Still pealed the bell ! the sound was joy—
  To labour's toil the dreamer ran ;
That bell he hated when a boy,
  But now he blest it as a man.
"Give crowns," he cried, "to kings alone ;
Let me possess the lab'rer's throne.

"Oh, ne'er let me ambitious strive
  High seats of pride and pomp to fill ;
For flowers that in the valley thrive,
  May soon be blighted on the hill.
Content shall be my aim alone,
With Independence for my throne !"

FAITHFUL LOVE.

She was gentle as the dove,
Every glance and word was love ;
Love sat beaming on her brow,
O'er her eyes hung Cupid's bow,—
Fringes drooped, like shadows meek,
From her eyelids soft and sleek ;
From her lips of ruby hue
Fell the sweetest honey-dew.
Peeping 'neath their rosy lining
Teeth, like pearly drops, were shining :
Smooth her lovely, rounded chin,
Where a dimple nestled in ;
White her cheek, and fair as snows,
Her warm bosom softly rose ;—
Still of charms *this* was the best—
Faithful Love dwelt in her breast.

Chide her ?   Ah, you could not chide !
She had not one spark of pride,—
Save the pride of doing good,
Which no scandal e'er withstood.
Blame her ?   What !   *Perfection* blame ?
Faultless she—she knew not shame,—
Save the shame she, 'gainst her will,
Felt for others doing ill.
See, she blushes !   Tell me, why
Her fair cheeks wear crimson dye ?
Why do clouds of vermeil deck
With warm glow her ears and neck ?
Ah ! such blushes words may raise,
Whispered in my sweeting's praise,
As her name by all is blest,—
Faithful Love dwells in her breast.

Have you seen the snow-flake quiver
Ere it touched the trembling river,
And beheld the trace behind,
As it wandered with the wind ?

Just so light her airy feet
Touched the ground with motion fleet ;
Just so faint—a shade of sound—
Fell her step upon the ground.
Flowers, the slightest, scarcely bent
As her footsteps o'er them went ;
Fragrance wooed her facile feet,
Where she trod the grass was sweet ;
As if wings of perfumed air
Followed beauty everywhere,—
Homeward fluttering to their nest
In my faithful sweeting's breast.

When she sung the birds grew still ;
Echo slept beside the rill ;
Though she heard my sweeting sing,
Imitation broke her string,—
Fearful, lest her awkward song
Might the soul of Music wrong ;
Fearful lest her mimic lay
Might such music drive away.
Philomela heard her strain,
Ceased her song, nor sung again ;
Conscious that her little throat
Ne'er could equal Beauty's note ;—
Listening still each thrilling tone
Wild and warbling as her own ;
Tones that heart and soul expressed,—
Faithful Love dwelt in her breast.

THE ANGEL'S PROMISES.

WHEN thine infant, in his cradle,
  Smiles with sweet and rosy air,
I, with wings of love extended,
  Will be standing watching there.

When the child hath grown to boyhood,
　　When he gambols o'er the lea,
Mark him, tired of play, and sleeping!—
　　Know, he nestles close to me.

When the cares of manhood cloud him,
　　Like a vapour sad and drear,
With my love I will enshroud him ;
　　Songs of hope his heart shall cheer !

Disappointment — Falsehood—Danger—
　　May his path of genius cross ;
I will whisper in his dreaming,
　　"Heaven is gained by worldly loss !"

When the snows of age shall crown him,
　　And deep furrows mark his brow ;
When his bright eye lacks its lustre,
　　And stern Time his form shall bow ;—

I will spread my plumes of glory,
　　Like a halo, round his head ;
And when Fate shoots forth his arrow,
　　I will raise him from the dead !

Folding near my breast his spirit,
　　As celestial breezes blow,
To the throne of bliss eternal,
　　Bear him far from mortal woe !

BEAUTIFUL FLOWERS.

BEAUTIFUL flowers ! beautiful flowers !
　　O how I love ye, fair stars of the ground !
Budding and blooming in paradise-bowers,
　　Robed in rich perfumes, by loveliness crowned.
Let not the honey-bees steal all your treasures ;
　　Close your soft leaves when the butterfly's near ;
List not the zephyrs, with love-breathing measures,
　　And heed not the twilight that woos with a tear.

Beautiful flowers! Beautiful flowers!
　Oft have I sought ye in wildwood and glen!
Breathing my spirit in odorous showers,
　Far from the envy and malice of men.
Morning came gathering the dreams of your slumber,
　Weaving a garland of perfume and light,
Decking her forehead with gems without number,
　Culled from the vi'lets and lily-buds white.

Beautiful flowers! Beautiful flowers!
　Loved for your sweetness, and mourned when ye fade;
Breathing a language of heart-stirring powers,
　Singing till fair things of earth are decayed.
Soft on a rainbow of fragrance ye wander,
　Painting the skies with the tints of your bloom;
Casting your leaves where the clear brooks meander,
　And whispering of spring from the winter's white tomb.

NINA OF HASELDALE.

I was sitting lonely, lonely,
　Where sweet flowers around me sprung,
Thinking of One only, only,
　And her name was Nina young.
O my fairy Fancy sweetly
　Sung to me a gentle tale;—
Robed my heart in joy completely—
　Of my Nina, lovely Nina,
　Little Nin of Haseldale.

What was Fancy saying, saying,
　When she breathed her gentle strain—
When the flowers were swaying, swaying,
　Bending blushing on the plain?
O my fairy Fancy told me
　That sweet Nina would not fail
In her snowy arms to fold me,
　And that Nina, charming Nina,
　Loved her lad of Haseldale.

I was sitting lonely, lonely,
   While the sun sunk to the sea,
Thinking of my Nina only,—
   Did my Nina think on me?
'Twas not Fancy's misty-dreaming,
   'Twas her form upon the vale;
And her eyes with love-light beaming,
   Proved my Nina, beauteous Nina,
   True to me in Haseldale.

KNOCKING AT THE DOOR.

FULL is our world of mystery!
   Strange phases of our times
Work wonders on the sea and shore,
   In near and distant climes.
The soul of Genius stricken lies,
   While fools are seen to soar;
O, many a one, by Fate undone,
   Stands knocking at the door.

Behold! a Monarch leaves his throne;
   The *Liberator's* nigh!
A thousand brave and noble hearts
   On Slaughter's field must lie.
While through the gloom of cannon-smoke,
   And 'mid the battle's roar,
Of crown despoiled, with garments soiled,
   That King seeks Friendship's door!

A lady, fair and beautiful,
   With diamonds once arrayed,
By false, designing man is lost,
   By lawless love betrayed.
Her cheek was once the roses' bed,
   Joy filled her bosom's core;—
Now see her lorn, with wandering worn,
   Knock at her father's door;—

While,—O the strange and sad reverse !
  The maid who with her dwelt
Hath at the altar, with her swain,
  In love and duty knelt.
Her lady-mistress, frenzied now,
  Seeks dark Destruction's shore ;
Her serving-maid, to Comfort wed,
  Knocks at the banker's door !

That banker, full of monied trust,
  And honest for a show,
Is hurl'd from wealth and affluence,
  To hoard with crime and woe.
His pomp and fame are lost in shame ;
  His frauds are counted o'er ;
Run is his race, and in disgrace,
  Knocks at the dungeon's door ;—

While the sweet children of his love,
  And partner of his bed,
With pallid looks of poverty,
  Are forced to beg their bread .—
Till friends grown weary of their cries,
  Relief will grant no more ;
Now desolate, in abject state,
  They seek the workhouse door.

Behold the picture's brighter side !
  An artizan you view,
Skilled at his trade, toil-undismayed,
  By shades of wreck or rue.
Firm, self-reliant on his craft,—
  For Labour swells his store,—
No bailiff grim e'er troubles *him*
  With knocking at his door !

And yet, *all* happiness hath clouds,
  As sunlight hath its shade,—
This life of mirth and misery,
  Of calm and storm is made ;

The Winter of old age is come
When Autumn's harvest's o'er,
And Death—the postman of our fate—
Comes knocking at the door.

'TWAS A' THE BRIGHT MUNE.

YOUNG Robin has ta'en his braw lassie to kirk,—
Sweet is the rose and the lily is fair ;
There's a bunch o' white posies in Robin's white sark,
An' orange-flow'r blossoms in Jeanie's brown hair.
The kirk-bells are ringin',
Ilk joyfu' heart singin',
An' gaily-dress'd laddies an' lassies are there.

Oh, brightly she glances her bonnie blue e'en,—
Sweet is the rose and the lily is fair ;
An' lightly she trips to the kirk on the green,
Her bonnie wee feet seem to tread on the air.
Noo, dinna be jealous,
Young maidens an' fellows,
But tak' off your bonnets—the minister's there ?

An' how did ye, Robin win Jeanie sae sune ?
Sweet is the rose and the lily is fair ;
"Hoots, awa !" quo' young Robin ; "'twas a' the bright mune,
An' a wee bit saft daffin', won Jeanie sae rare.
Sae tak' my example—
My courtship's a sample
O' what can be dune, gin ye dinna despair."

Jeanie's minnie an' daddy sit gladsome at hame,—
Sweet is the rose and the lily is fair ;
For their bonnie wee douchter has altered her name,
An' mauna be ca'd "a young glaiket" nae mair.
Sae sit ye down gaily,
Let joy never fail ye,
An' welcome, right hearty, the new-wedded pair !

LOVE'S LAST PRAYER.

GIVE me back, give me back, the bright moments of gladness,
　When gay o'er the field in my childhood I strayed ;
When morning appeared void of sorrow and sadness,—
　When night in fair star-beams of joy was arrayed.
Give me back, give me back the gay hours I have squandered !
　Sing, sing to my heart the dear ditties of glee !
O, the love-tales repeat you oft breathed as we wandered,
　When twilight was robing in silence the sea.

Give me back, give me back the fond words of devotion,—
　Affection's soft glances,—the kisses of peace !
The soul-heaving bosom, the sighs of emotion,—
　The vows that your love with your life would but cease.
Give me back, give me back every truth-breathing token
　That honour and virtue can only bestow !
But alas ! you can never restore my heart broken,
　Nor cause its faint pulses with life-streams to flow !

SWEET FLOW'RETS WILD.

EVER I've loved the flow'rets wild ;
They were my treasures when a child ;
In seasons when these flowers were seen
In grassy nook or hedgerow green,
Then wandered I in happy hours,
And culled the simple, wayside flowers:
　Sweet flow'rets wild ! sweet flow'rets wild !
　O give me flowers, and I'm a child !

As Memory leads me to each spot
Where grew the blue Forget-me-not,
And guides my gay and careless feet
To daised meads and cowslips sweet ;

Once more a child I seem to be,
For flowers are beams of Memory.
 Sweet flow'rets wild ! sweet flow'rets wild !
 O give me flowers, and I'm a child !

The flow'rets fair a language speak :
The daisy tells of beauty meek ;
The sweet blue blue-bell rings out Love's strain ;
The cowslip breathes its pensive pain ;
The primrose points to childhood's hours ;
The eglantine to tuneful bowers.
 Sweet flow'rets wild ! sweet flow'rets wild !
 O give me flowers, and I'm a child !

O ne'er let Care's dull poppies steep
My thoughts of childhool's days in sleep !
But let the blossoms of the pea
Bring dreams of pleasure back to me.
Let mountain-pinks my hopes sustain,
And wild plum-bloom my freedom gain ;
 Then, flow'rets wild ! sweet flow'rets wild,
 My heart shall hail thee as a child !

———

THE PEOPLE OF GREAT BRITAIN.

O, THE people of Great Britain, with the native sons of Wales,
Have oft been sung, by old and young, in ballads, odes, and tales;
Still, still we praise Great Britain, and the reason soon is shown,
For when we raise Britannia's praise, we loudly chant our own.

John Bull's a sturdy Englishman, and bids his Lion roar,
When foes, on secret mischief bent, come prowling near his door ;
Still, brave John Bull's a kind old boy, with open heart and hand ;
He gives to all, the great and small, full freedom in his land.

O, the people of brave Scotland, to their Queen are leal and true ;
The valour in them seems to spring from hills o' "Mountain Dew ;"

The spirits of their mighty chiefs rise from their grave-repose,
And hover round their heathery ground, like steam abune their
    brose.

On hill and dell they gather well, in kilt and tartan trews,
Wi' thistles i' their bonnets blue, to fight they ne'er refuse :—
They never flinch from war an inch ; they'll either do or dee :—
O, the people o' braw Scotland are the chiels that *will* be free.

O',the people of Green Erin are the sprigs for fight or fun ;
From jig or reel they scorn to wheel, or from their whisky run.
And when the pipes are playing loud, who then can dance so gay?
Och ! the Irishman takes *one wise* plan—he drives all care away.

Tho' e'er so poor, his cabin door to strangers open stands ;
He welcomes you with honest brow, and grasps you by the hands ;
Then, as a lover of the fair, he's ever foremost seen—
No wonder he's so fain and free to fight for Erin's Queen.

O, the Nations of Great Britain ne'er will bow to one compeer ;
For every man's a soilder now, or Rifle Volunteer !
Now the Rose of merrie England mid the Scottish Thistle blows?
And the Shamrock of ould Ireland round the Oak of England
    grows.

How proud must be VICTORIA of her Islands in the sea !
And proud should be her subjects of their native Islands free.
The Englishman of hearth and home ; the Scotchman of his clan,—
And of his country beautiful, the true-born Irishman.

SHADOWS ON THE HEART.

I STOOD near a pillar by Time overthrown,
With weeds and wild flowers and moss overgrown,
As the Dawn looked in sadness on tablets of stone,
    As if she would say,
  " Thus Hope fades away,
When our hearts' best affections lie shadowed in clay. "

The Sun rose on high in the clear azure sky,
But the shades of that pillar bade Noonday "good-bye,"
  As if they would say,
  " There is Faith in God's ray,
When the Spirit leaves Earth and her cradle of clay."

The Sun sank to sleep, and the shadows of Gloom
To a darkness increased of the Night in a tomb ;
While the weeds and wild flowers lost verdure and bloom,
  As if Time should say,
  " Human joys thus decay,
But Eternity cometh with shadowless ray ! "

IN MEMORIAM.—HEDWORTH WILLIAMSON,

Obit April 24, 1861 ;—Ætat 64.

WHEN good men vanish from our loving gaze,
And the cold tomb becomes their place of rest,
Our eyes are veiled by Sorrow's humid haze,
And sighs of sadness heave each faithful breast.

When good men die, the love we feel is spoken ;
Each gentle look, soft word, and action fair,
Hang round our hearts, as gems round Friendship's token,
By memory embalmed, like Childhood's prayer.

A good man dies, and grateful tears are shed ;—
The orphan mourns, the widow wails in woe !
The poor and old his bounty clothed and fed,
Look round in grief, and know not where to go.

Such was the loved and lost of WHITBURN HALL ;
A man of Virtue vanished from the earth ;
Noble, yet meek ; beloved and mourned by all,
But most by those who proved his sterling worth.

His heart and home are shadowed by a shroud ;
His noble sons bend low in manly grief ;
But she, his light, his love, sinks 'mid the cloud,
And mourns as one that ne'er shall find relief.

O, woman fair ! of comforters the best !
When Sickness held his heaving heart in thrall,
When every pluse beat languid and oppressed,
Thou, gentlest Wife, wast near to solace all.

He died, as good men oft are seen to die,—
As flowers and children fade and lose their bloom—
Not with a sudden dark'ning of the sky,
But stealing, like the twilight, into gloom.

    *   *   *   *   *

The tears we weep fall in the moaning sea ;
O, let them, Ocean, to thy surface rise !
That when God's rainbow hangeth over thee,
They may be proved Love-tokens in His eyes.

"KATE LO'ED HER JAMIE."

KATE lo'ed her Jamie mair than a'
The kintry laddies e'er she saw ;
There beamed sic kindness in his e'e ;
His temper was sae gay an' free ;
An' then the lays he wrote an' sang,
When seated shady woods amang,
Stole o'er her gentle, virgin breest,
Like mornin' breakin' i' the east.
"Whisper, saft breezes, that wander the lea,
  That nane but my Jamie is welcome to me ;"

Kate lo'ed her Jamie mair than a'
Frae mornin' till the e'enin's fa',
On him she thoucht—for him she pray'd—
An' dreams o' nicht his form display'd.

Her troth she plighted—brak' the ring—
An' waited but the comin' spring
Her vows o' luve to seal an' sign,
By nuptial rites and words divine.
" Whisper, saft breezes that wander the lea,
  That nane but my Jamie sall e'er marry me !"

Kate lo'ed her Jamie mair than a' ;—
Though mony a spring had fled awa',
An' mony a winter-storm had pass'd,
Syne Kate had seen her Jamie last.
She wadna' sing—she wadna' say,
But pined in silence day by day ;
She tented no' the tales o' scorn,
O' lovers fause that ne'er return.
" Whisper, saft breezes that wander the lea,
  An' bring back my Jamie lang parted from me !"

Kate lo'ed her Jamie mair than a' ;—
An' now the white an' drifted snaw
Lay heap'd, like faem upo' a wave,
Cauld, drear and dowie, on her grave.
For Jamie to the wars had gane,
An' fightin', fell on battle's plain ;
Still true was Jamie to his Kate,—
He blest his love an' bow'd to fate.
" Whisper, saft breezes that wander the lea,
  That the sauls o' true lovers ne'er parted may be !"

THE WARRIOR AND CHILD.

An Incident in the Italian War.

THE far-sounding trumpets, the deep-rolling drums,
Were mingled with voices exultant and loud,
While *vivas* and cries, "See, the Conqueror comes !"
Re-echoed, like thunders, from castle and crowd.

Majestic the hero his charger bestrode,
　　And grandly on nobles and ladies he smiled ;
O, his heart with affectionate joy overflowed,
　　As he bent to receive a fair wreath from a child.

He raised the young girl in her vesture of white,
　　And placed her small feet on his saddle with pride,
While tears glowed, like gems, in the warrior's sight,
　　As the child, like a dove, nestled close to his side.

Round the neck of the Victor she wound her white arms,
　　And kissed his rough visage again and again ;
O, what were all conflicts—War's rudest alarms—
　　When love, such as this, hailed his march from the plain !

A showering of garlands of odorous flowers ;
　　A raining of tears of most exquisite joy ;
A scattering of roses from Gratitude's bowers ;
　　A chorus of rapture without an alloy !

And thus into Milan, 'mid cheers of the crowd,
　　The fame-crested hero, of conquest beguiled,
Made his entrance, like morn on the car of a cloud,
　　His glory the wreath of an innocent child !

————

GOD SENDS ALL THINGS FOR OUR GOOD.

STRUGGLING 'mid the human strife
In the battle of this life,
Let us manfully proceed,
Nor the frowns of Fortune heed.

When I'm lonely 'mid Life's throng ;
When I'm jostled by the strong ;
When the sorrow and the gloom
To my saddened bosom come ;—

When stern Poverty and Pain
Waste my form and rack my brain,
Let me always look on high,
And God's providence descry.

Watching kindly from above,
With His sleepless eyes of love ;
Then elate my soul shall soar
Far above Earth's sterile shore.

Oft I hear the Spirit say,
" Mortal, struggle on thy way !
Life's best efforts are not vain ;
Steadfast to thy trust remain !"

From the dawning of the skies,
Till the star-beams ope their eyes,
Light and Love I still behold,
Rainbow-wings my breast unfold.

Then Life's woes and cares depart ;
Hope sits smiling on my heart ;
Gloom is changed to Glory's flood ;—
God sends all things for our good!

LOVE AND HATRED.

IN this world of joy and sadness
Hatred is a vice of madness.
Why should man contemn his brother ?
We were made to love each other.

Life, at best, is but a dream,
Transient as the meteor's gleam ;
Waking hours are full of strife,
Sleep alone is peace in life.

Smiles commingle with our tears ;
Pleasure hath her doubts and fears ;
Pain seems kindred to our fate ;
Why should we poor mortals hate ?

Soon our pains and pleasures pass,
Like the breath on Folly's glass ;
Sunshine, song, and jocund mirth
Flit, like shadows, o'er the earth.

Clouds and darkness come with night ;
Hope's fair morning brings us light ;
Noonday ushers Evening's ray,
Soon in mists to fade away.

Hasty greetings cheer the heart,
Then "farewells" bid love depart ;
Pleasure leaves us, cometh Pain ;
Naught, save Memory, will remain.

Friend and foe together meet ;
Love is seen dark Guile to greet ;
Thus the scenes of life pass on,
Till Time saith —"The play is done !"

Let this world of moody madness
Change its glooms for smiles of gladness ;
Let no man despise his brother ;
Let us cherish, love, each other.

WOMAN'S DEVOTION

She sat by my bed wi' her hand in mine ain,
An' hushed wi' kind whispers my heart-heavin' pain ;
Whiles, like dew on the lilies, the tear-draps wad sway
Down her bonnie pale cheeks sairly wasted wi' wae.
She watch'd me for weeks ; she wad sing me to sleep ;
She wad kneel down to pray, but sune rise for to weep ;
For the hope o' her bosom grew faint in its gleam,
When I moan'd in my slumber an' raved in my dream.

The fever that bound my puir body an' brain,
That rack'd me wi' anguish, that madden'd wi' pain,
Increas'd in wild fury ; I lay on my bed,
Unconscious an' prostrate, like ane that is dead.
Lang days, langer nichts, there was naebody seen
To wet my parch'd lips, an' to wipe my clos'd een,
For my ain bonnie lassie, wha nurs'd me in wae,
Had pass'd frae this world, an' was sleepin' in clay !

I'm sittin' in grief by the grave o' my love ;
I'm gazin' in tears on the bright mune above ;
I'm longin' to leave the green earth for the skies;
But how can I quit the cauld bed where she lies!
O my ain faithfu' lassie ! lang watchin' an' care,
Affection, devotion, ha'e buried thee there !
An' here will I bide, like a tree in the gloom,
For my heart hath its roots in the soil o' thy tomb !

PRACTICAL JOKES.

I AM quite out of love with you men,
    You are *minus* both feeling and sense ;
Else you ne'er would annoy a poor girl,
    And then laugh at your follies' expense.
That I'm very good-natured, you own,
    To rebuke you I fain would decline ;
Would you leave a young maiden alone,—
    Quite a different course should be mine.

Last Sunday to chapel I went,
    As I thought, with a volume of prayer,
Which no sooner I opened when lo !
    'Twas the "Poems of Burns," I declare !
I closed it in shame and dismay,
    But mamma took the liberty then
To find out the "Psalms for the day,"—
    O, what fun for you *practical* men !

There's a season for laughter and fun,
   But a chapel's no place for a " lark ; "—
My respect for young Austin is gone,
   As I told him last night in the " Park."
Ladies' fancies by fashion are ruled,
   And crinoline-skirts may be vain—
Still, what right had Fred. Peel to insert
   Fusées in my crinoline-train ?

I've been married I know not how oft,—
   I was drowned in the Thames t'other day,—
I eloped from the Hall with my page,
   And was captured to Gretna half way.
Now I don't think my conduct and style
   Such tales in the least guarantee ;—
Ah, you twirl your mustachios and smile,
   But such frolics are odious to me.

I detest all such practical jokes ;—
   And, remember, such creatures I ban !
I can never encourage mad folks,—
   I shall ne'er wed a mischievous man !
I should dread that some day—for a "spree,"
   He might give me a dose in my drink ;
O, a sensible husband for me,
   Or I'll die an old spinster—I think !

THOUGHT.

As the silkworm's toil produces
   Shining threads for robes of grace,
Still bestowing for our uses
   Webs which Beauty loves to trace ;
So bright Thought that worm resembles,
   Clothes with costly silks the Mind,
Valued webs of sense unfolding,
   While it decks the soul refined.

THE BRIGHTER SIDE.

TROUBLES are better for us all,—
   A zest to life they give;
The faithful need not fear to fall,
   The just regret to live.
The sea forever bright and still,
   Were but a painted charm;
And vainly great the pilot's skill,
   If Ocean knew no storm.
Things may look dark; so doth the night—
   And clouds the morning hide;
The sun will surely come in light,
   And show the brighter side.

The Winter wreathes his brow with snow,—
   The flowers no longer bloom—
But Spring shall bid the blossoms blow,
   And trees their leaves resume.
The fairest gem in caves marine
   'Mid darkness long may hide;
But Time shall show its priceless sheen,
   And Beauty's brighter side.

At all times choose the brighter view,
   The dark side comes of woe;
Times may be hard, but looks of rue
   Good seasons ne'er bestow.
Why droop our heads, like trembling trees
   Borne down by Winter's pride?
O let us hope for Fortune's breeze,—
   Contentment's brighter side!

As Day in clouds his journey ends,
   In silent gloom to dream;
So Man, the dreary grave descends,
   Where Darkness reigns supreme;—
But as the Day from gloom shall wake
   And cast Joy's radiance wide;
So shall Man's soul Earth's woes forsake,
   For Glory's brighter side.

HAVELOCK IS DEAD.

"Where are your men of might? your grand in soul?
Gone, glimmering through the dream of things that *were !*"
BYRON.

SOLDIERS ! Brave Havelock's dead ! His corse, behold !
   Ungash'd and bloodless from the deathly fray !
Soldiers, look on your General's body cold !
   Who slew him thus ? Can ye, brave warriors, say ?

Was it Siriasis, the Fiend of Fire,
   That scorch'd his brain and cast your hero prone ?
Or the grim Cholera-giant, gaunt and dire,
   That stretch'd your Havelock mute and chill as stone ?

Havelock is dead ! The hero of Cawnpore,
   Lucknow's great ægis ; England's pride and boast—
Shall never lead your hosts to conquest more !
   Havelock is dead—your glory's Star is lost !

Give way, brave men ! A widow in wild woes,
   Rushes with bursting heart her *own* to claim ;
Upon her husband's breast her form she throws—
   Kisses him oft, and shrieks her Henry's name !

Oh ! who can speak the agonies that dwell
   In that lorn, stricken bosom, prostrate there ?
Who can her burning brain of anguish tell,
   Or feel the torture of her soul's despair ?

Be gentle, soldiers ! Loose her fingers fair
   From his white neck around which now she clings !
Stay ! she grows calm, and breathes Hope's blissful pray'r ;
   O come, Faith's angel, shield her 'neath thy wings !

Now, in his martial vesture, soldiers brave,
   Bury him deep beneath the Indian sun ;
Remember, as ye leave the warrior's grave.
   He did complete the task he had begun.

Men of the Wear, come forth ! and on his sword
    Swear that his name shall in each breast repose ;
That ye will love the native Chief of Ford,
    So long as life-blood through each bosom glows !

But he shall stand before ye, men of Wear,
    Array'd in warlike majesty and grace ;
On Building Hill his statue shall appear,
    And crowding thousands shall behold his face !

The advent'rous seamen, from the strife and storm
    Of the huge waves, with tearful eyes shall gaze
On Havelock's moon-lit, marble-mantled form,
    And hail the beacon with a hymn of praise.

Sweet flowers around the statue's base shall grow,
    And laurels green his monument entwine ;
Then all who love the hero's name may know
    The Malakoff is Havelock's hallowed shrine.

YE STARS THAT SHINE.

Ye stars that shine, like joyfu' e'en,
    Frae heav'n's saft forehead, bright an' clear,
Let no' your twinklin' smiles be seen,
    While I bewail my absent deàr !
An' thou, pale mune, behind some cloud
    O, wand'rin' darkness, hide thy charms,
While I enfauld the snaw-white shroud
    O' my lost Mary in these arms !

Oh, change your steps, gay, dancin' stream ;
    Some mournfu' measure now assume !
While I o' by-gane pleasures dream,
    As bending o'er my Mary's tomb.
Hang down your heads, ye flow'ry trees ;
    Ye hollow rocks, repeat my mane !
Come, Grief, on ilka dewy breeze,
    An' weep, my Mary, lost an' gane !

LOVE UNKIND.

I saw the Violet sleeping
  With tears upon her cheek,
While stars were gently keeping
  Their angel-watches meek.
Of what the Flower was dreaming
  I ask'd the wandering Wind;
"The Violet's tears are streaming,
  Because her love's unkind."

I saw the Lily drooping
  In lovely slumber pale,
And near her fairies trooping
  On moonbeams o'er the vale.
I asked why drooped the Lily,
  And why so pale she pined?
Fays answered, "Love is silly
  To weep at thoughts unkind."

I wandered on the morrow
  The weeping flowers to cheer;
The Violet showed no sorrow,
  The Lily shed no tear;
For Hope came to the flowers,
  As sunbeams kiss'd the Wind;
And birds sung from the bowers,
  "No more is Love unkind."

TOOTHACHE AND HEARTACHE.

For toothache and love there's no pity,
  'Tis useless to grieve and complain;
I had *both* when I courted young Kitty,
  And alas, for my double-fang'd pain!
    My swelled face was twining;
    My heart was sore pining;
O what could I do with twin torments, like these?
Let the dentist and Kitty my maladies ease.

With a face, like a firkin of butter,
    Tied up with a white linen clout,
I sought my fair girl in a flutter,
    As the tooth-twister chanc'd to be out.
      I gazed on my lover
      Some hope to discover :
" O Kitty, relieve this poor heart, if you please,
  And the dentist is certain my toothache to ease !"

The dentist my stump soon extracted,
    The swelling was quickly allayed,
But my heart, now that Kitty attack'd it,
    Swelled higher with love for the maid.
      " My beautiful Kitty,
      Have mercy and pity !"
" Agreed !" she rejoined, as I sunk on my knees ;—
So we married—and toothache and heartache had ease.

"THE TIDE'S COMING IN."

" Oh, gentlefolks, pray, let me pass on my way,
  For my love I must meet at the pier-end to day !
The moon's at the full, and the clock has struck three,
And my lad will be waiting his Mary to see.
I have deck'd my brown hair with long ribbons of blue,
For my lad is a sailor and loves colours true :
The 'kerchief he bought me is tied 'neath my chin,
And my Willie I'll meet now the tide's coming in !"

Poor Mary ! 'tis Fancy that madness now cheers,
That points to thy love through the vista of years ;
Affection's mild moonbeam lends shape to a cloud,
And kindles new life 'neath the folds of a shroud !
She sits on a rock murmuring songs to the sea,
" O Willie, my sailor, is coming to me !
I will wave the blue 'kerchief now tied 'neath my chin,
And hail my true love, for the tide's coming in !"

She kisses her ring, throws her arms o'er the deep—
"Oh, did he not promise his vow he would keep?
'Tis his bark I now see through the mist of my tears,
He is coming! he knows I have watch'd him for years!"
Poor Mary! thy dreaming is happy, yet vain!
'Tis long since thy sailor was drowned in the main;
Still hoping, live on, sweet Contentment to win,
And sing thy wild song—"Now the tide's coming in!"

A MODEL HUSBAND.

"So you wish me, dear Lucy, the man to describe
    That my heart would delight to confess?
Now I won't sketch his person—description were vain—
    Though it ought to be something to bless.
But it never shall be for his mould nor his mien
    That my love on my choice I'll bestow;
To my vision his heart and his mind must be seen
    To be all that we sigh for below.

"First, he must be a pillar on which I can lean,
    Aye, and cling to, in storms of this life;
In ambition an eagle, in meekness a dove,
    And his nest the fair fame of his wife.
Then, the love he confers must be wide as yon sky,
    And as firm as yon mountains to me;
His heart the full flood of his soul must supply,—
    Nay, his love, like the ocean, must be!

"Round this column of might wild affections shall twine,
    And this eagle the myrtle shall bear!
In the nest of this dove the green laurel shall shine,
    For Contentment shall ever dwell there.
Thus the noble and tender, the glorious and kind,
    Ennobling and chast'ning the whole,
Like the statues of gods by the moonbeams enshrined,
    Shall be blent in my Chosen One's soul."

THE GOLDEN GOBLET.

GAY Pleasure came smiling with goblet of gold,
    By Rapture replenished, for Gladness to drink,
But ere to his lips the joy-cup he could hold,
    Pale Envy and Jealously poisoned the brink.
The nectar to bitterness changed in a minute ;
    The gold became dross, and its beauty was o'er ;
And nought, save the drugs of dark Hate, remained in it,
    For the love-stream had vanished that filled it before.

The seraph of Charity fluttering near,
    With a breath of rich fragrance the dust gathered up,
And, bedewing the ruins of Joy with a tear,
    From grains of pure gold formed a beautiful cup.
The sides were encircled by roses of Prayer ;
    The handles were olives of Peace and Content ;
Round the base twined a chaplet of lily-buds fair,
    With the daises of Modesty curiously blent.

" But where," Pleasure sighed, " is the nectar divine—
    The magic that raises poor mortals from earth ?
In this goblet bright pearls and rare diamonds shine,
    But no fountain of Joy in this chalice hath birth."
" In these pearls," said the seraph, " Repentance behold !
    These jewels the virtues of angels contain ;
Here Faith, Hope, and Meekness lie nestled in gold,
    While the nectar thou praisest is Madness and Pain."

———

THE GALE AND THE FLOWERS.

ONE Summer's eve, a love-sick Gale
    Came to my garden sighing,
And lingering, near a Lily pale,
    Complained that he was dying.

" O let me rest on thy white breast,
    In love for thee I'm pining !"

The Lily sighed, and thus replied
To this young Gale's designing :—

" O gentle Gale, my cheek is pale,
And Evening's eyes are closing ;
Do not my trembling heart assail
By love-words interposing.

" Thou can'st not rest on my white breast,
For angels there are sleeping ;
They come to me, for Purity
Is ever in their keeping."

The am'rous Gale then left the pale
And Spirit-guarded treasure ;
A Rose he found with beauty crowned,
And lingered there with pleasure.

" O let me rest on thy soft breast,
For thee my heart is pining."
The Rosebud sighed, and thus replied
To this warm Gale's designing :—

" O gentle Gale, would'st thou prevail
With one so young and tender ?
I do believe, thou would'st deceive
The heart that love could render.

" Thou can'st not rest on my soft breast,
So leave love-words unspoken ;
For angels fair, with holy prayer,
Have won my soul's best token."

The night-dews fell on dale and dell,
The moon and stars were shining ;
And near each flower in Beauty's bower
An angel was reclining.

The Gale, dismayed, no longer stayed
Near flowers by Spirits guarded.
'Tis thus in life, where Guile is rife,
That Virtue lives rewarded.

WHEN FIRST I AWAKENED MY LYRE.

WHEN first I awakened my lyre
   To strains of young love and delight ;
My bosom was fraught with a fire
   That burned, like a star, day and night.
O, the sweetest of beautiful girls
   Presided as queen o'er my lays ;
My harp-strings were made from the curls
   That fell o'er her shoulders, like rays.

The zephyr with musical wings
   Had fain with my harp wantoned free,
But I hid in my bosom the strings,
   Lest the zephyr my rival might be.
The bees came in swarms to her lips,
   Such sweet roses delighted to find,
But my kiss covered up their red tips,
   And the bees fled away on the wind.

O, her voice was a song to my soul ;
   Her smile was a sun to my breast ;
Her sigh o'er my heart gently stole,
   Like an angel's with pleasure oppressed.
E'en the thought of her form and her face,
   Though now I am olden and grey,
To my spirit wafts glory and grace—
   O, I walk in a paradise gay !

———

OUR SAILOR BOY.

My son, Robert William Robson, was drowned in the Chinese Seas, in an
   attempt to save a cabin boy, who had fallen overboard.

OUR Boy is on the sea, far away,
On bounding billows free, far away ;
   From all the loved at home,
   He wanders 'mid the foam,—
But sailor-boys must roam, far away.

The restless, heaving wave, far away ;
Is oft the sailor's grave, far away,
    When the fever-tainted air
    Wakes the wail of wild despair,
And the weak, unpitied prayer, far away.

When pillowed on the main, far away,
He dreams of home again, far away ;
    His parents' forms he sees
    Beneath the waving trees,
And feels his native breeze, far away.

The voices of the deep, far away,
Disturb the sea-boy's sleep, far away ;
    He wakes in midnight lone,
    On his billow-crested throne,
And mourns Joy's vision flown, far away.

Dark night and tempest wild, far away,
Surround our only child, far away :
    O God ! whose mighty hand
    Rules air, earth, sea, and strand,
His help and refuge stand, far away !

To India's burning clime, far away,
He ploughs Thy seas sublime, far away ;
    Grant, in Thy mercy, Lord,
    That by Thy potent word,
Our son may be restored, far away !

STELLAR IDEAS.

Stars we may suppose to be
    The fruits of light on high ;
The sky, a grand and spreading tree,
    Whose produce ne'er can die ;
In every season, budding bright,
By day, unseen ; in darkness—light !

Stars are diamonds round that Hall
  Where shines Jehovah's throne,
With dazzling splendours covering all
  The vastness of Love's zone.
Behold the glorious roof on high
To which Earth's chastened spirits fly !

Stars are lamps to guide our way,
  Amid life's clouds below ;
Our hearts to raise when gaudy Day
  Lies 'neath old Ocean's flow ;
The beacons to each wandering sense,
The sleepless orbs of Providence !

FROM CHILDHOOD'S HAPPY TIME.

FROM Childhood's happy time
  My Lilla dear I knew ;
But years had pass'd since I had last
  Looked on my Lilla true.
With sad and boding heart,
  I sought the well-known spot
Where, hand in hand, we loved to stand
  Beside her humble cot.
She was gone ! she was gone ! she had left me alone,
Mourning my Lilla, with comforter none !

The cot no longer stood—
  My Lilla's peaceful shrine—
A waste was there, where flow'rets fair
  Long loved to intertwine.
The beauty of the place,
  Like Childhood's dream, had fled ;
The wandering gale, with requiem wail,
  Sang of the lost and dead.
" She is gone, she is gone, she hath left me alone,
Mourning my Lilla, with comforter none !"

I sought the churchyard old,
   And there, alas! I found
A simple stone with grass o'ergrown,
   And daisies margined round.
My Lilla's name was there,
   As on my heart and brain ;
I mourned and wept, and as I slept
   The angels sung this strain—
"She is gone, she is gone where sad sorrow there's none,
 And a crown of bright glory thy Lilla puts on."

MY HAPPY HAME.

LET Monarchs prize their gilded thrones,
   When courtiers bend the knees,
My humble hame's to me more dear
   Across the bounding seas.
The croon o' luve an' innocence
   Is worth a conqueror's fame :
O gi'e to me, across the sea,
   My lang lost, happy hame !

My hame has charms o' sweet content
   To princely domes denied ;
The sleep o' peace to Labour sent,
   Invoked in vain by Pride.
'Tis there my bairnies gather round,
   An' oft repeat my name :
O gi'e to me, across the sea,
   My dear an' happy hame !

Braw Castles pleased the Chieftan's pride
   Whar batter'd trophies hang ;
An' deeds o' fire frae minstrels lyre,
   Delight the festal thrang ;
But gi'e to me the cot o' peace
   Abune a' earthly fame ;
O let me flee across the sea,
   An' hail my happy hame !

LOVE AND MEMORY.

WHERE are those sunny moments
   That glanced their golden wings before us ?
Where are those pearls of gladness
   . That Childhood's fingers scattered o'er us ?
      Gone ! gone ! forever gone !
      Like a rainbow's melted throne,
      Leaving weeping clouds alone,
      And the pearls crushed on the stone !

Where are the smiling faces
   That, like fair peaches, clustered round us ?
Eyes bright, and smooth cheeks glowing,
   And words of holy love that bound us ?
      Gone ! hushed—for ever still !
      Like the sunset o'er the hill ;
      Like the lark's last loving trill,
      Ere Eve sleeps silent—chill !

———

THE FLOWER ON THE STREAM.

A BONNIE blue flower bloomed gay by a stream—
   Life is a painting of shadow and glow,
And childhood's the dawn of a beautiful dream,
   O, a flower's soft smile is the sweetest we know !
Gay 'mid the grass woke this perfume in blue ;—
Why should its fragrance the dark shadows view ?

A rude breeze awoke, and the hailstones came down—
   Life is a vision of sunbeams and rain,
And the smiles of existence oft end in a frown—
   And the flower lay broken and bruised on the plain :
Torn from its stem by the pitiless blast,
Beauty and perfume evanished and past.

Now hast'ning away to its doom in the sea—
Life trips in joy on its paths to the grave,
But grief chills the heart of the hopeful and free—
As the stream swept the flow'ret to Ocean's wild wave:
Hurried along from its loved native bed,
The bonnie blue sweet one lay scentless and dead.

THE LAMP OF LIFE.

O, THE lamp of life, new lighted
   In the infant's wandering gaze,
Seems, like dawn of timid Morning,
   Struggling through a misty haze.
Higher now, it brighter groweth,
   As the spring of Youth beams forth :
O, the lamp of life bestoweth
   Gladness to the Child of Earth.

Now the lamp of life is glowing
   Gloriously in Manhood's noon ;
Shadows faintly pass, unknowning
   Aught, save light and love in June.
Cloudless are the paths of heaven,—
   O, the lamp of life burns gay !
Now existence seems but given
   Ne'er to feel life's oil decay.

Ah ! the lamp of life is waning !
   Darker shades flit round the flame ;
Age begineth his complaining,
   Asking whence the darkness came.
Fainter—feebler—shorn of splendour,
   O, the lamp of life burns dim !
Now no oil new light can render,
   Death's dark shadows round it swim.

VOWS OF TRUTH.

Vows of Truth are rashly spoken,
Oft to be by Falsehood broken ;
Like the strings that music hold.
Snapp'd by fingers rudely bold.

Vows of Truth and heart-devotion
Often spring from Guile's emotion ;
Born of Frenzy and Romance ;
Ending like the meteor's glance.

Vows, when by Affection plighted,
Are as chains of gold united ;
Time shall fail their links to sever;
Faithful hearts beat true forever.

Vows of Truth should e'er be given
As the bonds 'tween earth and heaven;
That, when Love's fair task is over,
Angels may their seals recover.

MY AIN WINSOME MARY.

As I wander'd yestre'en by the banks o' the Doon,
The green sward beneath me, the starlicht abune,
I thoucht o' my Mary, an' won'nert if she
At hame, wi' her minnie, was thinkin o' me.
The breezes were balmy, the munelicht was fair,
White cluds o' the lift skimmed like birds o'er the air ;
I thoucht, wi' my Mary, how blest I could be,
Gin that nicht she sat crooning luve-ditties to me !
O my ain winsome Mary, my dear, airtless Mary,
She's my ain bonnie lassie; my Mary for me !

The blackbird an' mavis had gane to their nests,
An' slept wi' their heads i' the doon o' their breasts ;
I thoucht o' my Mary, an' lang'd sair to see
Her bonnie saft cheek nestlin' snugly to me.
Flow on, siller stream, 'neath the mune's tender rays,
An' bring me the daw o' the joy-yieldin, days,
When Mary, lo'ed lassie, united shall be
To the chain o' affection she's cast aroond me !
O my ain, winsome Mary ! my dear, airtless Mary !
She's my ain bonnie lassie ; my Mary for me !

CLOUDS ON THE HOUSEHOLD.

Wearily, wearily all the long day,
  Drearily, drearily all the dark night,
The Dying One, pale as the white sheet, lay
  Wearily longing for heaven's own light.
Answering sadly the moon's soft smile,
  Beaming at midnight her forehead upon ;
Panting and praying, her bosom the while
  Fervently breathing "'Thy Will be done !"

Three boys around her are moaning and weeping ;
  Beside her an infant lies cradled in peace ;
But Death holds her fast in his ransomless keeping—
  Angel of Darkness, oh, give her release !
See, her lips moving, like roses at even
  Breath'd on by kisses from spirits of light ;
"Father of Mercy, whose throne is in heaven,
  Oh, guide my four orphans in virtue aright !"

Infancy wakens with querulous crying—
  Oh ! hush thee, sweet blossom disturb not her pray'r !
The spirit that long for its rest hath been sighing,
  Now soars with the seraphs from earth and its care.
Cold is her brow, and her lips have no motion ;
  Still is her breast, like a snow-cover'd ocean ;
Cold as that snow is the hand that should press thee,
  Poor motherless baby ! who *now* shall caress thee ?

There's a black ribbon over the soft features flowing ;
   The cross of salvation lies close at her breast ;
There are orphans bereft, of their future unknowing,
   And the priest who proclaims that her soul is at rest.
Cover the mirror ! it beams as in gladness—
   And yet nought but woe on its surface we trace ;
Cover its brightness with love-mingled sadness,
   For it often reflected her beautiful face !

Kiss her, my babes ! a last kiss is endearing—
   Kiss her pale lips ; bid your mother adieu !
Mute is her voice once so gentle and cheering,
   And, alas ! she no longer hath kisses for you.
Hark ! from yon turret the death-toll is sending
   Dirge-tones of sorrow ! oh, bid her farewell !
What heeds the iron whose heart is now rending ?
   And the sexton draws life from the sound of that bell !

Laughter and ribaldry rise from the people
   While the sad knell ringeth round the old steeple ;
Chariots roll gaily to pleasure and riot—
   Whose death ever calmed a rude world into quiet ?
See, the gay lark in the bright heaven soaring !
   How gladly he sings, for there's joy in his nest ;
His young ones are not a lost parent deploring,
   Else mute were the strains of his woe-stricken breast.

In the dull room where the dead is reclining,
   One there is left in deep anguish repining ;
One who is praying in darkness and sorrow
   For a wife who will never more wake on the morrow !
Not all the tears, hapless mourner, now falling
   From thy red eye-lids, though weeping for aye,
Ever can rouse her to wake at thy calling,—
   Oh ! Love lies unheeding ; Death's night knows no day !

Wearily, wearily pass his lone hours ;
   Drearily, drearily ! Earth seems a tomb—
Kneeling and weeping forlorn in those bowers,
   With the sunshine once gilded, now shaded in gloom.

THE GRASS IS GREEN AN' BONNIE.

(Music by Henry T. Leslie, Mus. Doc.)

O, THE grass is green an' bonnie,
   Wi' its blades o' shinin' dew,
Wi' the gowan an' the cowslip,
   An' the primrose peerin' through.
There the laddie lo'es to wander
   'Mang the saft an' dewy grass,
An' at e'enin' mid its freshness,
   To woo his ain, dear lass.

O, the grass is green an' bonnie,
   Whar the whimplin' burnie flows,
. An' on the hill-side sunny,
   Whar the bloomin' heather grows:
Whar the lambs are friskin' gaily,
   Whar the shepherd slums at noon,
Whar the kine are feeding daily,
   Wi' the lav'rocks sang aboon.

O, the grass is green an' bonnie,
   Whar the lav'rock findeth rest,
Whar the mousie comes to cater
   For the young anes in her nest.
Whar the callants play at cricket,
   An' the lasses boo' the ba',
Whar the bairnies row an' tumble—
   O the happiest o' them a'!

O, the grass is green an' bonnie,
   Though it aft maun sadly wave
Aboon the breasts o' mony,
   As they slumber i' the grave.
O, then blessed be its verdure,
   An' hallowed ilka blade
That draps the pearls o' Sorrow
   O'er the spot whar Love is laid.

L

MERCY'S MONITOR.

Let us think on the poor when dread winter appears,
 And shiv'ring misfortune lies chilled in the snow ;
When the finger of frost petrifies the warm tears,
 And freezes the blood in the pulses of wo ;—
For, believe me, the hand that shall tenderly lead
 The houseless and outcast to comfort and joy,
Or that lifteth the wretch from the dunghill of need,
 Shall bloom in the spring that no storm can destroy.

Let us think on the poor when our purses are full,
 And sunny prosperity brightens the hearth ;
Let us tender a share of the apples we pull
 From the branches of riches to gladden the earth ;—
For, believe me, these seeds of benevolence given,
 In gratitude's bosom fair buds will unfold ;
And a thanksgiving tree will ascend to high heaven,
 Yielding fruits in good season more precious than gold.

AN ADDRESS TO THE BEETHOVIAN SOCIETY.

When Music from the skies came down in light,
And from the ocean's gloom arose in night ;
Touched with her rainbow hues *chromatic scales*,
And gave the *weight* that in all *bars* prevails ;—
Sought the bold *breve*, with note long-sounding, clear,
And to the *minim* gave the *crotchet's* ear ;
Then the sharp *quaver* near the *semi* stood,
Till grand Beethoven proved the work was good.

 Beethoven ! Prince of mighty Concord great !
Lord of the Fugue, the Counterpoint in state !
Grand in sonatas, excellent in song,
Tho' once pronounced by critics to be wrong.

Strict codes of music oft he disobeyed,
But genius all the critics sneers outweighed :
The fifth consecutive, the chord suspended,
The seventh on earth, in heaven the song was ended,—
Proved that all length and breadth of music's grasp,
Were but the souls that still elude the clasp.
E'en *deaf* was he, unconscious of a sound,
Filled the whole world with music's gems around :
Gave to the burning spheres a lovely zone,
And stamped Beethoven's self a music-god alone.

Beethovians, rise, and with true pith and merit,
Lend to the world a show of music's spirit ;
Blend with harmonious voices one acclaim,
And sing in harmony BEETHOVEN's name !
Oh, that the shade of him, whose soul reposes,
On music's bed—a softer couch than roses--
Could, with this magic, be with us to night,
And to the Stephensons bring concord bright ;
Grasp hand with hand, and heart to heart unite,
Strike loud your chords ;—Beethoven is all might !
Oh, let us bathe in waters of delicious glory,
The founts of sounds by which men may adore ye !
Rush to the chorus of exulting chords,
As if the singers were not slaves, but lords,—
And pile on scales of everlasting tone,
The chorous of ourselves, Beethoven's friends alone !

Now to the task ! Piano lend your strings !
We are Beethovians ! We are music's kings !
We are the concords from a glorious key,
The souls of song, the sons of liberty !
Then let this meeting, which we've dubb'd the first,
Be, as a child of beauty, loved and nursed—
The swaddling clothes will soon be sent adrift ;
For as a lark, our music gives the lift ;
Raises our throbing hearts to strings of worth,
Played by chaste angels far from sin and earth,
And to the gates of harmony divine,
We lose ourselves, and shirk the bonny Tyne.

LITTLE CHILDREN.

FLOWERS of faith, of hope, and bliss,
Made to fondle, love, and kiss,
Heaven smiles in your looks and bloom,
Earth to hallow and perfume.
Children! O, I love ye well!
More than my poor verse can tell ;—
When ye sport the flowers among,
When ye lisp your artless song ;
When ye play, or when ye rest,
Ever lovely, ever blest!
How can mortals fail to love ye?
Pure ye are as skies above ye!
Wearing still the stainless white,
Inside plumes of angels bright.
Ye are spirits new from God,
Free from earth's attainting clod,
And if prayer can keep ye blest
Lock heaven's gems within your breast.
Lift ye from the snares of crime,
Guard your virtue through all time ;
Let your guardian saints beseech
Love and grace and heaven for each.
Children! bless ye! ne'er to fall,
Peace and glory crown ye all!

———

LOVE'S REMEMBRANCE.

WHEN the moon, in summer early,
 Comes smiling o'er the hills ;
When the flowers spring fresh and pearly
 Beside the rippling rills ;
When the lark on high is soaring,
 On trembling pinions free,
And his strain of rapture pouring,
 Then I will think on thee.

When the summer noon is shining,
And still the sultry air ;
When the flowers for rain are pining,
And bees are humming there;
When a sheet of silver glowing
Appears the slumbering sea ;
When the streamlet scarce is flowing,
Then I will think on thee !

When the summer day is dying
Behind the distant hills ;
When the birds to rest are hieing
With love-notes in their bills ;—
When the flowers of peace are dreaming,
When moonlight robes the sea,
And the twinkling stars are beaming,
Oh, I will think on thee !

EVERY HOUSEHOLD HAS ITS ANGEL.

EVERY household has its angel
Hovering watchful round the hearth,
Guiding through the parents teaching,
Smiling 'mid the children's mirth ;
Whispering to the baby sleeping,
Singing with the cradle-song ;
Near misfortune kindly keeping,
Chiding when regret is wrong.

Every household has its angel
In the sweet and gentle wife,
Shedding dews of love around her,
Beaming like a star of life ;
Patient in her heart's distresses,
Loving in affliction's hours ;
Constant in her sorest trials,
Blessing home with Love's fair flowers.

THE BLIGHTED BLOSSOM.

"Tak' me till me hame, mither !
  Tak' me till me hame !
For like some wayward, wanderin' beam,
  My licht lies quench'd in shame !
Spier no' for the peace o' mind,
  For the glance o' glee ;—
Sorrow's shades are on my cheeks,
  An' tear-draps flood mine e'e.

" Ask the tombstane i' the Kirk
  For the heart it hides,
Spier no' for the boat o' joy
  Aneath the treach'rous tides.
Tak' me till me hame, mither !
  Tak' me till me hame !
Hide me frae the licht o' day,
  An' let me dee wi' shame !"

SELF-RELIANCE.

Why at Fate make such wry faces ?
  Groaning never bringeth peace :—
Buckle bravely to the traces,
  Time at last shall bring release.

Should a wandering hornet sting thee,
  Crush not every honied hive ;
Should *one* path to sorrow bring thee,
  Choose *another* road,—and thrive.

Why at life's mischances bluster ?
  Swearing never mended luck—
All your manly courage muster,
  Winning horses head the " ruck."

Rail not at the ocean roaring,
   Whistling Hope the storm may still ;
He who sighs for lofty soaring
   Must keep winding up the hill.

Life affords a faithful warrant
   To successful enterprise,—
But your boat will stem no current,
   Should you helm and oars despise.

Resolution is a giant,
   Naught his progress can impede ;
Man, upon himself reliant,
   One day surely shall succeed !

SHE WAS SAE FAIR AN' YOUNG.

WHEN she was wed till her braw young lad,
   Her years were just saxteen ;
But she was daft for the braw young lad,
   Gif he a laird had been.
Bonnie she was, an' aye sae young !
   Aye sae young this bonnie wee thing !
What did she see at the daft young lad
   That she raimed an' sighed for a gowden ring ?
Young an' fair, wi' her bonnie brown hair,
Lassie, ye'll rue, for the married hae care !

When she was wed till her braw young lad,
   She ran frae her father's ha' ;
To follow the feet o' her braw young lad,
   She left hame-comforts a' ;
For naething had he, the puir young lad,
   O' money, or gear, or land—
Still content was she wi' her braw young lad,
   She was wife till his heart an' hand.
Young an' fair wi' her bonnie brown hair,
Hech ! but they kist an' they cuddled fu' rare !

FRIENDSHIP.

WHAT so precious to the heart as a kind and constant friend?
One that casts aside the dart which the evil world may send.
   'Mid woe's grieving, loved, relieving,
   Dark misfortune ne'er deceiving;
   When men jeer you, ever near you—
   What so precious as a friend?

When the ruthless fangs of scorn wound the spirit, breast, and
  brain,
Causing gentle minds to mourn, what so sweet as friendship's
  strain?
   Ever singing, steadfast clinging,
   Hope and Joy to mis'ry bringing;
   Gently tending and defending
   Poverty in grief and pain.

When the minstrel's home and wife, wreck'd and lost to want
  descend;
When the fiend of scowling strife comes domestic peace to end;
   What so cheering and endearing,
   What so like God's love appearing?
   What so glorious, so victorious,
   As a true, firm, faithful friend?

REGARDEZ LA LUNE.

Regardez la Lune is the burden of my song,
For to' her mystic lamp many rays of truth belong;—
From the rising of her beams to her cloudless, nightly noon,
She is preaching wisdom's words, then O man, regard the moon.

Regardez la Lune when she smiles on ocean's breast,
When like an angel fair, she approaches care opprest;—
Behold the clouds of gloom, how they catch each soothing ray;
Thus the sombre shades of grief from all hearts should pass away.

Regardez la Lune, how she walks 'mid starry beams,
To upraise our hopes to heaven, as our angels do in dreams—
In her gentleness and love, looking down on those who die,
That all may mark the rest where the chastened spirits lie.

Regardez la Lune!   Ha! the giant storm awakes!
He tears old forests down, and the mirror'd sea he breaks;—
And scattering in his wrath tempestuous arrows wide,
He roars along the rocks, and he dashes through the tide.

Regardez la Lune when thick darkness veils her light,
How calmly still she moves through the howl and rage of night!
Unheeding raving winds and leaping hills of foam,
Oh, far above the rolling cloud, for no stormy earth's her home.

Regardez la Lune, in her fulness and her wane,
See the rounded orb of wealth, and the failing hope of gain;
In her night of exile dark from her sisters of the sky,
See the grave of early love, yet of hope that may not die.

Regardez la Lune, for again her crescent shines,
Like a silver branch of peace 'mid the skies' glittering shrines;
And blessings round that light in full tides are seen to flow;—
O, man, lose not that flood, for the neap brings want and wo!

THE ANGEL OF THE FLOWERS.

"The memory of a beloved child is a vision of the blessed."

" Mother, you weep beside my grave,
     Your tears will drench the flowers
That you have planted on my breast
     To mark life's fragrant hours.
You must not mourn! I'm gone to God,
     My *clay* is only yours.

" Mother, sweet flowers I loved to give
    To you and friends on earth ;
My Lilies breathed their purity,
    My Roses blushed Love's worth ;—
But *all* flowers die, like little Ann—
    Save those of heavenly birth.

" Mother, look up, and mourn no more ;
    And, on my next birth-day,
My spirit-steps shall near you be,
    To chase your grief away :—
I'll bring you amaranthine flowers,
    That never can decay.

" I'll bring you Lilies of pure Faith,
    And Violets of Prayer ;
I'll bring you Snowdrops of sweet Hope,
    And Gilead shall be there :—
I'll bring you God's Forget-me-not,
    To banish Woe's despair.

" Then weep no more for little Ann !
    Oh, could you see her now
Walking through groves of glittering gold,
    With gems upon her brow,
You would lift up your praise to Him
    Before whom angels bow ! "

LOVE FANCIES.

SHE was like a gentle bird,
Whose sweet song with love is heard,—
To all other songs preferred,
    Mellow, soft, and clear.
She was like a beauteous child,
Innocent and undefiled ;
When she whispered, spoke, or smiled,
    Angels leaned to hear.

She was like the star that glows
In the morning on the rose,
When the flower its dew-gem shows
   Sparkling on its breast.
She was as the setting beam
Slumbering on a placid stream ;
Like a seraph in a dream—
   Lovely, calm, and blest.

THE WINTER OF LIFE.

I WALK along the street,
   But the faces there I meet
Wear not the looks of former love for me ;
   Cold the smile and the salute,
   Eye and tongue are strangely mute—
What a dreary thing an old man to be !

   Young hearts are like the flowers,
   Loving green and fragrant bowers,
They will not grow beside the withered tree ;
   Like butterflies they love
   Sweet blossoms of the grove,—
What a dreary thing an old man to be !

   I mingle with the gay,
   And forget my locks are gray,—
That wrinkles with my forehead have made free ;
   The young go flaunting past,
   Scorn's eyes are on me cast,—
What a dreary thing an old man to be !

   Ah, youth ! the preacher, Time,
   Shall come with words sublime,
When you have trod the vale of years, like me ;
   And then you will discover,
   When all life's joys are over,
What a dreary thing an old man to be.

Yet let us not lament,
Nor pine in discontent,
The Arch of Love encirles you and me ;—
And the rays of God's own bow
Shall gild our Winter's snow,
For a soul in bliss an old man may be.

IN MEMORIAM.—JOHN PRITCHARD.

BEHOLD, the Temple of Shaksperian might
Dazzles by beauteous forms of love to-night !
The young, the brave, the honest, and the free,
Are there with bosoms jocund as the sea
When moonlight flutters o'er the laughing wave,
And ripples sparkle as the sands they lave.
In this vast temple Music on her throne
Sits, like some empress, potent and alone :—
She, by her wand of magic, chains the soul,
And binds the savage by her sweet control.
Hark ! how the dulcet flute assumes the sway ;
And now the trumpets lead the mazy way ;
The jealous drum in measured starts will bray ;
To mark the violin in wild chromatic play,
Increasing harmony and chords by grasps,
The Canto and the Tenor love by clasps.
But now the thunder of the fugue is o'er,
And Silence slumbers on her tonic floor.
Hark ! how applause prolongs harmonic sway !
But see ! the curtain rises for the play !
One solemn figure on the stage is seen,
Sad are his looks and abject is his mien ;
The big round tears, like gems on stainless snow,
Stand melancholy in their speechless woe.
" Where are the actors ? whither have they fled ?"
The solemn figure speaks these words,—"*John Pritchard's dead!*"
What ! hath the noble Roman Father brave,
Sought his Virginia in the caverned grave ?
Hath the swart Moor to Desdemona flown ?
Hath Lear for sweet Cordelia wreckt his throne ?

Hath Cassio's dagger Brutus robbed of breath ?
Doth the pale Antony recline in death ?
Is Tybalt slain, and Romeo in the tomb ?
Oh, night of horrors ! Day of Thespian gloom !
Duncan and Banquo rest on pillows red,
Macbeth is king no longer—*Pritchard's dead !*
Nay, nay, it cannot be ! I hear the swell
On Switzer Alpines—" Hail to William Tell !"
The tidings of his death can ne'er be true—
He totters on in crimson cloak, the Cardinal Richelieu !
Besides, the Bosworth battle-field is won—
Yes, yes, but Richard's dead—*his* day is done !
Oh, melancholy Jacques, that we should know,
With all thy wond'rous skill—thou liest low ;
Then let the angels, ever bright and fair,
Take thee, oh ! Pritchard, to their loving care ;
Let them with thee in robes of virgin white,
Speed from the earth and plunge thee in delight.
But come with me, and let us leave the stage,
And with Realities at once engage.
Let us who loved our friend departed dear,
Shed o'er his early grave a heartfelt tear :—
His nobleness ye knew, his manly worth,—
His sterling virtues—things too scarce on earth !
Remember still his towering form, his face,
His sunny smile, his speech of glorious grace ;
And all the charms that nature yields to man,
When proud Perfection shows her prosp'rous plan ;—
But as the master-tongue of Avon spoke,
Life's but a candle brief that dies in smoke :
The noblest conqueror descends to clay,
And stops some hole to keep the wind away.
Still shall we cling to Pritchard's honoured fame,
And raise the arch of Friendship o'er his name ;
On Love's high altar ceaseless lights shall burn,
And mystic roses bloom around his urn :—
The Temple's pillars shall his deeds display,
As brethren thread the tessellated way ;
While the great organ shall the requiem swell,
To him we knew too shortly—yet loved well.
  Now, then, thou gentle partner of his life,

His lode-star lovely, his young, faithful wife,
Dry thy wet cheeks, and let the rainbow-beam
Of everlasting glory be thy theme.
Tears shed for love are gems, but we should know
Bounds there should be for every mortal woe.
Above thy grief, God's clemency remains,
To soothe thy anguish, solace all thy pains :—
Death is the lot of all ; by Hope be led ;
Tho' all seems dark, thy husband is *not* dead !
His spirit lives, and hovers round thee *now ;*
Let Mem'ry frame his soul—then kneel and bow !
And when the summer comes, with roses red,
When all the storms of wildest woe have fled,
When halcyon bliss again comes to thy breast,
And angel-dreams proclaim thy Pritchard blest,—
Then to his tomb, and sigh thy soul away,
That thou may'st meet him in eternal day.

THE BARD'S LAST TESTAMENT.

When cold within my grave I rest,
The daisies growing on my breast,
When moonlight marks with mournful rays
The pillow where your Bard decays ;
Say, wilt thou breathe a sigh for him,
And, with Love's tear, thine eyes bedim ?
For Oh ! thou know'st he loved thee well,
As lays of truthful tomes may tell.

Ere the dark angel of my doom
Shall lead me to the land of gloom ;
Ere this warm heart shall cease to glow,
And life-springs through its art'ries flow,
My last fond pray'rs for thee shall rise,
On wings of Hope beyond the skies,
That thou on earth may'st find a friend,
When all my cares and sorrows end.

No worldly wealth, no gems, no gold,
Can I bequeath, for none I hold ;
No castles, lands, estates, I own,
My Legacy is love alone!
And should my soul have leave to stray,
Unseen through time, as sages say,
Thy peace and joy shall be my care,
To watch and bless thee everywhere.

And should the memory of thy Bard
Grow faint and die in his regard,
Should his poor lays e'er cease to charm,
Affection wake, or Friendship warm,
Still o'er thy head his watch shall be
To guide, console, and comfort thee,
Till kindred spirits, we unite
In regions of eternal light.

————

THE HEART'S OBLATION.

God's altar is the mountain's peak,
  His minster's dome is air !
Why should I cold cathedrals seek,
  When I can worship there ?
While incense of earth's grateful flowers
  Receives creation's hymn ;
Vast clouds of golden, gorgeous towers
  Above me soar and swim.

Stained windows of the opening-day
  Cast glory round my head ;
Woods wave their censers as I pray—
  For Nature's mass is said.
No crucifix I need to bind
  My thoughts to Him I love ;
His crown of thorns yon sun hath shrined,
  His cross beams bright above.

Angels,—but not the painted things
　　That man to sense hath given,—
Not earthly beauties, with white wings,
　　But seraphs blest from heaven,
Stand round me and within me dwell,
　　Kindling Devotion's urn
With rapt, pure thoughts.　What tongue can tell
　　How God in clay can burn ?

Bow down ! Adore, thou child of earth,
　　Thy heart, mind, soul, bow down !
Praise Him who gave thy spirit birth,
　　Thy dust a deathless crown.
God's altar is the mountain's peak,
　　His minster's dome is air !
The hill of Hermon I will seek,
　　And meekly worship there.

———

IN MEMORIAM.

Dedicated to Sir Rowland Stanley Errington, of Sandhoo.

"Loved, lost, lamented one ! my heart is broken,
　　Lured to despair ! and yet I should not grieve,
When all the angels' voices, sweet, out spoken,
　　Command me in thy virtues to believe ;
For thou wast holy.　Still bereaved am I !
Can Hope's loved lay a mother's loss supply ?
　　　　　　　　　　　　　　Oh, never more !

" Beauteous thy baby face, like hallowed prayer,
　　Fell on my heart, so full of gentle calm,
That Love abandon'd every thought of care,
　　And filled my soul with beatific balm.
Now love is lost, inanimate, and cold,
　　Shall I again in life such joys behold ?
　　　　　　　　　　　　　　Oh, never more !

Lisping and laughing, clinging to my breast,
　　Like rainbows to white clouds of dewy woe ;
I see thee, as a birdie in its nest,
　　And fain would bind thy wings lest thou should'st go.
I cannot bear the parting, yet must part !
Shall I again e'er clasp thee to my heart ?
　　　　　　　　　　　　Oh, never more !

" When flowers awake, the world looks beautiful ;
　　Then Summer's wings above them are outspread ;
All seems of fragrance fashioned, nothing dull.
　　Life dwells 'mid beauty.　Ah ! my flower lies dead !
I only hold the semblance of its worth !
Can gentle nature raise thee from the earth ?
　　　　　　　　　　　　Oh, never more !

" Shall childhood's dreams of daisy-mantled meads ?
　　Revisit those dim orbs now closed in death ?
Shall the wild buds she clustered into beads,
　　E'er blush again beneath her balmy breath,
While clinging round her warm and lovely throat ?
Shall I again e'er list my pet-bird's note ?
　　　　　　　　　　　　Oh, never more !

" Shall her sweet looks rest on her mother's face,
　　While her ripe lips distil affections dew ?
Shall her white teeth, the pearls of witching grace,
　　Pierce, like the light, the ruby casket through ?
Shall her long, lovely locks embrace the gale,
And with their glossy wings on zephyrs sail ?
　　　　　　　　　　　　Oh, never more !

" Shall the meek moon, and peace-reflecting eyes
　　Of the blest stars gaze down upon the chaste
Communion of fond hearts, whose fall and rise
　　Of purest love the holiest raptures taste ?
Shall her soft whispers meet again that ear,
Bent low to listen, pleasure-bound to hear ?
　　　　　　　　　　　　Oh, never more !

" But are the roses in her cheeks quite dead ?
　　The lilies in her bosom faded ? gone ?

Hath her tongue's molodies forever fled ?
　　Of all her soul's love beacons, are there none ?
Shall not my daughter, like a white rose rare,
Spring into life, and sweeten all the air ?
　　　　　　　　　　Oh, never more ?"

　　　*　　　　*　　　　*　　　　*　　　　*

Yes ! deathless roses on her cheeks shall glow,
　　The fairest lilies shall her bosom deck ;
Her songs in sweetest melodies shall flow,
　　And amulets of joy enfold her neck.
Bright robes angelic shall CLAUDINE invest :—
Mother, weep not ! thy daughter liveth blest,
　　　　　　　　　　For ever more !

HAIL TO THE HOMES OF ENGLAND !

WHILE Freedom roams our mountains on bold, unfetter'd wing ;
While Peace dwells near our fountains, of England let us sing :
The birth-place of true glory, of Science, Art and Song,
Renowned and brave o'er land and wave, the pride of Valour's
　　　　throng.
Hurrah ! hurrah for England ! the Island of the Free !
Hail to the homes of Britain ! Old England, hail to thee !

Where is such love domestic as in our country fair ?
The modest, the majestic, the loveliest forms are there.
The gems of wealth and grandeur, the pearls of priceless worth,
Are found to shine, as in a shrine, on England's peerless earth.
Hurrah ! hurrah for England ! the Island of the Free !
Hail to the homes of Britain ! Old England, hail to thee !

The rose of England bloometh in honour's guarded bowers,
For Valour's prowess doometh to death encroaching powers :
And while the waves of ocean our island-home surround,
For Beauty's charms, for Arts and Arms, her like shall ne'er be
　　　　found.
Hurrah ! hurrah for England ! the watchword of the Free ;
Hail to the Queen of Britain ! Old England, hail to thee !

THE OCEAN-BURIED.

Sorrow sits with sad eyes streaming,
　Gazing on the heaving main ;
Not one hope of young Love's dreaming
　E'er shall glad her heart again,
For the billow is the pillow
　Of her sailor true and brave ;
Her heart's pleasure, hope and treasure,
　Slumbers silent 'neath the wave.

Why did he, her loved one, leave her
　Lonely in this vale of tears ?
Why did Hope smile to deceive her,
　Blighting joys of future years ?
Her fair bosom, like a blossom
　That no spring can e'er restore,
Now must languish, fade with anguish,
　For her love she'll view no more.

On her breast distressful, heaving,
　Rests her love in pictured art,
All unconscious of the grieving
　Of her trusting, gentle heart.
While the billow is his pillow,
　Far across the Indian main ;
Never, never, shall she ever
　See his living form again.

To her dreams his form in gladness
　Rises from the placid main,
She awakes to daily sadness,
　For the fleeting dream is vain.
His gay smiling, woe beguiling,
　Vanishes with morning's ray ;
And the shining silver lining
　Of Joy's Vision melts away !

Where his kiss and fond caresses ?
　　Where his words of truth and love ?
Who can soothe her soul's distresses ?
　　Who can now her grief remove ?
To her sighing, no replying
　　Cometh from the sea again ;
She is weeping, he is sleeping
　　Far beneath the Indian main.

Vain were all her accents lowly ;
　　All her prayers to heaven were vain ;
She must bow to wisdom holy,
　　She shall meet her love again !
Yes, his spirit shall inherit
　　God's bright sea without a shore ;
Where true pleasure, without measure,
　　Shall her broken heart restore.

———

THE POET'S PHOTOGRAPH.

THE Poet, like the rest of men, his mission must fulfil,
Which is to heave Fate's heavy stone up steep Parnassus' hill ;
And when this huge and heavy stone just reaches this high plain,
Out comes Ill-Luck, a giant grim, and hurls it down again.
The Poet is a preacher stern, with living very small,
And though his sermons seldom pay, they often fill a stall ;
Whatever dues to him belong, of profit-tythes he's fleeced :—
O, who would not Apollo be when Mercury's a priest ?
The Poet is an eagle bold, and cleaves the clouded skies,—
He gazes on the dazzling sun with strong and piercing eyes ;
But there the likeness of the bard and soaring bird's reversed,—
The eagle by his talons feeds—the bard by talent's cursed.
The Poet culls the dainty flowers ; he saileth on the floods ;
Leaps with the fountain's ecstacy, and dwelleth in the woods ;
Launcheth his barque of hopeful song, nor dreads the roaring fall ;
Singing with lark and nightingale, though oft he singeth small.
The Poet claims Thought's kingdom vast ; his regal throne, the
　　Mind ;
He sitteth on the rainbow's arch, careereth on the wind ;

But ah! Imagination's dish, too oft, is his sole fare!
Though he on earth would gladly dine, if men would tell him
  where!
Now all these unpoetic ills from Genius might be ta'en,
Were Wealth to help the struggling Bard the Hill of Luck to gain;
Were every man to pay love's tythes, and to the Bard be kind,
Then, like the eagle, he might feed on something more than wind.
Yet, why complain that earthly gifts are not to Genius sent,
Is fame not worth the best of these that seldom bring content?˙
The Poet claims of earth no share, save where his bones may lie;
The world that he hath made his own—is Immortality!

THE BAIRNIE'S LAST WORDS.

" My mither dear, 'tis simmer noo, the flowers are fu' o' bloom:
Fresh, bonnie gowans dress my bed, ah, sune they'll deck my
  tomb.
The sweet-lipp'd things ye canna see,—for tears are in your een—
Smile saft, an' a' around my head, the hawthorn's spreadin' green.

" 'Tis simmer noo; the weanie birds wi' sangs come me to greet,
An' still your tear-draps, mither, fa', like rain-dews, on my sheet.
I fancy, tho' I'm lyin' 'lane, I'm gath'rin' bonny flowers;
Sae sweet they smell, I'm sure they come frae God's ain angel-
  bowers.

" An' when I sleep, fine leddies stand, my little couch around;
Wi' sunbeams on their doo-like wings, their brows wi' star-licht
  bound;—
Abune the hills they lift me far, an' singin' as they rise,
Show me the gates o' Heaven, like flames that open to the skies.

" Last e'en, when I was wae wi' pain, O, mither, sad to bear!
My hands I clasp'd—I prayed an' slept, an' saw the queens ance
  mair.
An' i' their midst, their King appeared, his face beamed like the
  sun;
A shinin' cross was in his hand, fu' bricht to gaze upon.

"A lamb was stanin' by his side—but whisht ! what do I hear ?
A sound, like waters rushin' past, as if the sea was near.
An' mirk the sun is turnin' noo—O mither tak' my hand !
An', hush ! there's music playin' saft, as frae some distant band !

"An' see ! the King comes wi' his cross ! O King, I am thine ain !
Tak' me awa', for I am sick an' weary wi' my pain !
My failin' breath is hard to fetch—O, mither, pray wi' me !
'*Thy will be done!*' Noo, mither, kiss thy bairn—for he mun dee !"

The mither bended law her knees, an' covered up her face,
While tears between her fingers thin cam' ane by ane apace.
She laid her bairnie's hand across his cauld an' pulseless breast,
While angels whispered " Greet na mair, wi' God thy hope's at
    rest."

SHAKSPERE'S TER-CENTENARY COMMEMORATION.

APRIL 23RD, 1864.

O, THAT my lyre were full of angel's dreams
    That, one by one, sweet strains I might awake
On Avon's banks, and woo her pensive streams
    To join my singing for her Shakspere's sake !
    But oh ! my breast no music now can make
That may be mingled with his lays divine :—
    Still to my heart his magic words I'll take,
And raise my voice, while choruss'd throngs combine
To crown the WORLD'S BARD-KING with wreaths from Coally
    Tyne.

A gentle Boy, of wond'rous aspect mild,
    Lay on the flow'ry sward of Avon's stream,
One hand beneath his cheek, as sleeps a child,—
    Smiling, like some young flower when Beauty's dream
Falls on its fragrance in the evening beam.
    The wand'ring winds were scarcely felt to blow,
    And o'er the heavens the Twilight led her team
Along the star-path, as the sunset glow
Warmed with a transient life Day's bosom faint and low.

Behold, in spirit, o'er that mild Boy's brain
  A gorgeous crowd of kingly visions float ;
What forms angelic mingled with the train
  Of human passions !   View each motley coat !
  Peace-lighting Love, Revenge with corded throat,
Dark-visaged Jealousy, Ambition wild,
  Gold-grasping Avarice with parchment note,
And all the demons e'er the earth defiled :—
Then wonder why in sleep that Boy of Avon smiled.

That Boy was SHAKSPERE, and his dream was Truth,
  God-made, God-sent.   Truth robed his mind withal.
Creation woke when this strange prophet-youth
  His words delivered in the sphere-gemm'd Hall
  Of the vast universe.   Then Pride must fall,
And bloody Usurpation felt his throne
  Crumble to fragments, while the 'leaguered wall
Of fancied greatness dwindled stone by stone ;
Thus Guilt shall be destroyed, and Virtue's power be shown.

With Shakspere every man and fancied thing
  Had proper place and glorious circumstance ;
Whate'er he saw from God-like Nature spring
  Stood high in character above romance.
  He, like the sun, awoke Progression's trance :
To crawling worms gave rainbow-glories rare ;
  Bade Love and Joy and fairy trains advance,
And peopled with his Genius, Earth, Sea, Air !—
O, who of all mankind with Shakspere can compare ?

He claimed the Globe in twofold plenitude ;
  The Thespian planet gave to him the light
Of Time's o'erwhelming glory.   From the rude
  First planking of that stage came forth the might
  Of his unrivall'd wisdom.   Thus the flight
Of long Three Hundred Years still leaves *one* Globe,—
  This firm-set, marble Earth, to prove his right
To its inheritance.   Bring forth Fame's robe,
And let poor cynics sneer, and Shakspere's failings probe !

He is great Nature's best interpreter ;
　His homilies are sculptured on the peaks
Of everlasting hills ; and, where the stir
　And tumults of the world prevail, there speaks
　The preacher-Bard.　Mankind, in vain, ne'er seeks
A text to prove what human passion feels ;
　' Shakspere's the soul's epitome.　All secret creeks
Of love, hope, sorrow, gently he reveals,
And schemes of dark despair that madness oft conceals.

　　　*　　　*　　　*　　　*　　　*

Three hundred years, and not forgotten yet ?
　Where are the heroes of his age and time ?
Where the vain bards who lived 'mid fume and fret
　Of what the world then thought and named sublime ?
　Where are their Dramas and their tomes of rhyme ?
Like unsubstantial visions, they have fled !
　While Shakspere's Temple, free from Age's grime,
Uprears its Pelion 'bove their Ossas dead,
Robed with immortal Praise, Heaven's glories round its head.

───────

SUNSHINE AND SHADOW.

In the midst of our pleasures, sad sorrow may shed
　Her tear-drops of anguish and pain ;
As the morning that rises with light on its head
　May weep e'er 'tis evening in rain.
Though the ocean look calm as a baby asleep,
　And gay vessels glide smooth o'er its path ;
Rude storms may awaken to vex the wide deep,
　And tempests howl furious in wrath.

Thus the dawning of boyhood, the noontide of life,
　And the ev'ning of age's decline,
Hath each its dark shadow, its turmoil and strife,
　And its season to weep and repine.
But, as storms yield a calm ; as the clouds bring the day,
　As sweet peace is the child of red war ;
So the evils of life have their rise and decay,
　Till our spirits inhabit love's star.

THE PILOTLESS BOAT.

A TINY boat I set afloat,
  Upon a stream of amber glowing ;
Away it went, like sweet content,
  With fragrant breezes round it blowing.

The flowers bent low to see it go ;
  Soft, verdant leaves its path arrested ;
While butterflies of countless dyes,
  Flew round its mast, as if they blest it.

Awhile it stayed, then off it sped
  Away along the streamlet dancing ;
The trout came by with golden eye,
  And showed his sides of silver glancing.

With graceful ease the waving trees
  Scattered their hawthorn-blossoms lightly ;
The boat sailed on beneath the sun,
  Like some gay heart, in measure sprightly.

The stream grows wide ; a stronger tide
  Carries the boat with quicker motion ;
While breezes blow,—as high and low
  The bark is rocked as on an ocean.

No flowers are there, no blossoms fair
  Salute the vessel onward sailing ;
Gone are the trees, and, by degrees,
  Thick clouds of darkness are prevailing.

The boat still braves the growing waves,
  As high they leap and dash beside it ;
In vain the sail obeys the gale,—
  There is no pilot-hand to guide it !

It topples o'er ! to rise no more !
  Its short-lived trip of joy is ended:
Thus Ships of Life oft run ashore,
  By Pilot, Virtue, unattended !

THE FAIR MAIDEN MIMOSA.

(LANGUAGE OF FLOWERS.)

A BEAUTIFUL lady sat at a lord's gate ;
   Nightshade and Rosemary, Lupine and Yew !
Her tears fell fast as the fair lady sate,
   Sighing and sobbing the dark night through.
Around her the dead leaves of Autumn were sighing ;
   The hawthorn was withered—the willow was green ;
And the wind through the black thorn and aspens was hieing,
   To whisper love's plaint to Anemone's queen.

Mimosa, the beautiful, mourned for her love—
   Love lies a-bleeding, and none to be kind !
And her moan was as soft as the lay of the dove,
   And her sighs gently sweet as the balm-breathing wind.
A little, pale star looked, and winked at her sorrow,
   And brightened the tear on her cheek as it shone ;
Then the fair fell asleep as the star said " good morrow !"
   And left the forsaken is silence alone.

Mimosa, the lovely, lay dreaming a dream ;
   That myrtles and roses were wreathed in her hair ;
That she sailed with her knight on a silvery stream,
   While strains of sweet melodies floated in air.
She awoke, on a couch sweet as kisses of peace,
   She arose, like the moon when the cloud-war is o'er ;
She was claspt by her Knight of the Garter and Fleece,—
   Ah, Mimosa, the beautiful, sorrows no more !

A LASSIE I WEDDED.

A LASSIE I wedded baith bonnie an' braw,
   She neither had riches nor tocher ava' ;
Guid sense she possessed, tho' her luck was but sma',
   By linkin' her fortune to mine, jo !

I neither had hooses, nor hame, nor a purse,
But she wed me, like ithers, "for better an' worse,"
Tho' she quickly fand oot that a Bard is a curse,—
For rhyme was a folly o'mine, jo !

For luck, I received a fair portion o' fame,
An', for hooses, a handle o' praise to my name,
But the profits frae sang were provisions sae tame,
That they gilded few follies o' mine, jo.

Still I *rhyme* an' I rant, tho' my *reason's* but scant,
For verse seldom fills the toom cogie o' want ;
Six feet i' the mools is the land they maun grant,
When they hide a' the follies o' mine, jo.

THE CHILD AND THE STARS.

CHILD.

WHAT are those lights suspended,
    Like lamps, from yonder skies ?
They look, 'mid wings extended,
    Like angels' glittering eyes.

MOTHER.

Those lamps above us gleaming
    Are worlds, and greater far
Than our vast Earth, whose seeming
    Exceeds Sun, Moon, and Star.

CHILD.

And hath each world now shining
    Its lands and seas, like Earth ?
Doth Want sit there repining ?
    Have Crime and Sorrow birth ?

Have stars their woods and mountains ;
   Their fields, their hills and dales ;
Their gardens, rocks, and fountains ?
   Can wise men prove these tales ?

MOTHER.

Nay, *prove* them, mortals cannot !
   Still we may hope in this,
That each bright, pendant planet
   Contains a home of bliss.

CHILD.

Then God these spheres created,
   His love for man to show ;
Why, though with sin we're mated,
   This earth's our heaven below.

Yon skies seem like an ocean,
   With gems spread o'er each wave ;
White clouds in gentle motion,
   The moon appear to lave.

Mother ! can rude gales blowing
   This sea of worlds annoy ?
Can storms, ships overthrowing,
   These beauteous orbs destroy ?

Doth loud and angry thunder
   Those fair stars drive away ?
Do lightnings render asunder
   The star-trees in dismay ?

MOTHER.

My child ! above the roaring
   Of storms on land or sea,
Those stars keep safely soaring
   For ever bright and free.

Some say, these beams are flowers,
  Whose fragrance never dies,
Blooming in angel-bowers,
  'Mid Edens of the skies.

CHILD.

O, say each orb's a spirit,
  Gem-crowned and shining fair,
That when I heaven inherit,
  You'll see me, Mother, there !

———

MOURNFUL TEARS ARE FALLING EVER.

WHEN we were young and careless,
  And round our mother play'd,
We thought not of the sorrow
  That soon our hearts would shade.
Amid Life's flowers we sported,
  Nor dreamt of winter's gloom,
When our dear, darling mother
  Would slumber in the tomb.
        Mournful tears are falling ever ;
        We on earth shall never, never,
        See our darling mother—never !

Her face was pale and gentle,
  Her eyes serenely meek ;
Her voice was low and tuneful,
  As when the angels speak.
She lay upon the bosom
  Of our weeping father dear ;
And dying, kiss'd and blest us,
  And left us orphans here.
        Mournful tears are falling ever ;
        We on earth shall never, never,
        See our darling mother—never !

Cold in the grave she's lying,
  The daisies on her breast ;
High in the holiest heaven
  Her spirit is at rest.
And now when memory whispers
  Of happy seasons fled,
We bow to hide our sorrow,
  And mourn our mother dead.
      Mournful tears are falling ever ;
      We on earth shall never, never,
      See our darling mother—never !

PRIDE, POVERTY, AND LOVE.

HE rolled 'mid wealth and splendour,
  His name a star of light ;
What honour men could render,
  They gave him as his right.
He loved a peerless creature,
  Rich, beautiful, and gay ;
In rapture he would meet her,—
  She proudly turned away.

And yet she fondly loved him,
  Her heart was all his own :
In secret she approved him,
  To him she loved unknown.
Reverses came : the glory,
  The grandeur of his state,
Sunk like a baseless story,
  And left him desolate !

His friends, like clouds deserted
  By beams of morning light—
Grew cold, and from him parted,
  And he sat lost in night.
" To think of *her* were madness !
  What heeds she how I pine ?"
When, lo ! 'mid want and sadness,
  Love's star was seen to shine.

She came ! that haughty beauty—
　　She soothed him in his grief,
And with her love and duty,
　　She brought him joy—relief !
And all her pride was banished,—
　　And now she may be seen,
Meek, patient ; pomp all vanished—
　　His faithful wife and queen.

THE WORLD WAS MADE FOR ALL.

O STAY the gory brand of War,
　　And still the shouts of slaughter !
Why should Columbia's beaming star
　　Be quenched by blood, like water ?
Why should your mighty rivers run
　　In battle 'gainst each other ?
Why should the father slay the son,
　　And man destroy his brother ?

CHORUS.

Let peace go forth to South and North,
　　Lest Ruin both befal ;—
Remember, strife robs love and life,
　　And brings disgrace to all.

The flag of Freedom waves not now,
　　As in your days of glory ;
No Independence clothes your brow,
　　Destruction stalks before ye !
Your spangled banner's trodden down,
　　Your stars no more are shining ;
The eagles of your old renown
　　In death are low reclining !

Why should the North forget her worth ?
The South discard her splendour ?
Let every man leal Reason's van,
Let Peace be Right's defender !
The slaves ye wish now to be free,
The demon War's destroying ;
What earthly use to make abuse
Of blessings worth enjoying !

O stay the brand, for, from our land,
By thousands, men are flying ;
The cotton-yields of countless fields
In wasted wealth are lying !
Hush, hush the horrid din of War ;
The groans of starving Labour !
Let grand good will God's word fulfil,
Let each man love his neighbour.

CAST ON THE WORLD.

WHEN cast on the world without mercy,
Like ships on a desolate strand,
We find that the waves round us roaring
Are foemen we cannot withstand ;
Still the stars of fair Hope may be shining,
Unseen by the eyes of Despair,
And the cloud with its soft, silver lining,
May float, as an angel, in air.

When cast on the world without mercy,
When friends from your bosom depart,
When Scorn, and Neglect, and Dishonour,
Stand ready with poisonous dart,—
Be valiant, as soldiers in battle,
Defying the arrows of Fate ;
Ne'er shrink from the conflict one moment,
While Truth keeps his post at the gate.

When cast on the world without mercy,
   When low and forsaken you lie,
When Want your sad bosom is rending,
   Despair not of help from on high.
Be patient, upright, persevering—
   O quench not Hope's beam in the breast!
Though life seems a pathway uncheering—
   The end of all travel is rest.

CHORUS.

Then keep up your hearts with true courage,
   For troubles, like darkness, decay ;
And the tears of regret, like a rainbow,
   Shall shine in the glory of day.

THE PUIR BARDIE'S WISH.

O ! GIN I had a purse o' gowd,
   An' hamestead I could ca' my ain,
I'd cheer the wand'rer on his road,
   O' wardly bitterness an' pain.
The cog o' reekin' brose wad warm
   The gaberlunzie's empty maw ;
'Twad cheer him through the peltin' storm,
   An' guide him through the driftin' snaw.
But, wae is me ! though *will* gaes free,
My *way* is barr'd by Poverty !

How cantie by the ingle's reek
   The wearie wife an' bairns I'd mak' ;
They'd wipe the saut tear off their cheek,
   An' bless me ilka bite they'd tak'.
My ain guid lass—for ane I ha'e,
   Wi' cumley face an winsome smile—
Wad soothe the bosoms sair wi' wae,
   An' wi' kind words their cares beguile.
But wae is me ! though will gaes free,
Our ways are barr'd by Poverty ;

Wad wealthy lairds an' leddies braw .
   Gie wi' kind hearts what they could spare,
Few mourners then need hug the wa',
   Or dee wi' hunger, grief an' care.
Grand Ha's wad prove the shelters sure
   For a' that puir men tak' i' tow,
An' Age content might then endure
   The weight o' years an' siller pow.
But wae is me ! their will's no' free,
An' thus earth groans wi' Poverty.

IN MEMORIAM.—RICHARD COBDEN.

Supposed to be spoken by his Friend, John Bright.

" How can I speak of him, my friend and brother,
   Like one whose heart knows nothing of his love ;
Who mourns his death no more than any other
   Man-victim doomed from this stern world to move !

" My tears come welling to my saddened eyes,
   From the warm fountains of my bursting heart ;
Choked are my words, for crowding, rending sighs
   Stay the soul's language I would fain impart.

" *Cobden is dead!* ah, what a solemn sound
   Booms, like a muffled bell, o'er sea and shore !
Nations in grateful sorow wail around,
   For he who proved their saviour is no more.

" Did he not weep for me as sick I lay
   In a far distant land, when secret foes
Strove to destroy my elective power and sway,
   To shatter hope, and blight my heart's repose ?

" He wept for me before a mighty throng,
   Who gathered to receive his welcome words ;
He wept for me with such affection strong
   That all hearts present felt sharp sorrow's swords.

" *Cobden is dead*, the father of the poor,
  Earth's benefactor to its starving throng ;
He left Cheap Bread at every workman's door ;
  He fed the feeble, and sustained the strong.

" He was a victor, on whose brow serene
  No blood-bedabbled laurels ever shone ;
Peace, was his watch-word, and his dove was seen
  Spreading its pinions o'er a tranquil throne.

" He was ambitious, but his only pride
  Was his dear country's weal ; his earnest prayer,
That Britain might be blest ; that far and wide
  The wings of Commerce should float free as air.

" As some bright star, unwearied round its course
  Moves calmly onward through the halls of heaven,
In undiminished sheen and equal force,
  Through azure skies, or clouds, by lightnings riven ;

" So Cobden round the sun of Faith and Love
  With industry unflagging, soul unbent,
Was seen a light in cloud and calm to move,
  While wond'ring nations blest him as he went.

" His words were lark-like, simple when they soared ;
  His thoughts were like some river deep, yet clear ;
A listening child might understand each word
  That men of wisdom crowding stood to hear.

" Lift up your voices, nations of the earth !
  Praise slaughtering chieftains on the ensanguined plain !
Blow loud your trumpets, let glad shouts go forth !
  Exult triumphant, kings and kaisars reign !

" But shall their warlike conquests, deemed so great,
  Accepted be before the Throne of Grace ?
Shall tyrant's names on Mercy's golden gate
  With Richard Cobden's take a kinglier place ?

"Hush, hush ! he sleeps in silence, while my tongue
    Forgets the gentleness that marked his own ;
Let not my love for him evoke aught wrong,
    Or write one word in anger on his stone.

         *   *   *   *   *

"Richard, my brother, thou shalt never die,
    While corn shall grow, or Free Trade blessings spread ;
While Peace and Truth shall dwell in harmony,
    And greateful millons by thy hands are fed !"

———

THE LOST STAR.

AMID the hosts of shining orbs that wander o'er the sky
    A silly star had lost its way in gloom,
And many were the dewy tears that sparkled in its eye,
    For darksome fear enwrapped it like a tomb.
        It sought the pathway whence it strayed,
        Alas ! an erring course it made
    Beneath the ocean and above the sun,—
        Essayed each point of wind,
        But still it failed to find
    The radiant home whence first its race begun.

'Tis thus 'mid spheres of pleasures bright the virgin trips along,
    Unconscious of the clouds that dim the day ;
She moves in joy and revelry amid the sinning throng,
    For guileful man hath led her feet astray.
        Then sad regrets and fruitless tears,
        And mem'ries of once happy years,
    In clouds of dark despair before her rise ;
        She seeks the stranger's shore,
        But home she finds no more—
    That star is lost to virtue and the skies !

O, FOR THE DAISIES!

O, FOR the daisies! when life's day is o'er,
    To mantle my grave with their blush-tinted light;
When the canker of sorrow shall trouble no more,
    And silence shall fold me in robes of the night!
O, beautiful daisies! your bosoms of gold,
    Your white wings, like angels', my refuge shall be!
Oh, cling to me, daisies, above the damp mould,
    And breathe, "*requiescat in pace*," for me!

O, for the daisies! but winter will come
    And bury their beauty in shrouds of the snow;
Their bright eyes shall slumber in chillness and gloom,
    Like the heart of the mortal that moulders below.
O, beautiful daisies! the spring shall arise,
    And steal from your bosoms their mantles of white;
Once more shall ye gaze on the sun-gilded skies,
    And hail the fair spirits in regions of light!

THE HUNGRY SEA.

RAIN! rain, thick, bead-like rain, rushed hurrying from the clouds,
Driven by the howling, wolfish wind that bellowed through the
    shrouds
Of a black-sided, struggling vessel in the boiling main,
While lightnings, like blue flames of hell, flashed whizzing 'mid
    the rain.
O, how the sailors cursed their fate, blaspheming to the skies!
Still dashed the surges madly on, and drowned their oaths and
    cries.
Struggling and heaving rolled the ship, the canvas fluttering flew;
And now the mainmast crashing fell among the yelling crew.
Dark, vast, and grim, the rugged rocks, like giants huge appeared,
The ship a wreck—a waste of hull—the granite gorgons neared;
And now amid the roaring storm the vessels rends in twain,
Shivered against the adamant, and scattered o'er the main!

Like watery fiends the billows fought, the seamen to devour,
Their horrid, foamy jaws agape in that tempestuous hour!
Down, down to darkling depths profound, sank mariners and bark,
A hungry ocean prowled for more, like some insatiate shark,
Leaping above the closing void, and roaring as in glee,
O, what a monster is the main! When shall be gorged the sea?
In that doomed ship, 'mid that doomed crew, a passenger was I,
And sore I battled with the waves, determined not to die;
My strength was like a baby's strength, the billows crushing fell,
And, like a plaything, hurled me up, then caught me 'mid the swell;
Down, down, and still down, down, my helpless body sunk,
As huge sea-demons thronged around, and seized my sinking trunk.
Piece-meal they tore me! Some with horns scooped out my glaring
    eyes,
Some crunched my bones with iron jaws, some battled for my
    thighs:—
One with a dark-red, horny throat ingulped my severed skull,
Then lashed his vast sides with his tail, and bellowed like a bull!
At length my carcass disappeared; my spirit then was free,
And from the prison of my flesh, my soul was in the sea!
Calm were the depths marine, like glass, pellucid, strangely still,
Blue glowed the briny atmosphere, transparent grew each hill;
Interminable forests spread undying freshness wide,
And glittering rocks high heaved their heads in everlasting pride.
Vast fields of coral waved like corn, and diamond caves were there,
And grottoes of a million shells and halls of rubies fair.
The pavements where the dolphins basked were one vast sheet of
    gold,
And 'mid a couch of rainbow pearls the sportive creatures rolled.
Palaces stood, like clouds of flame, the mother streams beside,
Where silver rain with amber mixed, and gold enriched the tide.
There gem-encrusted diadems, that earthly pomp had borne,
Lay near the whitened skulls of kings that had these treasures worn;
Piles of red armour strewed the deep, their tenant-warriors, where?
And gleaming shields, moss-grown and old, and battered helms
    were there.
But who can number all the sights that lie beneath the sea?
'Twould be like counting days and nights in round Eternity!
Count all the sand-grains on all shores and sun-motes in the beam.—
Behold! I waken! all is fled—*my shipwreck was a dream!*

DEATH OF PRESIDENT LINCOLN.

SCARCE had the pulses of a nation's heart
   Begun with joy to leap, and from the tongue
Sent shouts exulting, and the Victor's art
   Had stayed the strife of foemen bold and strong ;—
   Scarce had the pealing bells, and chorussed song
Of million-voices with th' artill'ry's boom
Thundered high hills and verdant vales among,
   Than Death stalked onward through the nitreous gloom
To stab the nation's heart, and hurl it to its tomb.

The faith was high in every patriot's breast,
   That War at last would on his buckler sleep ;
That every soldier in a peaceful rest,
   Would dream of home, and wake at home to weep ;
   That Monitors would scour no more the deep ;
That swords to reaping hooks, that strife to peace,
   Would be transformed, and Union keep
   His grasp of Friendship, never to release
His bonds of brotherhood, till Time himself should cease.

Hope, in her rainbow wings, stood bright arrayed,
   A tear of thanks in each uplifted eye.
"Now, praised be Heaven, the storm is past," she said,
   When crashing thunder from the cloudless sky
   Fell blazing at her feet, amid a cry
Of suffocating grief—"*He's dead! He's dead!*"
The nation shrieks her wail of agony !
  .His widow wanders by her Lincoln's bed
   With bosom woe-distraught, with reason almost fled.

Lincoln is dead! the man whose prudent skill,
   Whose wisdom, firmness, led a nation great
Through scenes of civil conflicts terrible,
   More dread than e'er convulsed European State ;
   Whom Scorn ne'er crushed, or flattery made elate ;
Who looked on failure and success as things
Common to good and evil ; wheels of fate
   That had their motions from contending springs ;—
   Lincoln is dead! the vultures close their wings.

Lincoln is dead ! the man whose name shall stand,
  Like a grand Pharos o'er th' Atlantic wave,
Above all patriots in this wond'rous land.
    Chosen of heaven, four million souls to save
    From bondage-chains, and from a living grave !
Hark ! how the wail of sadness rends the vault
Of th' upheaving skies ; Washington shall crave
    The crown of Mercy's tears.   Shall Britain halt
    In her vast love of Right, or reckon Treason's fault ?

No ! no ! the dead is sanctified ; the assassin's ball
  Hath oped the gates of glory to his name !
BOOTH, in his madness, saw old Lincoln fall,
  But never dreamt that from the ensanguined shame
Of his vile murder would a Phœnix rise,
    To change its gore-blot to a sheet of flame,
On which the lightnings of th' avenging skies
    Would cast him down to hell-depths of dread blame :
Would write tempestuous scorn and countless obloquies !

Assassin ! fool ! the drama is played out,
  Has Cæsar tumbled down at Pompey's feet ?
Thou, wretch, shalt be crime's blazon, and the scout
    Of all good men, who shall from thee retreat,
    As some mad dog, the nuisance of each street.
" *Thus always with the tyrants,* " was thy cry ;
Greater than thou no tyrant can we meet ;
    A blighting blast upon thy name shall lie ;
    For thou cans't ne'er repent—the demons lock the sky !

The widow ! Oh, that name for wretchedness !
  That desert-blast ; that springless waste of death !
Where verdure never comes the heart to bless,
  Or lend the perfume of affection's breath,
To wake the kiss of love, or love's caress.
    Lincoln is dead ! the widow cries "*for ever !*"
Her heart within a sea of wild distress ;
    Her mem'ry rushing on a raging river ;
    Her eyes fixed on one dead, mind, soul, heart, brain, to sever!

Sweet Queen of England? widow unconsoled !
  Thou do'st with Lincoln's relict sympathise,
Although thy heart sleeps with thine Albert's cold,
  The spirit of thy love is seen to rise,
  Like birds from earth, to wake the slumb'ring skies.
Thou art a mother, Queen ! and thou can'st feel
  What only mothers can. Thy missive flies
  As rays from Sol's bright scintillating wheel,
  The mourning world to warm, thy greatness to reveal!

Who shall accuse the South of thy dread slaughter?
  Lincoln, the honest, firm, arise, and say !
Did not thy foes pour life-blood out like water?
  Were they not noble in each horrid fray?
  Thou wast of maniacs wild the only prey?
But thou art gone ! the sun still shines the same ;
  The evening gloom precedes the glorious day.
  Thou'rt gone to dust ! from dust arose thy name ;
  The rainbow is from God ; to God resign thy fame !

THE LOVED AND THE LOST.—IN MEMORIAM.

HERE, mid the Jesmond tombs of death,
    I sit, and sadly ruminate
    On bygone days so full of Fate,
So plague-struck with Doom's icy breath.

I see my first-born child,—a girl
    Blooming to womanhood, lie dead,
    Masses of beauty round her head,
And loveliness in glossy curl.

I see my boy—my first dear boy,
    Stricken by death just at that time
    When Youth and Strength are seen to climb
The flow'ry hills of Hope and Joy.

I see two cherubs, blessed things
  That sleep in death, like virgin snow,
  Sinless, unheeding care and woe,
Greater and mightier far than kings.

I look again, but oh, mine eyes
  Are full of tears and streaming grief ;
  Where shall I find hope, joy, relief ?
Above me hang the gloomy skies,—

Below me yawns the gulfing main,
  And there a noble youth I see
  Struggling with wide Infinity,
But struggling, oh, alas, in vain !

Mad waves !   Why did ye drown my boy ?
  I had but two my heart to bless,—
  And whisper future happiness,—
But thou'rt accustomed to destroy.

The snows of age fell o'er my brow—
  Still *one* child lived my home to cheer—
  He to my heart was ever dear—
But, oh, my God !   *I'm childless now !*

Thy mother takes my hands in hers
  And solace, to my woe bespeaks ;
  Tho' grief is coursing down her cheeks
And agony her bosom stirs.

Weep with me; widow, young and fair,
  Thou loved'st thy husband with a faith
  That followed him thro' life till death,
That still breathes forth affection's prayer.

Oh, fold thy children to thy breast,
  And think of him whose love for thee
  In weal and sad adversity
Was by his kindest acts expressed.

He was—but, no ! I will not weave
    The web of woe around my breast ;
He's dead, and wherefore should we grieve
    When well we know his soul is blest ?

I have no children ! *all are gone!*
    Gone, gone ! Sad word that rends my heart !
Child-comforters I now have none,
    And readier thus with life to part.

Yes, I have grand-bairns, bless them all !
    They shall replace my children dead ;
May Heaven's blessings o'er them fall,
    And Hope's bright bow shall still be spread.

THE ORPHAN'S GOLDEN DREAM.

Weary, oh, weary of wand'ring all day,
Sighing and fretting her young heart away,
Emma, the orphan girl, slumbering lay
    By the side of a soft-flowing stream.

Pale were her cheeks, while her bright, glossy hair,
Floating around her, like Hope in Love's prayer,
Kiss'd off the tear-dews still lingering there,
    As she smiled in some beautiful dream.

There was her mother, with looks of delight,
Seated before her in vesture of white ;
Crowned, like an angel in virtue and might,
    In a kingdom of bliss undefiled.

Emma, young dreamer, arose in great haste,
Hung round her mother whose neck she embraced,
Gazing in wonder on beauty so chaste,
    While the mother looked love on her child.

" Mother, dear mother ! you look like a queen !
Rolling in riches 'mid glories serene—
Who would now think that a pauper you'd been—
   Or that ever you begged for your bread ?

" Where is the shroud that in death you were dress'd ?
Where the jet cross that you wore at your breast ?
You are a lady, and live on the best,
   Oh, how have you 'scaped from the dead ?

" Homeless, I wander, a beggar forlorn,
Sleeping in byeways, and rising at morn
Hungry, and dreading the cold night's return.
   Oh, mother, I faint as I speak ?

" Let me remain with you ! Here I can rest !
Free from starvation, with care ne'er oppress'd ;—
Take me, oh, take me again, to your breast !
   Tis a refuge from want I now seek !"

Ah ! she awakens ! Joy's vision is vain !
Sad to the orphan comes life's grief again ;—
Still there is hope, for a beautiful strain
   Breathes from the soft-purling stream.

" Onward and upward !" the voice seems to say,
" Trust in Thy God, child, and walk in His way !
He will protect thee till cometh that day,
   When Time shall not mar Emma's Dream !"

DREAMING OF THE RAINBOW.

DREAMING, I saw the sunlight
   Salute the raindrop's lips,
As the shadows of the evening
   Awoke from their eclipse,
Blushing their hues of sea-shells
   That sing beneath the ships.

And, lo ! an arch of beauty
  Arose from out the mist !
Gems of all tints were glowing,
  Where'er the sunbeams kissed :
The topaz, ruby, sapphire,
  And purple amethyst.

Soon as this dome of diamonds
  The earth appeared to span,
There breathed bright aspirations
  From heart and soul of man :
And prayers, from grief and anguish,
  Through crowds of mortals ran.

The sailor bless'd it, circling
  Above the storm-spent main ;
The farmer, in its glowing,
  Beheld the ripened grain :
He knew the deluge flood-gates
  Were ne'er to ope again.

The soldier viewed the topaz,
  And sighed for glorious fame ;
The amethyst's clear purple
  Clad high Ambition's name ;—
Oh, that rainbow crowned the Emperor
  With an imperial flame.

That Arch spoke like an angel,
  To dying hearts of clay ;
For there was consolation
  In each chromatic ray ;
Each gem-hue seems to whisper
  The advent of Joy's day.

Hope ruled there for a season,
  But ah ! the segment broke !
And gems, like opals clouded,
  Seemed gleaming through a smoke,
And mingling indistinctly,
  Like the whirling chariot-spoke.

The poet knelt enraptured,
    The rainbow's wings to view ;
And deep, wild strains he rendered,
    Each sun-created hue :—
But, like his dream, all faded,
    And nought remained but dew !

—————

OPHELIA.

BEHOLD the meek Ophelia, pale as snow,
    And in her gentle hand bruised buds of Thought—
Remembrance—Love.   The melody of Woe
    Is hers, most musically wild, and fraught
    With the heart's requiem, tender and untaught.
She scatters flowers upon her father's shroud,
    And gems them with her tears.   Thus heaven's bright bow
Paints the descending rain-drops on the cloud,
    Blending the ruby with the sapphire's glow.
    But whither now doth sweet Ophelia go ?
Fair, flowery chaplets, from the brook to cull,
That she in death may seem more beautiful.

—————

ROBERT CHAMBERS.—IN MEMORIAM.*

HANG down thy hoary head, oh, Father Tyne,
    And let thy sorrows mingle with the wave ;
For ruthless Death his claim will ne'er resign,
    Nor render back thy son, thy Champion brave !

O'er thy broad bosom, like a streak of light
    Shooting along the starry depths of heaven,
How oft, oh Father, hath he blest thy sight,
    And to the hearts of thousands rapture given !

—————

* A magnificent monument of Prudham stone, sculptured by Mr. Burn, of Newcastle, now stands in glorious beauty over the ashes of "honest Bob," in Walker Churchyard.

Have not thy verdant hills with jocund mirth
  Reverberated to th' exulting crowds,
When thy brave boatman in his skiff came forth,
  Like some May-monarch 'mid his golden clouds ?

Have not thy daughters fair, with bosoms white,
  And sun-kiss'd tresses, and with beaming eyes,
Come thronging to thy banks, in wild delight,
  To watch their fav'rite oarsman gain the prize ?

Call forth thy Naiads ! Let them weep with thee !
  Let Love's soft rain fall dimpling thy calm streams,
Till Hope shall rise in beauty from the sea,
  And shed on every tear her rainbow-beams.

Oh, Tyne ! Thou never hadst a son like him !
  So placid, yet so brave ; so famed, yet true !
A wine-filled goblet, gen'rous to the brim ;
  A trusty captain, king of every crew !

Did he e'er barter once his noble soul,
  Or risk his Independence by Deceit ?
Did interest e'er his manly heart control,
  Or gold seduce him to a vile defeat ?

Oh, never ; no ! E'en when the surge of death
  Struck fierce and chill against his sinking frame ;
When fell disease had check'd his bounds of breath,
  He struggled onward, upward, for his fame !

And he hath reach'd the goal of glory now,
  Though pale he lies beneath the churchyard sod ;
For thousands at his grave were seen to bow,
  While Mercy gave him to his Maker, GOD !

Oh, Tyne ! didst not thine eyes run o'er with joy—
  The joy of grief—to see the moving crowds,
Draped in their sable garbs, attend thy boy
  To his last resting place among the shrouds ?

There came the Order of the Sleepless Eye,
    With polished Pillars of the Temple Grand ;
The Lights of Truth, the glorious Mystic Tie,
    And all that fills the boundless sea and land.

There glowed loved hearts of Friendship, Union, Love,
    'Mid flowers and fruits gathered in Paradise ;
There beamed the blessings from the heavens above,
    With every excellence on earth that lies !

Then, Father Tyne, were seen thy skiffsmen bold,
    The " Albion," " Northern," and the " Elfin " crews ;
Take them, sage Patriarch, to thy watery fold,
    And teach them how the oars of peace to use.

But lo ! a marble tomb is seen to rise
    On the green grave where he we mourn reposes !
And see ! the name of Chambers greets our eyes,
    Crowned with a wreath of everlasting roses.

FOR EVER AN' FOR AYE.

My todd'lin, wee bairnie cam' lauchin' like flowers,
When their lips, fu' o' sweetness, peep oot 'mang the bowers ;
An' grippin' my coat wi' her fat, dimpled fist,
Held up her saft mou' to my ain to be kist.
The bairnie I lifted wi' joy to my arms,
Like a birdie, she nestled there free frae a' harms ;—
Noo the lips o' that wee thing lie covered wi' clay,
An' her kisses hae vanish'd for ever an' aye !

Gowden threads was her hair o' the saftest o' silk ;
Her forehead an' temples—oh, whiter than milk !
Her e'en were twin vi'lets, in dew-di'monds set,
Oh, her bonny round face I can never forget !
Her cheeks, dimpled pleasures—wee cups o' delicht—
The minglin o' blossoms, the reed an' the white ;
But the cheeks an' their roses hae sunk te decay,
An' the blossoms lie wither'd for ever an' for aye.

She laucht i' the sunshine, an' played on the sands,
An' scoop'd weeny wells wi' hor bonny white hands ;
Cull'd smooth pebbles an' shells by the marge o' the sea ;
Wi' delicht in her breast, an' a smile in her e'e.
The starn had just lichted their lamps in the sky,
When sudden an' shrill rose my bairn's fearfu' cry ;
The hand o' deeth's angel had striken his prey,
Her life-glee is ended for ever an' aye !

On her grave I ha'e planted the sweetest o' flowers,
An' oft I bedew them wi' heart-rainin' showers ;
A white marble stane at her head I ha'e set,
An' there you may read the lo'ed name o' my pet.
A green, droopin' willow abune her grave hangs,
Where the sma' birds at e'en sing their sweetest o' sangs :
Oh, cease your gay warblins! I'm weary wi' wae ;
For my bairn's sang is hush'd noo, for ever an' aye !

I sit i' the gloamin ; an' fancy I see
The face o' my bairnie wi' luve in her e'e ;
Her hair still is shinin', her forehead's still white,
Where a croon o' fair di'monds is flashin' wi' licht.
She points wi' ae finger as if she would show,
That happiness dwells not in *this* world below ;
Then as she ascends on a heavenly ray,
I ken God will keep her for ever an' aye ;

BONNIE NELLIE.

BONNIER than the rose in June, sweeter than its breath ;
Safter than the ruby lips o' buds that blush beneath,
Nellie was, and Nellie is, though she is no' mine,
I maun speak the holy truth, o' a' God's works divine.

Ha'e ye seen a milk-white lamb, sleepin' nigh its mither ?
Ha'e ye seen a shinin' star brighter that ilk ither ?
Sic a lamb my Nellie was, sic a star she shines ;
She was spotless as the plume an angel's wing that lines !

Ha'e ye heard the lavrock sma', to the rainbow sing?
Ha'e ye seen him swiftly fa' earthward on the wing?
Nellie sung to Love and Hope—will she sing again?
Yes, she sits abune the bow chantin' glory's strain.

When my heart is sad and sair wi' the world at war,
I gae out to sigh an' stare at a bonnie star.
Blindin' draps stand in my e'e, maun I then despair?
Never! for the star I see is Nellie shinin' there!

FRIENDSHIP'S GARLAND.

By a wreath of Friendship circled,
By love's chaplet on each brow,
Let all doubts that round us darkled
Be transformed to gladness now.
Like the lark from earth upspringing,
We will leave sublunar care,
And with soul-tuned voices singing,
Waft affection everywhere.

Let our words, like moon-light stealing
To the glooms the caverns know,
Send their accents mild, appealing
To all rugged hearts below.
Let not winds or Hatred waken
Angry tumults in the breast;
Come, Love, sooothe the bosom aching!
Sing its sorrow into rest!

Let our hearts to one another
Be united in Love's chain—
Let not selfish motives smother,
Or divide our faith again!
Then this world would be an ocean,
Where God's pearls may thickly lie;
Where true Honour, Love, Devotion,
And strong Friendship cannot die!

THE LILY AND THE BUD.

'Twas yesterday "The Lily of the Plain,"
Woke my rude harp among the Tyneside strains ;
To-day my lyre shall tell of sweeter lilies
Than ever blossomed on the plains of Fars.
So, come with me, and I a flower will show
That rocks all sweets to rest, and leaves a bud
To bless the world with fragrance, oh, divine !
That lily grew, no, not on the banks of Nile,
But in a little place called Nazareth,
Christened by Christ ; for He, poor child, was born
In a mean stable there.   But as God's rays
Of everlasting glory glow on gloom,
And shame the clouds of Ignorance and Pride,—
So did this Lily's beauty gem the souls
That bowed before it in it's lowly bed.
The shepherds sung loud songs and hailed this Bud,
That fluttering left the Lily's side.   Great kings
Salaamed before this Bud, that looked and smiled
On gifts of gold, of frankincense, and myrrh.
Angels composed new songs to hail this Sweet,
And the young stars danced joyfully that morn
When this dear Passion-Flower first saw the day
Of life and light and the redeeming Cross.
This Bud, more beautiful than Sharon's Rose,
Grew gracefully beside the Virgin Lily,
And filled the earth and heavens with perfumed love.
The sick and leprous wretches, worn with woe,
Crawled, like lank worms, to feast their fading eyes
On so much beauty, chastity, and peace ;
And having suck'd the perfume of this Bud,
Like bees that steal their honey from sweet flowers,
Rose cured, rejoicing, laughing at past griefs,
And blessing God in raptures of the heart.
Blind men came, feeling out their path of Hope,
And went home weeping tears from opened eyes ;
Yea, the white shroud of death was cast aside,
And dead men leapt, like spring from winter's thrall,
To bless their Saviour-Flower with outstretched arms.

But hark ! the jocund bells have noisy grown,
And wag their clanging tongues of merriment
Against the metal sides of mirth and joy !
Why, this is Christmas Day !   Oh, fool am I
Not to remember that Salvation's Bud
Bloomed in the snow and crimsoned on the cross !
Let me, and you, bend low and kiss the rood
Where hangs the chaplet of Eternal Love !

THE TURQUOISE AND THE RUBY.

Inscribed to the Right Hon. the Earl of Durham.

An angel, full of grace and love,
Descended from his sphere above ;
His embassy to earth was peace—
To bid all war and discord cease.
His wings were spread above a world
Where Slaughter's banner was unfurled ;
And soon his plumes of rainbow-light,
The gloom of battle put to flight.

The angel's crown was starred with gems,
Priceless above earth's diadems :—
The Amethyst and Emerald green ;
The Sapphire's cerulific sheen ;
The Chrysolite and Topaz' gold ;
The Jasper—Hyacinth, behold !
But lo ! still brighter on his brow,
The Turquoise and the Ruby glow !

A castle's ancient towers appear,
Fast by the marge of winding Wear ;
And from the turrets, high and bold,
A banner floats in blue and gold,
While sunset rays these words illume :
" *Le jour viendra,*" the day will come !
" The day *hath* come !" the angel said,
And through the castle's portals sped.

What sees he there ?   Twin cherubs fair !
Joy ! joy ! a sweet, celestial pair !
The spirit thus the babes addressed :—
" Meek lambs of beauty, take your rest !
Chosen of Heaven !   Your names shall be
A watchword to the good and free ;
As twins in birth, so time shall prove
The Lambton-twins as Peace and Love !"

Thus said, and kneeling lowly down,
The angel, from his dazzling crown,
Two gems removed—the Turquoise blue,
And then the Ruby's blushing hue.
One babe's soft arm the Turquoise bound,
The other's wrist the Ruby crowned ;
On each the angel breathed a prayer,
And left the jewels shining there.

"DO ALL THE GOOD YOU CAN."

Written in the " People's Park," Building Hill, Sunderland.

A GENTLE, fair-haired, little girl
    About the " Park" was playing,
Her rosy cheek and sunny curl
    Had graced young love a-Maying,
She sang a sweet and simple song,
    And thus the burden ran :—
" Let knaves and fools delight in wrong,—
    Do all the good you can !"

Was this an angel who addressed
    My spirit in its grief ?
The words were comfort to my breast,
    And Hope smiled on relief.
A confidence, ne'er felt before,
    To nerve my heart began ;
The fair girl's song was Wisdom's lore,—
    " Do all the good you can !"

When friends are false—the world unkind—
　When Slander utters lies—
When Envy paints Affection blind,
　And Folly scorns the wise ;
Forgive the treach'ry of thy foes,
　You'll frustrate Envy's plan ;
For Scandal's henbane yield the Rose—
" Do all the good you can !"

When Sickness or Misfortune pines,
　Beneath the blight of Fate ;
Removes the ills that Want entwines
　Around the desolate !
Lead with thy best benevolence
　The everlasting van ;
Perform thy deeds without pretence,
　And do what good you can !

Be as the sun on all to shine,
　The dew on each to fall ;
The sea reflecting truth divine—
　The sky to cover all !
Live in the world the world to bless,
　Be faithful man to man ;
As you would purchase happiness,
" Do all the good you can !"

———

VICTORIA AT THE TOMB OF NAPOLEON.

THE thunder-spirit roared,
The lightning flashed its plume,
The cloud-pent waters poured,
And Evening reigned in gloom,
When, solemn as the beat
Of castle clocks at night,
Went forth the measured feet
Of nations famed in fight.
And now the torches glare
Athwart the Hall of Doom,—

Victoria standeth there,
Beside Napoleon's Tomb.

Round her crowd Frenchmen bold,
Who loved the dead as heaven,—
Warriors with gray locks, old,
Who oft in war had striven ;
They come our Queen to show
The Sepulchre of One
Who had been Britain's foe,
But now all strife was done.
A sadness fills the place,
Deep Silence sleeps in gloom,
The torch-light on each face
Bent on Napoleon's Tomb.

There stood with saddened pride
The living power of France ;
He gazed on death and sighed—-
Then gladness marked his glance.
He look'd on England's Queen—
His thoughts were on the Past ;
He scarce believed the scene—
Yet prayed it long might last ;—
While stood our Queen with grace—
A rose of modest bloom—
The tear upon her face,
Beside Napoleon's Tomb.

And yet it cannot be
That Queen Victoria, meek,
Hath crossed the bounding sea,
Her love for France to speak !
Yet strains that grandly swell
From voice and pipe unseen,
To France the tidings tell,
And chant " God save the Queen !"
The torches' ruddy rays
His trembling tears illume,
And Louis inly prays
Beside Napoleon's Tomb.

Well might the thunder's song
Amid the hills resound,
And lightning's flashes throng
At such a time profound !
Well might the joy-fraught skies
With gratitude run o'er,
To see that old Hate dies,
And Rancour wounds no more !
To know that England's wars,
With France repose in gloom ;
Behold ! the peaceful stars
Shine on Napoleon's Tomb.

Oh ! France, well hast thou proved,
By deeds of grateful kind,
That she, by Britian loved,
Is now with thee combined!
Splendour, and pomp, and power,
Were to Victoria given ;
Thy " Welcomes " as a shower
Of rainbows fell from heaven ;
Thou led'st our Queen with pride
To fountains fête and dome,—
She left the blaze, and hied
To view Napoleon's Tomb.

" The bonnie English Rose "
A fragrant sigh hath shed ;
The Eagle hath repose
Among the noble dead.
Hail, generous thought, sublime,
That prompted this display !
A deed which worlds of time
Can never waste away !
Age shall record with pride,
And youth the tale resume,
Of her who mourned beside
The FIRST NAPOLEON'S TOMB.

LINES

Supposed to be addressed to the Statue of " Hermione" in Shakspeare's
"Winter's Tales."

(Inscribed to Joseph Durham, Esq., Sculptor, London.)

"HERMIONE ! how mild thy look !
How meek and motionless thine air !
· Oh ! thou art more than marble fair !
A lily painted in a book,
On a rose-tinted 'leaf so rare
That butterflies from flowery nook,
And honey-bees, come fluttering,
To pause love-stricken on the wing !

" Thou art death-robed, Hermione,
And yet thou art not like the cold
And Fate-doomed beauties we behold !
Death seems to breathe, like life, in thee!
Sure thou hast never pressed the mould
That openeth Eternity !
There is a radiance on thy shroud,
Cloud-like, but warmer than a cloud !

" Thine eyes are glancing with the light
Of angel thoughts ; and language seems
To float upon our ears like dreams
Of vocal rainbows, fair and bright !
Hermione ! chaste moon, whose beams
Resemble more the day than night,
Open thy long-closed lips of love,
And let thy bosom, joy-heaved, move !

" Before thee, on my bending knees,
With willing heart, I lowly kneel!
'Tis false to say thou can'st not feel !
Can human art mould limbs like these ?

And who shall smile when I appeal
To Shakspeare's golden memories ?
E'en *then*, as *now*, ''tis stone !' they said ;—
Their words were false—thou wast not dead !

"When rested dark Suspicion's gloom
Of love unfaithful ;—when the shade
Of envious breath thy love betrayed,
Thou camest forth, in spotless bloom,
An angel virtue—truth-arrayed !
Thou did'st but mock the bondaged tomb,
Rising, like morn, love's ' Tale' to tell
How thou had'st loved—how long—how well !

"No longer can I brook delay
To whisper what I loved in thee ;
And thus I rise from bended knee,
In thy small, soft-lobed ear to say,
That thou art Truth, Hermione !
How cold thy cheek !   Ah ! art thou clay ?
Art but the *semblance* of the just
Alone ?   I will not yield my trust !

" Where is the sculptor that hath dared
To give a statute pulse and heart,
And to mere marble *soul* impart ?
Was ever skill to this compared ?
Hermione ! hath mortal art
A spell like this ?   What ! hath it shared
Creation's will, to call from stone
What only breathes in heaven alone ?"

To *marble*, sooth, the gazer spoke,
And still believing, as he gazed,
That she, long dead to life, was raised ;
Till stern Conviction slowly woke,
And then the sculptor's work he praised.
DURHAM ! what soul did'st thou evoke,
To aid thee in thy wizard-spell,
Of carving WINTER TALES so well ?

THE FLAG OF FREEDOM.

"The meteor-flag of England
Shall yet terrific burn!"

CAMPBELL.

BANNER of England! deathless Flag, that floats o'er land and
    sea ;
Beacon to Valour's glorious deeds—bright badge of liberty !
Proud as a lion in thy strength, thy prowess ne'er shall fail,
Beneath thy foot Oppression lies, and tyrant despots quail.

Like a cloud-sweeping avalanche, hurled from its dazzling throne,
Thine arms can deal destruction round, and make the world
    thine own.
Omnipotent on mount and main, terrific in thy wrath ;
What foe shall dare approach thee, Flag? red ruin strews his
    path !

Tempest, and storm, and iron hail, from battle's hostile crowds
Pass hurtless! thou wert never scathed—thy seat is 'mid the
    clouds !
Like a strong eagle soaring high, majestic thou art seen ;
The sun of fame blinks not thy gaze ; thy look is calm—serene !

The stars—those everlasting spheres—thy meteor-radiance know ;
The winds of heaven thy wings salute, and bid thee onward go.
The bounding billows love to bear thy glories o'er the deeps ;
And forests wave their arms with joy above high mountain steeps.

Exulting warriors shout thy praise, and follow in thy flight ;
For thou, old Flag, hast led them on to conquest in the fight !
Clasped to the dying heroes' hearts thy silken plumes shall be ;
And where, the foe can strike a blow to loose love's grasp on
    thee?

Yet mournfully and droopingly thy crimson folds are cast
O'er hearts like HAMPDEN'S, NELSON'S, MOORE'S, that faintly
    throb their last !

Like angel Hope, with rainbow wings, thy mingled hues appear;
And calmly then the brave ones die—they know that bliss is
    near!

Flag of a thousand years! once more thy signal shines from far;
And British valour gathers fast* to swell the ranks of war.
But death to him that hath evoked thy spirit o'er the wave;
For dire dismay shall mark his way and shame shall dig his grave.

———

GENTLY CHIDE POOR MORTALS FRAIL.

GENTLY chide poor mortals frail,
Strive their faults to smother,
Let kind words with all prevail,
Deem each man a brother.
He that doth mankind despise,
Loses many a bosom-prize,
Clings to clay and robs the skies.

Friendship is life's golden chain,
That the frail should tether;
'Tis the bow spread o'er the main,
Clouds and light together.
He must toil to win earth's gems;
Love must bind Faith's broken stems;
Mercy wears God's diadems.

Write man's errors in the sand,
Sighing as you trace them;
And each wave, with gentel hand,
Pitying, will efface them.
Let your words, like fragrant wind,
Bear reproof in accents kind;—
Keep no malice in your mind!

———

* This was written in May 1854, at the commencement of the
Eastern War.

"THE STORMY PETREL."

DARK roll the eddying clouds above, like mountains o'r the deep ;
Like lions wild with manes of foam, the crowding billows sweep.
The spume of vengeance on their lips, in thunder's voice they
　　roar ;
As the hurricane howls fearfully, and rainy torrents pour.

A gallant vessel struggling heaves, like a wrestler 'gainst his
　　doom,
Now skyward hurled in vengeful might, now downward dashed
　　in gloom.
The captain bold, and seamen brave, await the impending shock ;
With hearts that scorn all quailing fear, though hurrying to the
　　rock !

All that the skill of man can do, or prowess e'er perform,
Seems but an infant's feeble hand, against the giant storm.
Vainly the life-boat mounts the surge, the sinking ship to gain,
She strikes ! her masts, like some frail reeds, float useless on the
　　main.

"Help ! help !" alas, there is no help ! the ship is rent asunder,
The lighting of the Fiend hath flashed, he laughs and rolls his
　　thunder !
Rockets, in vain, whizz through the gloom, one moment, 'tis too late !
The struggling brave are in the wave, the victims to stern fate.

See ! see ! a human form appears, the messenger of Hope,
Mounting the mad, careering surge, he bears salvation's rope.
The " Petrel " spreads his sweeping wings, he nears the stranded
　　barque ;
The spray dashed o'er his gallant head, a rainbow o'er the Ark !

"Help ! help ! oh, help !" "There cometh help ! bear up my
　　trusty men !
Here, clutch this rope ! hold on my braves ! There's life for ye
　　again !"
Oh, that glad cry of gratitude exalts the " Petrel's " form ;
Salvation's cable is made fast ; there's mercy in the storm !

Men, captain, boy, with tears of joy, along the line move fast,
Till every soul, 'mid ocean's roll, hath gained the shore at last.
"Hurrah! hurrah!" The Storm-Fiend glares in disappointed
 wrath;
The dripping crew have all escaped the tempest's horrid scath.

Then glory to the "Petrel" bold, who snatched ye from the
 grave
And honour be to Hodgson's* name, who risked his life to save!
Shout, ye true sons of Neptune, shout, till all the welkin ring,
And crown him with a wreath of gold,—the "Petrel" is your
 king!

———

STANZAS TO ENGLAND.

When the summer-cloud floats on the far-seeming west,
And the night-mist begins to appear;
When Twilight sinks languid on Evening's cool breast,
To the lone, rocky cave I draw near;
And there I muse sadly by Ocean's dim strand,
And watch the waves kissing the shore;
As I think of those gone from their dear native land,
And dear friends they may never meet more.

But shall I, my dear England, my mother! my joy!—
The boast and the pride of my heart!—
Forsake thee? Oh! never! I hailed thee a boy,
And still honoured and cherished thou art.
I have shared in thy glories—I'm one of thine own;
My soul is now centred in thee;
Like the breath of the dying my love shall be shown;
Hail England! Fair Queen of the sea!

———

* Joseph Hodgson, of Sunderland, is by trade a ship carver, and is a person
of most singular intrepidity. He has saved numerous lives in imminent
danger of drowning. He is in possession of several gold and silver medals,
which have been awarded him for his courage and humanity, among which
we may note a gold medal from Louis Napoleon, Emperor of the French,
for saving the master and crew of the "Trois Seurs." The above poem
alludes particularly to this circumstance.

STANZAS FOR MUSIC.

SILVER Moon, now shining bright,
Pity me, a hapless wight ;
Tell my only love to-night,
    Here I weeping lie !
Tell her that mine eyes are sore,
With the hot grief running o'er ;
Tell her, here I shall deplore,
    Here remain to die !

Silver Moon, one moment stay !
Ne'er my words of sadness say !
See ! my sweeting moves this way,
    Dancing in thy beams !
Come to me, of loves the best,
Ah ! I feel thy bounding breast !
Mortal never was so blest—
    Rapture crowns my dreams !

THE DYING LOVER.

COME hither to my side, bonnie Mary,
An, let thine e'en be dried, bonnie Mary !
Though faint I lie an' weak,
Ae kiss on thy saft cheek,
My luve for thee will speak, bonnie Mary.

Oh ! lang I've lo'ed, an' weel, bonnie Mary,
As thy faithfu' heart maun feel, bonnie Mary ;
To thee I've aye been true,
But my days are ended noo,
Death's hand is on my brow, bonnie Mary.

Luve's but a gowden dream, bonnie Mary,
A rainbow on the stream, bonnie Mary:
Oh! my dream o' luve is gane,
Hope's bow is turned to rain,
Life's joys are fleet and vain, bonnie Mary.

Oft hae I sung to thee, bonnie Mary,
Beneath the hawthorn tree, bonnie Mary!
For thou wast a' mine ain,
The muse o' ilka strain,
But I'll never sing again, bonnie Mary.

There's silence in the air, bonnie Mary,
The mavis sings nae mair, bonnie Mary;
The birdie on ilk tree,
Has closed its weary e'e,
To fa' asleep, like me, bonnie Mary.

———

THE DESERTED WIFE.

Like the nicht, when the stars frae high heaven depart,
Is thy puir wife deserted wi wae in her heart;
Like a cloud lanely left on the brow o' the hill,
Is thy grief-wasted Patie forsaken an' chill.
The lammies are gane to their sleep i' the fauld,
An' cosy they rest while my bosom is cauld;
Oh! the wean at my breast sabs wi' sickness and pain,
For my Johnny has left me, an' I am alane.

I was ance like the gowan, that lifts its glad e'en
To the bright sun o' joy when life's sky is serene;
I was ance like the cowslip, when simmer is young,
Like the lambkin I played, like the lav'rock I sung.
Noo, a blight's on the gowan, the cowslip is dead,
The lambkin is slain, and th' lav'rock is fled;
An' the dream o' life's hope like a shadow is gane,
For my Johnny has left me, and I am alane.

The robin cam' singin' ae morn to my door,
But a crumb was na left him to feed as before ;
He plumed his red breast, an' he peck'd at the pane,
Till weary wi' tappin' he left me alane.
Ah, Robie, puir birdie! you're just like the lave,
Your luve-sangs ye chant woman's kindness to crave ;
But if Poverty tell you hame comforts are gane,
Like my Johnny you slight me, and leave me alane.

Noo, the lamp is fast failing, the oil is a' spent,
The wail o' my wee thing comes mournfu' and faint ;
There's nae clock noo to tick—there's nae stroke o' its bell,
The lang, weary hours o' dark sadness to tell.
Like the lamp is my life—like the oil is my wean—
An' like time I shall pass as I never had been ;
Oh! shine, leddy mune, on my grave when I'm gane,
Sigh ye winds, an' tell Johnny in death I'm alane.

SONG OF THE MASON.

A MASON am I, of the ancient trade,
    With my plummet, and bevel, and square ;
Of mortar and stones I raised my thrones,
    And build up my mansions rare.
Foundations I lay 'mid the tough, brown clay,
    Then like steps to the clouds I rise ;
Like a wise, good man's are the mason's plans,
    For he gives his best work to the skies !

Ye mounds huge and vast, that for ever shall last,
    Ye pyramids glorious and grand ;
By the chisel and line ye were lifted divine,
    And ye sprung from the mason's hand.
Let vain fables retire ! it was Art, not the Lyre,
    That heaved mighty Thebes to the sun,
Built Babylon's walls and Nineveh's halls,
    Alas, for magnificence gone !

The pinnacles high we enthroned in the sky,
   Like an angel the dome spreads its wings !
The breeze-shifted vane glitters bright in the rain,
   While the lark a sweet canticle sings.
The stone saint in his niche, and the tracery rich,
   The arches like branches that grow ;
The knight that lies grim, in the still cloister dim,
   The craft of old masons doth show.

A shout and a cheer for the chimneys we rear,
   Whence the smoke of the furnace ascends ;
For the bridges we cast o'er the dark waters vast,
   For the docks, the brave mariner's friends.
High levels we lay for the mighty railway,
   Where the engines run swift overhead !
Oh ! the mason hath shown, he works wonders in stone,
   As he buildeth for quick and for dead !

WAITING FOR THE TIDE.

A CHILD I saw beside the ocean playing,
His wooden spade had scooped a sandy cave,
To which, in his small hands, without delaying,
He bore with glee his tributes from the wave.
The yellow pit was filled to overflowing ;
The rosy creature viewed his work with pride ;
Anon the sea came stealing, onward growing—
His joys were buried in the rising tide.

A gentle maiden lingered near me, sighing,
With wet eyes gazing on the heaving sea ;
Oft to her sight a prospect-glass applying,
And sadly murm'ring " Where can Edward be !"
When, just as patient Hope began to fail her,
A white-wing'd ship, exulting, she espied ;
She wept for joy, and blessed her coming sailor,
Who, like his love, had waited for the tide.

I passed a cottage whence the wail of wourning,
Broken by sobs, fell on the evening air ;
To learn the cause my steps were bent returning,
A gray-haired man and old lay dying there.
"Weep not !" he said, "my soul is on the ocean,
Where God's my compass—chart—my helm—my guide !
My port is Heaven ! See ! see ! the ship's in motion !
Oh ! long I've wearied waiting for the tide !"

MORNING, NOON, AND NIGHT.

Morn, like Childhood, rises brightly,
    Walks with gladness from his bed ;
Life's dim shadows chasing lightly,
    Rays of glory round his head.
Verdant mountains—crystal fountains—
    Flow'ry meadows—Ocean-strand—
Dance delighted—joy-united—
    Hope and Love go hand in hand.

Noon, like Manhood, fame-surrounded,
    Glows in clouds of splendour bright ;
Soars amid a sky unbounded,
    Swims within a sea of light.
Robed imperial, mind ethereal,
    Priceless diamonds deck his crown ;
Life's best pleasures yield their treasures,
Pouring floods of rapture down.

Night, like Age, by gloom encircled,
    Sinks within th' eternal sea ;
Now with stars the heavens are sparkled,
    Point where Age's home shall be.
Head grown hoary—moonlight glory—
    Silvers o'er Life's ebbing wave ;
Peace decending marks Time's ending,
    Calm he sleeps in honour's grave.

THE LAST APPEAL.

"My last appeal to thee I make,
We've oft met here in days gone by ;
Thou wilt not now my words mistake,—
I come to bless thee—and to die.
This spot is hallowed—this green dell
Is consecrated by thy feet ;
Here I must sigh a last farewell,—
Here never more in life to meet !

" How I have loved thee none can show,—
No language can my heart reveal ;
'Tis not a common pang I know,
'Tis agony—'tis death I feel !
I love—*have* ever loved thee only !
Though like the lamp that gilds the urn,
Burns my soul's flame, forsaken, lonely—
Of joy, of hope, of reason shorn !

" My love is not an impulse glowing
With transient fervour in my breast ;
'Twas childhood-born—still daily growing—
'Twas nursed mid sweets in perfume's nest.
Day unto day increased the flowers,
That thou had'st planted one by one ;
Devotion grew with gathering hours,
And ripened 'neath Affection's sun.

" Oh ! often, hand in hand, far roaming
By daisied mead and tangled wood,
With thee I've wandered when the gloaming
Lay sleeping on the placid flood.
Here is the spot where oft I've pillowed
My youthful head beside thine own ;
When round thy neck mine arm was twining,
And thine around me softly thrown.

"No lark that in the sunshine dwelleth,
And roams among the crystal fields,
And to the listening rainbow telleth
The unknown joys that Nature yields,
Was e'er so happy as that creature
Thou once didst name thy chosen mate ;
But now, like Etna's smould'ring furnace,
Scorched is his brain—he's desolate !

"I left thee with thy vows repeated,
That thou would'st ever faithful be !
Why hath the sun the morning cheated,
And failed to glid the darkened sea ?
Returning with a love unaltered,
My name unsullied by a crime ;
I sought thee—but thy language faltered—
Thou had'st deceived me in that time !

"'Tis done ! the bitter words are spoken,
The last fond link that bound our hearts,
By a deceitful tongue, is broken,
And with this sigh my soul departs !"
He lies beside the shining river ;
His heart hath mouldered into clay ;
The maidens mourn his sorrows ever—
The false one pines in grief away !

THE SIGHTLESS, MITHERLESS, BAIRN.

"OH, tak' me faither, by the hand, an' lead me cannilie,
An' let me feel my mither's grave, the spot I canna see !
I'll drap me doon amang the mool, an' kiss the damp, cauld clay,
The lanely bed where mither sleeps, for ever and for aye !

"Oh faither, dinna greet again ; ye're sabbin' waefu' noo !
Ye canna speak your bairn to bless, your heart is ower fu' :—
Bend doon an' let me wipe your e'en, ye ken I lo'e ye weel !
Though I'm a puir an' sightless bairn, I ha'e a heart to feel.

" Lang, lang my mither's name I heard, when sick an' pained she
    lay ;
When to her side I felt my steps, to kneel me doon an' pray.
Her saft, thin fingers smoothed my hair, an' patted my wee head ;
Oh, faither, how for sight I prayed, to see her ere she dee'd !

" Nae mair she'll bring me buttercups, an' gowans frae the dell !
Her welcome flowers I couldna see, their names she bade me tell.
Their leaves like velvet felt sae saft, an' oh, their smell was rare !
1 lo'ed them when my mither lived, but noo I lo'e them mair !

" I hear you read o' gowden suns, an' o' the mune's pale licht ;
O' siller streams, green hills, an' woods, that never blest my sicht !
But when I dream, then, faither dear, bright angels fair an' mild,
Bring me braw croons an' gowden harps, an' ca' me their ain child.

" Our minister has aften said, that Heaven's sae fu' o' luve,
That nane amang the sons o' men its happiness can prove ;—
That neither heart, nor tongue, nor e'en, can think, or say, or see
What God hath for the gude prepared, oh, is that place for me ?

" Noo, faither, when your bairn is laid in death by mither's side,
Let every sab o' wae be stilled, an' every tear-drap dried ;
For then my mither's face I'll see, her lips wi' luve I'll kiss ;
Wha wadna thole life's darkness here, for bright, eternal bliss ?',

The father's ta'en his puir, blind bairn, an' led her cannilie ;
She's kneelin' by her mither's grave, an' sabbin' bitterly !
An' noo she draps doon on the mool, but a' the bairn can say,
Is "bonnie mither come to me, oh ! leave the kirkyard clay !"

THE BEGGAR LADDIE.

A Callan' cam' tirlin' the pin,
    His claes were a bundle o' duds ;
His breeks didna keep his sark in,
    An' his sark sairly needed the suds.

He cam' to the yett wi' his pock,
  Puir mannie! his powie was bare,
His cheeks seemed like peaches in smoke,
  An' his heelies were hacked an' sair.

"What want ye, braw laddie, wi' me?"
  Said the canty guidwife to him.
He glower'd wi tears in his ee',
  An' the guidwife's een grew dim.
"I'm wantin' some water to drink,
  For hunger an' thirst I feel;
I'm dizzy an' like to sink—
  Will ye thicken the water wi' meal?"

"Hech! meal in the water, my man,
  The bonnie clear spring wad spoil!"
"Deed, no! if wi' milk frae yon can,
  Ye'll mix wi' the meal and boil,
Wi' a pickle o' saut·an' spoon,
  When the crowdy is ready, I'll sup;
An' I'll show ye, guidwife, how soon
  A laddie can whallop it up!"

Then the mistress she gaed ben,
  An' ca'd on her dochters three,
"Noo, lasses, you're wild for the men,
  Just come an' this puir bairn see!
Ye may marry some ne'er-do-weel,
  An' your bairnies may come to want;
They may beg for water an' meal,
  When your guidmen's pouches are scant?"

The dochters leuch'd loud at the dame,
  Says Elspie, "our mither's clean gicht!"
But they fand she was no' to blame,
  Like a warlock she proved a' right;—
For they wedded, an' bairnies they had,
  And their men for drink wad steal;
Oh! aften they thocht o' the lad,
  That begg'd at the yett for meal.

FALL OF THE ANCESTRAL TREE.

Thomas Henry, Second Baron Ravensworth, of Ravensworth Castle,
Died March 7th, 1855, aged 80 years.

"He fell to earth, but left his memory green."

GRIEF veils her face ; deep sighs her bosom rend ;
She mourns the widow's stay, the orphans friend ;
The poor man's hope,—his constant, sure relief ;
While Gratitude sits mingling tears with Grief.
And yet, why sorrow when a good man dies ?
Why wish to hold Benevolence from the skies ?
Why strive to bind his soaring spirit down ?
Why rail at death when angels yield the crown ?
His blameless actions sanctify his dust ;
His name and memory live among the just ;
For through the seasons of a lengthened span,
Revered he lived, and died a friend to man.
His secret virtues none but angels know ;
His generous deeds to suffering want and woe
Are breathed in grateful prayers o'er many a hearth,
To bless the name and house of RAVENSWORTH.
  When tender lilies, fragrant, fair, and young,
Are, by rude breezes, on the desert flung ;
When summer grapes are from their tendrils torn,
Earth's wasted sweets and blighted buds we mourn :
But when the noble oak with length of days,
Snow-crowned by time, in wintry age decays ;
Sheds his frail branches, gently, one by one,
Like rain-drops falling in the setting sun ;
'Tis as the eve of life—the waning year—
That must be seen ere light and Spring appear ;
As death's cold robes must shroud the mortal clay,
When Life Eternal bears the soul away.
  Come, Love, erect thy temple, raise thy throne ;
Create a shrine, and make that shrine thine own ;
The dead we mourn Affection's boon shall share,
And RAVENSWORTH shall slumber sweetly there.

"𝕳𝖊𝖗𝖊 𝖑𝖎𝖊𝖙𝖍 𝖙𝖍𝖊 𝕺𝖆𝖐 𝖔𝖋 𝕽𝖆𝖛𝖊𝖓𝖘𝖜𝖔𝖗𝖙𝖍."

THE POET'S MONUMENT.

TELL me, Who builds the Poet's Monument?
  'Tis he who lendeth help when Love and Hope,
  The golden flowers on fairy Fancy's cope,
Are with the *living* minstrel's musings blent;
'Tis he who bringeth to the Poet's hearth,
Unasked, the elements of grateful worth;
Cheers his dark hours when Poverty appears
To drench with mournful, agonizing tears,
His home—his wife—the children of his heart;
'Tis he who bids the fiend of Want depart,
And weaves around Woe's weeping group content:
  He buildeth *well* the Poet's Monument!

He builds his own and Friendship's Monument
  Who brightens every cloud Misfortune rolls
  Around the Poet's head, and Fate controls:
Turning the current of Life's accident
To smoother channels. He who, like a wave,
Effaces every impress Scandal gave;—
Who, like a noble Christian, looks upon
The doom of OTWAY, KEATS, and CHATTERTON,
As sacrifices—victims to Neglect;
Stands forth the struggling Poet to protect
With heavenly shield, in arms benevolent;
  Buildeth his own and Love's high monument!

Behold! I stand by BURNS's Monument!
  His pulseless heart lies 'neath this sculptured pile
  Say, can Carrara's blocks evoke one smile
From his cold lips? Prometheus' fires are spent!
Else, could he burst the bonds of mighty Death,
The world had rung with his declaiming breath!
Nations that gathered on the banks of Doon,
To render Scotia's Bard their homage boon,
Like scattered fawns, had fled; while BURNS's tongue,
Toned in deep grandeur, had pronounced men *wrong!*
  Poets want *bread—not stones*—for genius lent;
  Cherish them *living*—then your Monument!

KATE MULLAGHAN.

Air—"Katty O' Connor."

From the swate little vale of the town of Kinsale,
    I have come here my luck to be chancin',
That my kind friends may see I am merry and free,
    And up to both singing and dancin.'
Poor father and mother, sister and brother,
    Paddy, my sweetheart, and Larry O'Sullivan ;
Dermot O'Leary, Terence M'Fleary,
    Were all left alone by Kate Mullaghan.

Och ! I've often been tould, when a child a year ould,
    That I danced on the floor so jintaly ;
And that Father O'Toole' said he'd send me to school,
    For my jiggin' beat piper O'Reily.
His Riverence blist me, and tenderly kiss'd me,
    While naggins of whisky he ordered all full again ;
" Pipers, play quicker, send round the liquor ;
    A fairy for dancin's Kate Mullaghan !"

Wid Pat Fin at the fair, how the spalpeens did stare,
    And he got into scrapes by the dozens,
For the boys left and right, for their Katty would fight ;
    I was claimed by a hundred full cousins.
"Katty Mavourneen ! Kate don't be scornin' !"
    Then the shillalagh would tip on a skull again ;
" Cushla ! I'm dying'!" Pat would be cryin',
    Och ! he was the boy for Kate Mullaghan.

To the weddin' of Ted, I was sought from my bed,
    Ted was married at five in the mornin' !
An' fait he was big wid myself for to jig,
    While his wife wid black envy was burnin'.
"Katty you're purty !" so Teddy did court me,
    Though he was tied to his wife Biddy Coolahan ;
" Say yes, an' I'll lave her ; no sin to decaive her !"
    But Ted could'nt blarney Kate Mullaghan.

Now I crossed the salt say, wid poor Pat t'other day,
  But in England no longer he'd tarry ;
An' as Paddy soon died—I can still be a bride,
  Och ! some broth of a Briton I'll marry.
Who's for the chance now ? see, I can dance now,
  Him that I pick on will never be dull again ;
Don't all be spakin'! there's one I'll be takin',—
  That's a boy to be true to Kate Mullaghan.

Wid some pigs an' a cow, there'll be meat you'll allow,
  An' I don't much object to good whisky ;
But the boy I shall take, must be true for my sake ;
  By my troth but his time shall be frisky.
An' if I have childer—no strife shall bewilder—
  I'll strive wid my husband for comfort to pull again !
Wid dancin' and singin', my cot shall be ringin' ;
  Now who buys the ring for Kate Mullaghan ?

———

THE WHITHERED WREATH.

My Mary bowed all hearts to love,
  She was so fair to see ;
And angels might have jealous been
  Of her soul's purity.
Now cold and white, as hill-side snow,
  She lieth on her bed ;
The flush of life is marble now,
  My beauteous flow'r lies dead.

Dark violet cups her gentle eyes,
  And rippling gold her hair ;
Her cheeks pale lilies, where the rose
  Smiled faint and sweetly there.
Oh! darkly dim her eyes are now,
  And 'neath her locks of gold,
The snow is lying on her brow ;—
  Love's beauteous wreath is cold.

WHEEDLIN' WILLIE.

Oh ! mither, but your bonnie,
Indeed, you're mair than cannie
The hair upon your cushat head's
    Like Jeanie's spool o' silk :
An', mither, when you're smilin'
I see the dimples coilin',
Like twa wee pearly buttons,
    In twa cups o' rosy milk !

Oh ! mither, you are bonnie,
The folk a' say you're cannie !
I'm glow'rin' in your dark blue een,
    An' what do I see there ?
Wee firey sparkles dancin',
Like pouthered star-dust glancin',
Noo, mither, let me gang wi' Jean
    To Inverury Fair !

Oh ! mither, you are bonnie,
You're unco' kind an' cannie !
But, whisht ! the lammie-wean I hear,
    How its fistlin' in the bed :
I'll gang an' sing him, mither—
An' croon some hymn or ither,
Aboot " Lie still and slumber,"
    An' God will guard his head !

For, mither, you're sae bonnie,
I lo'e you mair than ony ;
But gin you greet I canna' sing
    The lammie-weanie' mair.
Come, mither, bonnie dearie,
I'll kiss you and sit near ye ;
I dinna want to gang *to-day*
    To Inverury fair!

Oh ! mither, but you're bonnie,
Sae kind to your wee mannie ;
Ae kiss o' your saft, velvet lips
    Dirls through my jumpin' breest.
I' th' world there's no anither
I lo'e sae like my mither !
The langer that I look at you,
    The mair my een can feast : —

For, mither, you're sae bonnie,
To puir folk kind an' cannie ;
Hoots ! Jeanie's sel' may tak' the road
    To glower at the glare ;
I'd sooner see you smilin',
A'n your cheekies' dimples coilin',
Than be the maister o' the shows
    At Inverury Fair !

THE ILLITERATE BLUE.

'Mong musty books and old,
    Huge and black-typ'd volumes,
Webs of the spiders rolled
    Around the dingy columns ;
A lonley student snored,
    Dreaming of love—not classics—
His head on a folio's board,
    His feet on some torn hassocks.

A fat, blue fly was there,
    Buzzing near piles of learning ;
Like an eel he wormed the air,
    All ancient wisdom scorning,
The FATHERS old he passed,
    And the tomes of warngling sages ;
By missals of Feast and Fast,
    With yellow and painted pages.

This blue fly 'lighted once
　　On a tome of ROGER BACON ;
He thought to feed—the dunce !—
　　On FAT, but was mistaken.
To PINDAR then he flew,
　　And to ANACREON'S bottle ;
But Odes were odious stew,
　　So he turned to ARISTOTLE.

To SAPPHO next he fled,
　　For Saph, was a blue-stocking ;
But found that she was dead—
　　A suicide—oh, shocking !
He climb'd on PLATO'S back,
　　To look at THEOPHRASTUS ;
Then flew o'er EUCLID'S track,
　　To " Death and Doctor Faustus."

" Of bones," says he, " I'll taste,
　　And have a fly at HUNTER ;
Then HOME I'll seek in haste,
　　Home proves mankind a grunter."
A kiss he blew to POPE,
　　And waved his wings o'er DRYDEN ;
Then, with a graceful slope,
　　This LIVINGSTON he hied on.

He glanced at CAXTON'S " Boke,"
　　Outside—he couldn't *read* it—
He got his claws on COKE,
　　But *law !* he didn't heed it.
HALLEY, no doubt, was bright,
　　And NEWTON quite astounding ;
But comets blink'd his sight,
　　And " Optics" were confounding.

He buzz'd to Erin's MOORE,
　　MONBODDO was so fusty ;
To BURKE he tried to soar,
　　For OTWAY'S lot was *crusty.*

ARCHIMEDES—that *screw*
    Blue scarcely cast his eyes on ;
To CHATTERTON he flew,
    And wept his fate by poison

O'er SAMMY JOHNSON'S books,
    Our fly was seen to straddle,
But oh ! what funny looks
    He threw on BOSWELL'S twaddle !
NOLL GOLDIE was a prize—
    JOSEPHUS was too Jewish,—
But STERNE was just his size—
    Because his tales were *blue*-ish.

Ah ! HOMER'S verse was grand,
    But Greek—he couldn't bear it ;
He did not understand
    How Englishmen could hear it.
Though BYRON, BURNS, and SCOTT,
    And SHAKSPEARE too, were clever ;
But all the ryhming lot
    Was his abhorrence ever !

Still on from book to book,
    Our wise blue-bottle travelled,
At *titles* long he'd look,
    But *subjects* ne'er unravelled,
Thus men live long and die,
    Like flies in halls of college ;
Though always on the *fly*,
    They're seldom flies of knowledge.

MEMORY'S ROSE AND RUE.

OH ! you remember sweet and happy faces,
Bright creatures of your childhood's early days,—
Where are they gone ? Of them you see no traces ;
They fled, like morning dew-drops, from your gaze.

Where are your playmates in the greenwoods roving ;
Climbing the bending trees to find a nest ;—
Where are they gone—the lovely and the loving ?
Alas ! they slumber on the earth's cold breast.

Where are those diamonds of your deep devotion ?
And where the pearls and rubies of each face,
Whose glance and smile enkindled fond emotion ?
Decay inhabits beauty's dwelling-place !

Oh ! those bright stars in rapture's skies were shining ;
Those buds of promise breathed from love's own nest ;—
Where are they gone ?   The buds round death are twining ;
The stars extinguished on the earth's cold breast !

Where are your dearest, truest, loveliest treasures,
That gave you all that can in life be given ?
That nurs'd your weakness—that created pleasures,
And like good angels, led the path to heaven ?

Where are they gone ?   The marble tablet yonder,
Like a white surpliced-priest, points out their rest ;
Where meek Affection loves at eve to wander,
And plant sweet flowers around each dear one's breast.

SHAKSPEARE IN HEAVEN.

METHOUGHT, a placid face and graceful form,
Stood radiant near the throne of endless Time,
Outliving ages and creation's storm,
And tow'ring like a cloud sublime.
He looked ambrosial sweetness in his prime ;—
No wrinkles ploughed his calm reflective brow,
That seemed transparent, like the heavenly clime,
Where skies are ever cloudless, and the snow
Falls in bright diamonds on the earth below.

A golden lyre was in his master-hand,
On which the cherub Melody looked down,
And playful angels touched its music bland,
For which they longed to give their holy crown,
As they knelt near this Minstrel of Renown.
The stars were silent, while his melting song
Breathed inspiration ; as if heaven had blown
The sweetest of her gales ; and Rapture's throng
Stood mute, entranced—e'en by a mortals tongue.

The prophet-Bard that erst of Salem sung—
The kingly-Minstrel stayed his trembling string,
And rapt above the rival Poet hung,
Forgetting heavenly joys in listening !
He seemed to hear the chords of music ring
As if each tone were thirsty for deep love,
And drank the nectar of th' eternal spring,
To make delight still happier, and to prove
That strains by earth despised find high reward above.

THE JUDGE OMNIPOTENT.

CLAD in his ermine and wig,
    And his robes of scarlet hue,
He sat on his throne, like Justice *alone*,
    As the prisoner loom'd to view.
Blue were the culprit's lips,
    And his eyes were sunken deep,
As if a dark hell kept fiends in his cell,
    To banish the murderer's sleep.

Hundreds of glittering eyes
    On the culprit's face were bent,
And the hangman there, with greedy stare,
    Smiled a horrible grim content.
The Judge look'd solemn and sad,
    The Judge sat wise and grave,
There was not one flaw for the lost by law,
    He wished, but he could not save.

Hushed was the court as death,
  While the words of doom were said
" I can offer no hope ; you must hang by the rope
  Till your body be cold and dead !"
Like ashes the sickly hue
  Of the prisioner's cheek was then ;
And his face was wet with a chill, death-sweat,
  Oh ! doomed of the sons of men.

He turned to the left and right,
  No help in this world had he ;
Each eye-glance there was a demon's stare,
  " Oh ! God, dare I hope in Thee ?"
He strove to murmur a prayer,
  Alas ! but he could not pray !
Old words he forgot—and his brain grew hot,
  And he groaned in deep dismay !

But, look to the Judge,* good men !
  On his breast hath sunk his brow,
He sits on his throne like Justice in *stone*,
  For his lips are silent now.
The culprit cumbereth yet,
  The earth he stained with gore ;
His Judge hath fled to a Throne more dread ;
  He never will judge man more.

———

TO THE SHADE OF BYRON.

I stand with thee upon the misty cliff
Of the forsaken Past ; and, by thy spells,
Wizard pronounc'd, forbidden breath inhale.
Ye congregated worlds, air-poised and vast,
Bright eyes that glitter in th' ethereal space,

---

*The amiable and accomplished Thomas Noon Talfourd, author of "Ion,"
and other exquisite compositions, died suddenly on the Bench in the manner signified in the text.

Why do you shine on me ? I was not made
To be a denizen of your immense
Rotundities ! With thee, poetic king,
Amid convolving mysteries, I pause ;
And from the dizzy promontory gaze
On fleeting, transitory dreams ! With thee,
When the stern Dioclesian of my fate
Sends forth his ruthless mandate, will I stand ;
When the sharp fangs of hunger gnaw my heart ;
When nature's softness turns to adamant ;
In that dark hour, beside Love's putrid corse,
That grins in horrid mock'ry of my grief,
On thee I call ! for in thy name there lives
A secret talisman to sweep the plague
And horror of my soul to healthier thoughts.
Me, in thy moody moments, thou dost please ;
And when the glittering lightning from the cloud
Flashes its vivid glance, I gaze in joy !
Not with such joy as cunning, spider minds,
Weave for the common motes that blot the sun ;
But with such exultation, that the soul
Grows great withal, and spreads her wings,
Brushing the dew-drops from the purpling East.

WHAT ARE KISSES LIKE ?

"What are kisses like ? do tell !"
Like a warm and ruddy glow
Of the sun on buds that blow,
Berries red and ripe that glow,
    Clinging like twin hips ;
Dew from hope and balm for woe,
    Let me taste thy lips !

"Say are kisses false ? do tell !
Doth not sometimes vile Deceit,
Kneeling at the virgin's feet,

When eye-glances melting meet
    In a dim eclipse,
Stab the heart he doth intreat ?
    Keep away such lips !"

Sweet ! of kisses *true* I tell,
Rosy buds of joy, of bliss,
Faithful, glowing, such as this,
When no sinful thought amiss
    Hope nor honour nips ;
When the lovers cry out " *Bis !*"
    For such soul-fraught lips !"

"This is kissing, then ? ah ! well,
But wilt *thou*, when I grow old,
Clasp me with such fervent fold ?
Will thy kisses not grow cold,
    Using scornful whips ?"
Never, sweeting ! till earth's mould
    Resteth on these lips !

SELECTIONS FROM MINSTREL'S MEMORIES.

THE GRANDMOTHER'S REPLY.

" How she looked in death " ask me not again !
  Calm as angels' breath, gentle as their strain.
Wax-like seemed the mould of her placid face ;
Nothing stern or cold, every feature grace.
She her eyes had closed, like sweet buds at eve ;
Had she life supposed made but to deceive ?
Flowers were in her hand, but you scarce could say,
Of the lilied-band, which were buds or clay.
One sweet flower was there, one bright, azure spot,
From her golden hair breathed—' Forget me not ! '
'Neath each drooping lid slept a dark-blue eye,
Like a star-beam hid by white cloud on high.
Dimples from her cheek were by cherubs taken,
To adorn the meek that with God awaken.
Though her ruby lips words of joy spoke never,
Smiles were near their tips ever and forever.
Some one lingering near kissed her, grief to smother,
But the tell-tale tear wrote the name of ' Mother.'
Why she wept and sighed, why her heart was heaving,
Why she ne'er replied to her kindred leaving,
Few would stay to tell,—but there's no denying
Bidding friends ' farewell,' whispers words of dying :—
And a mother's heart by her troubles broken,
Leaveth friends to part, all adieus unspoken.
Could she but have seen, near her lost One kneeling,
Angels bowed serene, she had stayed such feeling.
Ah ! but who can stay founts of Nature flowing ?
When Love lies in clay, thoughts to tears keep growing.
How she looked in death, ask me not again !
Calm as angels' breath, gentle as their strain."

Oh, beautiful is Nature in all forms !
   In her green garments and her wedding flowers ;
In tranquil Summer and in Winter's storms ;
   Scattering her pearls of frost or golden showers ;
   Yea, beautiful is Nature in all hours ;—
But lovelier far when Love his throne assumes,
   When happy hearts unite their mystic powers ;
When Spirit-children gladden earthly glooms,
And bear the smiles of God upon their shining plumes.

Gems hidden from the world are riches lost.
   Imprisoned Grace is Beauty in her grave.
Ye dreary piles where Solitude's pale ghost
   Sat like, a pelican above the wave,
   Aud its heart's blood to hungry Folly gave ;
Ye now are tenantless and desolate !
   Bleak winds around your empty chambers rave ;
Rank weeds grow wild, and rust corrodes your gate,
And ye shall fall, like leaves, before the blast of Fate !

Then 'mid your desert places, shall arise
   Stone-columned palaces and crowded streets ;
Arcadian Marts of busy Enterprise,
   Shall stand on ruins of your dark retreats.
   Fountains shall scatter diamonds 'mid the sweets
Of fruits and fragrant flowers.   For the throng
   Of dark-cowl'd Friars, vendors of rare meats
Shall consolation yield the old and young,
The healthy frame confirm; and make the feeble strong.

And, for the mental appetite, vast Halls,
   And for the goodly, Churches shall be seen ;
Science shall rule where now the reptile crawls ;
   Smooth, tesselated paths shall clothe the green,
   Rank herbage of the solemn fruitless Dene.
Athens and Rome and Greece shall grace the soil:—
   The statue's towering front of Grey serene
Shall on the necromantic changes smile,
As fast before his view shall soar each classic pile.

A humble Boy who gazes on this waste
   Out from the casement in a neighbouring lane,

Hath in his mind these transformations traced,
   Laid down each street and plann'd each vast domain,
   Beholds the mighty fabrics crowd the plain.
His native Town he sees with glory crowned ;
   He knows his spirit-promptings are not vain ;
His heart he feels with raptured joys rebound,
And hears the name of GRAINGER, like Fame's trumpet, sound !

    *   *   *   *   *

A mother's love flows with each milky-rill
   Into her offspring's hearts, becoming there
Affection's future fountains, whence distil
   Most precious drops of Nature's treasures fair,
   The dew-gems on the angels' golden hair.
A mother's love without a mother's breast,
   Is like a rose bereft of sun and air ;
A bird without its parents' song and nest ;—
O ! list a MOTHER'S LAY, her love is there express'd.

———

   " Come, then, fair children, let me sing
      A little Song, Love's roundelay,
   To you, sweet blossoms of life's Spring,
      The promised buds of rosy May.
   Come, bend on me your sparkling eyes,
      And harken to my voice alone ;
   Come, place your hands of tiny size
      Within your darling mother's own.

   " When you are sick and suffer pain,
      Doth she not soothe your little woes ?
   Doth she not sing the the lulling strain
      To charm your bosoms to repose ?
   Doth she not shield you from all foes,
      And, like an angel at your side,
   Her wings of meekness interpose
      'Gainst all the ills that youth betide ?

" But she may die and leave you lorn
　　Amid the cares that life surround ;
Ah, then will come the days to mourn,
　　For none, like her, shall e'er be found.
Friends kind and faithful may abound,
　　The memory of your loss to smother,
But you'll ne'er find on God's own ground,
　　A friend so faithful as a mother.

" Then, children, love her fondly now ;
　　Cling to her breast while life remains ;
Cherish the soul's most treasured vow,
　　To list her words and soothe her pains ;
That when the sad funereal strains
　　Proclaim that she is cold and dead,
Her spirit from the heavenly plains,
　　May hover round your board and bed."

　　　*　　　*　　　*　　　*　　　*

The father of our future Poet lay
　　Like a white figure, motionless, in bed.
A reverend supplicant with locks of grey,
　　Bent on his knees and hid the tears he shed.
A " De profundis, " oft the old man said.
The dying one, his cherished, only child
　　Was wearing fast away.   His voice was dead ;—
His eyes were of their outward vision spoiled,
But heaven was in his gaze, as he on angels smiled.

His fav'rite and his namesake Josè, woke,
　　Beheld his grandsire kneeling, and the tears
Shining upon his furrowed cheeks, that spoke
　　Of bitter grief, filled Josè's breast with fears.
　　The silence of the room, like death, appears :
Anon, a sound of choking leaves the bed,
　　That seems to shiver as the boy uprears
With wonder and alarm his little head ;
Then rise the sobs of Woe, 'mid whispers, " *He is dead!*"

　　　*　　　*　　　*　　　*　　　*

THE FATHER'S BURIAL.

Slow sinks the sun on his gold-tinted pillows ;
   Soft sighs the breeze 'mid the grass on the graves,—
Motionless, mournful, and tomb-crested billows—
   Death's silent ocean of petrified waves !

Shadows, like fingers uprais'd in hush'd sadness,
   Steal o'er the tombstones, like dreams of the past ;
Sunbeams ! how can ye smile on in your gladness,
   Where dark mounds of Death o'er Affection are cast !

Willows are bending their branches in sorrow ;
   Daisies are shedding their tears of regret ;
Butterflies flit, as in fear, o'er each furrow,
   No lilies are there, and the daisies are wet.

Calm in the glance of the day waning slowly,
   Stands the old church with its time-wasted spire,
Like a sage prophet, hoar, hallowed and holy,
   Its vanes birds of Peace in the glow of Love's fire.

Enter, and breathe humble sighs of devotion ;
   Kneel where your ancestors worshipp'd of yore ;
Leave the wild tumult of life's warning ocean ;
   Venite ! Oh, come, let us kneel and adore !

Through the stained windows the sunset is throwing
   Mantles of beauty o'er statue and tomb ;
The cross of yon angel in glory is glowing,
   And the chaplet she bears seems to blush into bloom.

O'er the priest's surplice a rainbow is streaming ;
   Violets rest on his volume of prayer ;
Altar, and arches, and chancel are beaming
   Beneath the bright hues that are lingering there.

Hark ! the deep tones of the organ awaken,
   Swelling to grandeur a beautiful strain ;
Soothing the bosoms desponding—forsaken—
   Melodiously lulling their anguish and pain.

Voices and organ are solemnly blending !
  List to the words ! What sweet comfort they bring !
Faith, Hope and Joy on that strain are descending—
  " Grave, *where* is thy victory ? Death, *where's* thy sting?"

     *   *   *   *   *

Sadly and slowly the mourners are moving
  Round the old Pile to a grave newly made;
Weeping the loss of the lov'd and the loving,
  That now in his cold, narrow couch must be laid.

———

Our Boy,—as youngsters should—his school attends—
  Proves apt at lore, though delicate at times:
But, as a nurse, he hath the best of friends
  In his old Gran'dam. Oh, if all the rhymes
  Her grandson e'er hath written ; all the chimes
Of song he yet may sing ; he still would fail,
  Though every strain were pæans from all climes,
Her lasting love to show; for 'tis a tale
Fraught with devotion—love—that angels might regale!

'Twas she, who in our Minstrel, woke the fire
  Of love poetic, and, in dreams more sweet
Than Eden's blossoms, shadowed forth the lyre
  Of future days. Behold him at her feet,
  Wrapp'd in a sunny cloud of joy complete,
Drinking the dewy songs that seem to flow,
  Like golden streamlets through a wild retreat,
Rousing his spirit to a fevered glow
Of inspiration, wonder ! *Why*, he did not know.

Oh, she could sing a sang o' auld lang syne,
  Wi' pithfu' tone, and lilt a cantie lay
I' Scottish verse, for she was o' the the line
  O' Hamiltonian* pride. Oh, mony a fray
  Wi' hielan' clans and southrons i' their day,

---

* The name of the author's grandmother, on the maternal side, was
Hamilton.

I' martial rhyme she'd tell ; and she could write
   A bonnie ballant in a decent way ;
   An' aft our Bardie rose before the licht,
To hear her croon wild sangs, an' Tales like *this* recite.

THE REED LEATHER SHOON.

I WAS ance fair and young ; I ha'e danced, I ha'e sung,
But my heart wi' sad sorrow has aften been wrung ;
I ha'e lo'ed—I was wed ; but its lang syne the head
That lay on my breast was entomb'd wi' the dead.
Then my dawtie, fair flower ! fell asleep in an hour,
When snaw-drifts cam' snelly an' wild i' their power ;
She was fand stark an' cauld, for the storm russled doon,
An' buried my bairn wi' her Reed Leather Shoon.

Ah ! ye gentles may smile, but ye canno' beguile
The heart o' a mither sad sabbin' the while !
There are tears that *will* fa', spite o' haly words a',
When we think on the lo'ed anes now slumberin' law !
Her hair, like saft gowd, doon her white shoothers flowed ;
Her een, like wat blue bells, sae bonnily glowed !—
An' auld gin I be, memory shines, like the mune,
Ah ! there lies my Nell wi' her Reed Leather Shoon !

'Twas a nicht o' wild wae, o' lament an' dismay,
When they brocht ben my bairn frae the drift where she lay !
O ! how could the snaw on sic gentleness fa',
An' bury sic comeliness lanely an' law ?
Years ha'e dwindled an' gane, still my heart's young wi' pain ;
O, aften I weep the auld sorrows in vain !
An' e'en i' the kirk when to pray I bend doon,
I see my sweet Nell wi' her Reed Leather Shoon.

I had frien's no' a few, but I couldna renew
The youth o' my heart to their kindliness due ;
Bonnie toddlers cam' there, hingin' roun' my airm chair,
Sae I craved their fond minnies to bring them nae mair !

I ha'e keepsakes at hand ; there's my puir Willie's wand,
An' the buckles o' siller he fancied sae grand ;
There's the ring on my finger ; but O, far abune
A' mementoes o' luve, Nelly's Reed Leather Shoon !

———

Rhyme without reason is a thing too common,
    Like quantity unqualified, perhaps ;
Or beauty without virtue among women ;
    A kind of lace to set off dirty caps ;
    A luring jingle in poetic traps :
Still rhyme is rhyme, and pleasing to the ear,
    As bell-sounds to the sheep ; to brewers, taps ;
Or any thing that we may fancy dear ;
As ladies' whispers sweet that all men love to hear.

Josè filled slates with volumes of sweet sound ;
    What sense was there the slates have never told.
He tried with pencil-sketches themes profound,
    And tinted verse with rainbows, young and old.
    Epics from Ossian from the Muses rolled,
Till half-a-dozen ledgers, meant for bacon,
    Or cheese, or butter—they for such were sold—
Contained the songs that might Apollo waken,
Should he have naught to do but be by cloud-ghosts shaken.

Of Love our poet sung.   O Venus tender !
    Doves, groves, alcoves, and all the rhymes *fornent*
This passion of the heart, this pulse of splendour,
    Were harp'd on ceaselessly with fire unspent ;
    Though love might well have asked, "What all this
        meant ?"
O Love, for shame ! did'st thou not fry his marrow ?
    Were not his knees to thee oft lowly bent ?
Did not he bare his bosom to thine arrow ?
Ah, soon he was popp'd off—the poor, poetic sparrow !

His dear girl's name,—mellifluous word!—was Mary ;
  His big girl's form was luscious, coarse and lusty ;
Her foot was like to nothing like a fairy ;
  And then her breath was sweet as bacon rusty ;
Her arm was such a one as well could dust ye,
Should you have dared against her once to wrangle.
  She was a maid ; a trifle old and fusty,
  Yet fit for love, or feats that love might strangle ;
Oh, she was Queen of Arts, the Juno of a mangle !

  Ah, the young rogue had other fish to fry !
  Another Eve of Beauty, rich and rare,
Had caught the apple of his sparkling eye :
  A lady gentle, with her golden hair,
  His soul had charmed, had woke his muse to prayer.
Her footsteps fell, like moonlight on the dew,
  Her voice was music, queenly was her air,
  And she was good ; so love strong in him grew,
And mangling Mary's wiles and kisses overthrew.

She knew the Minstrel loved her, but what then ?
  Who was this Youth, unknown to her, that bowed
With heart and soul amid the ranks of men ?
  Some nameless pilgrim in th' admiring crowd ;
  Some twinkling beam that viewed her from its cloud.
She knew him, as the spirit knows its frame ;
  An earthly casket that may be allowed
  To hold soul-beauty and its deathless flame,
Then yield its treasured gem and sink to dust and shame.

" O tears of love ! what rainbows in the heart
  Your shining diamonds form, when Memory
Flies o'er the clouds of thought, with holy art
  Painting her glowing pictures fair and free,
  Of what thou wert, and what thou still must be !
My Henrietta lost, yet ever near
  My spirit's ken ; thy beauteous face I see
  In visioned dreams ! Ah, now thou dost appear
With smiles, like summer stars, my hapless heart to cheer !

" Thy golden hair in rippling brightness flows
  Adown thy falling shoulders, like a stream

Viewed through an amber glass. Thy bosom's snows
  Bring forth twin buds that 'mid rare fragrance dream
  Of roses in the garden of the chaste : they seem
Too beautiful for garish day, and hide
  Their ruby faces 'neath the glorious gleam
Of Purity's white wings, lest lustful Pride
Should pluck them from their hills, and cast their beauties wide.

" I gaze on thee when angels trembling kneel
  Before the altar of Eternal Love ;
And when the priest heaven's joys would fain reveal,
  On thee I gaze, as on Love's throne above.
  Around thee I behold fair spirits move ;
And while the raptured organ breathes delight,
  And strains mellifluous, like sweet seraphs, rove
'Mid clouds of incense, on their pinions white,
Sole thought art thou of bliss ; sole object in my sight !

" And tears, hot tears, have straggled down my cheek,
  As I upraised my humble voice in song
When mournful chants of solemn ' Holy Week '
  Awoke responses from the choral throng.
  O Salem, Salem ! did thy plaints belong
But to the Jews alone, not to my heart ?
  Or did the lover do thy prophet wrong,
When in his ' *Lamentations* ' taking part,
He thought too much of Self to mourn thee as thou art ?

" When sables mantled o'er the sacred Rood,
  And clothed the ' Crucifixion,' like a bier,
The ' *Stabat Mater* ' rising to a flood,
  From the afflicted Mother's swelling tear,—
  Naught did I know but that some angel near
Bewailed with her the anguish of that time.
  Can angels weep and not with wings appear ?
In sooth, they can ! aye, weep and soar sublime,
When clay becometh soul, and loving is no crime.

" To me, poor Minstrel, music hath stange spells,
  Potent as God's own choir. My soul e'er dwelt
With holy harmonies. The glorious spells
  Of HANDEL, HAYDN, and MOZART, are felt

Within my heart, as if archangels knelt
My soul beside, and bowed earth's passions down.
O music! teach my clay to thaw and melt,
And waft to heaven its tears, to form a crown
Glist'ning with gems of light, adorning man's renown!

. "O Henrietta, first pure fire that rose,
Like Abel's off'rings, from my burning breast,
Thy name within this bosom ever glows
In adoration of thy virtues blest.
Thou art an angel in the realms of rest;
And spotless as thy life on earth, shall be
Thy mem'ry in my soul, of love the best.
Thou art my guardian Spirit on the sea
Of mortal strife,—in death my advocate thou'lt be!"

Were we to quote forever we should fail
Interpreters of Jose's heart to be;
Were songs of her from him to load each gale
From groves of balm, and hills of Araby,
They would but echo his untiring tale
Of love and adoration vainly given.
For how could he with birth and wealth prevail?
As well might he have with some seraph striven
To pluck her plumes of light, and check her flight to heaven.

From heaven to earth, once more, we now descend:
Our poet and plane-dealer takes the cane,
Becomes the pedagogue, and strives to blend
The sweets of learning with correction's pain,
And at one swoop, a swarming school to gain,
And daily bread, which planes did not supply:—
Nor were his efforts altogether vain—
Soon pupils gathered in a noisy fry,
As many a one could prove who dwelt as neighbours nigh.

*   *   *   *   *

"Farewell ye planks of beech; ye planes, farewell! *
Farewell, the whirling stone and forge of fire!

---

* The Author served his Apprenticeship as a Planemaker in Newcastle.

Ye chopping-blocks, hatchet, and 'bursting' mell,
 Ripping and cross-cut saws, let me retire !
 No more can I your teeth and 'set' admire.
Ye Coopers' Jointers, Try and Jack, adieu !
 Hollows and Rounds ; ye Grooves, Mamma and Sire ;
Ye Mouldings-base, I now have done with you !
Ye Mother-planes, farewell !   Green plains I now shall view.

 " Ye Smooths, farewell ! whereon my muse essayed
  Apprentice lays ! where are your shavings now ?
How many lyrics from the beechen shade
  Have gone to Lethe ?   Where's the 'Pilgrim's Vow ;'
  The Sonnets to ' Belinda's blushing Brow.'
Where all the verses on your glossy *soles ?*
  Sand-paper Sapphics ?   Written, I allow,
 'Gainst parchment 'prentice-bonds—consumed in shoals,
To give the faggots life, ignite the ' roundy coals !'"

 " Oh, let me snatch one fragment from the fire,
  Ere the beech-shaving-scrolls depart forever !
One humble Offering from my trembling lyre,
 A Simple love-song to my native River,
 Adapted to an air that fadeth never !
And sung by native voices coarse and fine.
  At seventeen years of age I deemed it clever,
Proud that the child poetical was mine ;
'Twas christened ' THE RETURN ; OR, EXILE OF THE TYNE.' *

———

MY CHILDHOOD'S HOME.

My heart's in the home of my childhood,
 The mem'ry of beauty is there ;
O give me one glance of that wildwood,
 Where once dwelt the lovely and fair !
The banks where I gathered her flowers
 Shall greet me with verdure and joy ;
The stream 'neath the dark hanging bowers
 Shall murmur the songs of the boy.

---

* This Song is given in page 33 in this Selection.

The moon is abroad in her splendour,
  The stars seem to float in delight,
The gale seeks the roses to render
  Love's fragrant and gentle "Good night!"
I watch for my love near the stream—
  Will she come as she came in her joy?
Alas! she hath gone as a dream,
  She sings no more songs to her boy!

The billows of ocean may bear me
  From love and the home of my heart,
But nothing from mem'ry can tear me,
  Or bid its gay visions depart.
The star of my manhood declines,
  And age lies like surf on the shore,
Still home in my dear native shrines,
  Speaks sweetly of Childhood once more!

OUR BABY LILY.

Our baby Lily's lying, hands across her breast;
Sleeping, but ne'er sighing, happy in her rest.
Snowy raiment round her, white lace o'er her brow,
Thus the angels found her; she is happy now.

Our baby Lily's dwelling you may ne'er behold;
Some one hath been telling you 'tis dark and cold.
We who loved her dearly cannot this allow—
We believe sincerly she is happy now.

Our baby Lily's features all confessed were fair;
One of those bright creatures born for heaven and prayer.
Face of beauty smiling, limbs like rounded pearls,
Voice most heart-beguiling, sweetest of babe-girls.

She knew not the sorrow human hearts that fades;
Knew not grief's to-morrow waiting sinful maids.
Led by some fair spirit,—none knows why or how—
Heaven she doth inherit—she's an angel now.

Like Autumn's dew upon the withered flowers,
   Impearling their sere leaves, but failing still
To call them back to Beauty's blooming bowers,
   Are parents' tears for home-buds pale and chill ;
   For the sweet voices mute that never will
Breathe their loved lispings to the list'ning ears ;
   But as the rainbow forms on yonder hill
With humid tints, now glows, then disappears ;
So Hope dwells in the skies and Grief forsakes her tears.

Babes are but blossoms that the slightest breath
   Rends from the parent tree ; they fade and die,
Leaving their fragrant mem'ries after death,
   Like angels' blessings, while the tear and sigh
   For their lost sweetness flutter to the sky :—
But when the boughs of youth, from which depend
   Rich, fruitful promises of future joy,
Lose their green honours, wither, and descend
To the dark, wintry grave, of woe there seems no end.

When seventeen summers had their beauty shed
   On a loved daughter and her brother fair,
They both were stricken, by Consumption, dead.
   Vain was the leech's skill—the parents care ;
   Hopes were wide scattered on the viewless air ;
The fruit of joy prospective from the tree
   Was rent, as by the lightning, and the prayer
That Health and Strength would Life's salvation be,
Fell on the ear of Doom, like drowning shrieks at sea.

Pale Grief intones her requiem o'er their graves ;
   Affection lingers ever near their tomb :—
Like a love-pharos o'er the mournful waves,
   Lightning the darkness of sepulchral gloom,
   Devotion's lamp glows in the urn of doom.
O Death ! O Desolation ! fold your wings !
   O Faith ! O Resignation ! now illume
The minstrel's spirit as he sighs and sings !
Gild with your chastened beams Misfortune's sombre springs!

THE POET'S HOPES.

MID all the penury, the want, the woe—
  Heart-bitterness of life—the gloom of Fate—
Cast o'er the poet's soul, grand thoughts still glow,
  Like God's eternal promise round the gate
  Of Paradise. Let him but watch and wait
Heaven's advent of these messengers of Love,
  With humbled knees and heart, and contemplate
The splendours of God's endless joys above,
His grief and mortal care shall from his bosom move.

Are not the skies the birthright of the Just?
  Let then the poet, be he e'er so poor,
Look upward through the cloud of human dust,
  And keeping faith with Progress safe and sure,
  A dwelling with the Good he shall secure.
For do you think the Spirit vainly given,
  Or that the world his mission can allure,
And that he liveth to be backward driven
Far from the throne of Grace, to be by demons riven?

Soiled, soiled, indeed, are many regal robes
  With mortal clay-taints of their passions strong,
That else had graced with glory tuneful globes,
  And shed most gorgeous light on verse and song ;—
  But holy angels have been wilful, wrong—
E'en with the blaze of bliss upon them cast,
  Have with their pride swept heavenly hosts along,
Like the red lightning-beams upon the blast!
When seraphs thus have fall'n—let mortals stand aghast.

The poet's mission is most high—divine ;
  He is, or ought to be, the word—the pen ;
The teacher—prophet, nations to combine
  In holiness of deeds all grades of men.
  Rise should his hymns on mount, in wood and glen ;
Be heard symphonious to the voice of Truth ;
  Rescue from Error's dark and bigot den

The fallen spirits chained by fiends uncouth,
And glean the growth of Hope, as corn was gleaned by Ruth.

What of man's scorn ? Did e'er the sun's bright face
  Grow dim because of hatred Satan showed
To his transcendent beams ? Is mankind's race
  Annihilate for sinning Eve ? Or, hath the road
  By hallowed steps of sainted ancients trode
To heaven and grace, become a barr'd up-track
  Because red Guilt o'er Ruin's pathways rode,
And drove the weak from Virtue's castle back ?
O why should poets quail when Ignorance looks black ?

In spite of contumelious taunts the bards shall live
  Amid the stars of loveliness for aye,
So long as they, the sons of progress, give
  Their seals of inspiration, and display
  Their spirits' mission to exalt our clay.
God is a Bard! His poems fill all space ;
  His verse resoundeth o'er the ocean's way ;
On the sky-cleaving mountains we may trace
Eternal Epics grand : O, infinite in grace !

Doth not the Book of Glory glow with song ?
  The stars are shining Lyrics from His hand ;
All the green earth an Idyll, and the throng
  Of woods and praries *one great poem* stand.
  His hymns are written fair in every land ;
And the proud Tempest, with exulting throat,
  Chaunteth His Odes with elocution grand ;
The thunder-voice repeats the Storm-King's note,
Which with a lightning-pen the Great Jehovah wrote !

On every flower and leaf, on bloom and bud,
  There is a gentle air of perfumed praise ;
The verse of heaven is heard in stream and flood ;
  And every surge is vocal with His lays.
  The verdant mead, the forest's tangled ways,
The leaping fountain and the mirror'd well,
  The Alpine snows, the jungle's dreaded maze,
The stormy deeps, where huge, green monsters dwell—
All, all God's verse contain ; all of His Poems tell !

And we, poor things, pass onward in our path
　　To nothingness, unheeding Nature's strains ;
We, sordid mortals, scorn in secret wrath,
　　His messengers as vain and foolish swains,
　　Or *stones* bestow in mock'ry of their pains !
What recks the minstrel ? Like the children three
　　Who scathless trod the flames and 'scaped the chains,
The poet-soul forever soareth free
The eagle of bright fame—the Bird of Liberty !

The poet's world is one by Mind created,
　　And far aloof from plodding crowds he dwells ;
The sea is his, where, Neptune-like, elated,
　　He bids the tritons sound their twisted shells,
　　And call the mermaids from their coral cells.
Tempest and calm he owns.　Oh, he can wake
　　The whale-like surges from their stormy dells,
And hurl whole fleets with one terrific shake,
Down to the Acheron of rocks—for fancy's sake.

And he can woo wild whirlwinds into sleep,
　　Bind the fierce Boreas with a silken line,
Make crystal mirrors of the raging deep,—
　　String in a wreath of pearls the flashing brine,
　　Dissolve the rocks to fleecy wool of sheep,
Set up the rainbow o'er the purpling west,
　　And pile the golden cloudlets in a heap,
Beauteous and glorious as the eternal crest
Crowning the brow of Love in kingdoms of the blest.

Imagination is a potent King !
　　Of foul rebellion, treachery and wars.
And all the engines red Revolt can bring
　　To hurl earth's depots from their gilded cars,
　　He knoweth not ; *his* throne is mid the stars ;
His subjects are young Fancy's children fair,
　　Strangers to foreign and domestic jars :—
Spirits are they of ever balmy air,
Without a cause to weep, devoid of mortal care.

Alas ! Imagination fails to fill
　　The pocket, or the stomach, with good store ;

And the strong waters of the Aonian hill
  Are not so potent with the system's core,
  As ripe, rich, luscious wines ; and, what is more,
Poetic streams do not with Gain agree,
  They will not cleanse the clay from cradled ore,
They will not send our ships with goods to sea,
But then the souls they freight enrich mortality !

         ,   *   *   *   *   *

Grey locks hang o'er his temples, and the fire
  Of once dark eyes begins to pale and fade ;
Yet shall he mourn ? His soul can still aspire
  To the blue arch by Heaven's Grand Master made,
  And roam mid planets glorious, undecayed,
His spirit-pinions spread, like angels, free,
  And with God-granted Intellect arrayed,
Now buoyant sails o'er Mind's unfathomed sea,
Rolling mid isles of earth around Eternity !

Oh, his deep thankfulness to Him, whose hand
  Holds in its hollow countless spheres of light—
Whose breath can make, or mar, worlds vast and grand,
  And melt the heavens, as wax, before His sight—.
  Shall never sleep till death and endless night
Fold in their marble robes the humble worm,
  That from its larva, dared to wing its flight,
Clad in the poet's rainbow-painted form,
To glitter in the sun—to flutter through Life's storm.

God of the rolling spheres ! Who, by Thy Spirit,
  Eternal, glorious, omnipresent,—vast—
Did'st cause the Bard, Thy workmanship, t' inherit
  A legacy that should for ever last,—
  A mental statue to outlive the blast
Of blighting Time, and all the viper brood
  Of haughty Pride—that dread iconoclast ;
Who fain would hurl to dust Thy gospels good,
And bury Mind and Soul beneath Gold's lava-flood ;

Disarm the fury of his impious rage !
  Stay his bared arm of sacrilegious spite !

Bring lightning from the Minstrel's holiest page,
    That he, like Elymas, deprived of sight,
    And rendered impotent of scathful might,
May fail to launch Hate's arrows at those men,
    Who, seated by Thy will on Wisdom's height,
Reveal Thy mystic teachings by the pen,
And from chaotic gloom create new worlds again.

Thou who hast hung aloft the starry globes,.
    And crowned with dazzling light Thy thrones of glory!
O'er Intellectual grandeur cast the robes
    Of evershining grace that Mind before Thee,
    Should an angelic minister, adore Thee!
Teach thy verse-prophets to confide in Thee,
    Heedless of scoffing scorn by vice made hoary!
Lift Thy Bards' hearts, as on a joyful sea,
That they may never cease to praise Thy majesty!

And when Earth's wilderness shall be no more;
    When clouds shall disappear where sorrow-slept;
When Ocean-tempests fail to rage and roar,
    When rocks shall fade where billows madly swept,
    Where shipwrecked seamen sad and wildly wept—
When the poor Bard lies peacefully inurned
    Beneath the sod where Love her vigils kept;
May the soul's flame, that in the Minstrel burned,
Be to its Source of Light in quenchless joy returned.

*   *   *   *   *   *

LOCAL POEMS AND SONGS.

DEETH O' THE AWD PITMIN.

THE wintor snaw wis on the grund, and frost-prents on the pane,
When Rawfy Dagg, yence Jarra's brag, wis hord to growl an'
    grane,
A big man Rawf, ne bettor meyd te battil thro' this life,
An' for a spree, Rawf thresht cheps, tee, but nivvor struck his
    wife.
" What ! strike the muthor o' maw bairns ?　No ! no !" wad
    Rawfy say,
" Let cocks fight cocks ;　the hens, poor things hes nowt te de
    but lay."
Noo Rawfy's gannin' fast te pot ! he's oney just alive,
But what can ye expect o' Rawf ? the man's torned eigty-five !

" Sally, hinny, sit aside us ; lang, maw bairn, aw canna last,
Beukt aw's for the dowley lonnin' ; thoo may see aw's sinkin' fast.
Where's wor Tom ?　Where's maw pet Emmy ?　Let me a' maw
    gran' bairns see ;
Let thim hae maw fareweel blessin' ;　let thim cum afore aw dee.
Is that thoo, my heart-joy Tommy ?　Last sun left me in this life ;
Iv a week aw lost five bewties ; then, O warse, aw lost maw wife !
Eig, poor Peg ! she went afore us ; faithfil was she te the close,
Monny a yen 'ill tawk aboot us, when in deeth aw cock me toes.

Eigty-five last Pankeyk Tewsdor ; aw's a tidy age, thoo sees.
Aw's ne yewse te mortil leevin' ; aw's a deed chuck i' the seas.
Divvint bothor mair wi' docktors ; aw's fair sick wi' fizzic
    smells--
Greet M.D.'s may a' be clivvor, but they cannet mond thorsels.

When a man's fair set for deein'—mettors nowt, the rich or poor,
Lord or Deuk—eigh, there's Lord Pruddor—he wis rich eneuff,
    aw's shoor !
Greet Northumborlin's dipparted—him thit owned beyth land
    an' gowld—
Deeth heeds nowt aboot fine tytils, doon he shuvs thim mang the
    mowld.

Tom, bend law ; heer maw confesshin, an' a warnin' frev us teyk,
Man, aw *was* a wild yung scoondril ; is we broo wor'e shoor te
    beyk.
Coits an' bools wis maw sowl plisshor ; cock pits then wis in
    thor prime,
Gallygeyt leeds te the gallis, leest it *did*, Tom, in maw time.
Things gets bettor ; foaks gets wyzor ; still thor's pitmin warse
    nor me,—
Warse! Lord save us, Tommy, devils cannet warsor be !
When awd wives, eigh, mevvies, grannies, hes te suffor sheymfil
    ways ;
Be the prissint beests o' Bedlim ; Dorhim lads aw cannot praise.

Aw liked drinkin' ; is for sweerin, like the gammit aw cud gan,
Noo aw see maw yuthfil madnis when its owor late, maw man.
Cairds an' gamlin wis maw hobby, cheetin' oft te win the main,
Thowts i' sic like blagaird ackshins borns, like het leed, throo
    maw brain !
Tommy, hinny, drop a' gamlin', thoo thit coonts a' pop-shops bad,
Gamlin' is the deevil's pawnshop, where men's sowls is lost, maw
    lad.
Divvent drink te meyk the' feulish ; ef thoo cannet guide thesel,
When thoo teyks a glass for cumfort, stop the whiskey an' the
    yell.

Oh, this fleem is like te chowk us ! Sally, hinny, gie's the' han's !
Thoo's been mair nor dowtor tiv us ; bliss the', darlin', where
    thoo stans !
Where's that wine the ownor sent us ? Just fetch here a little
    drop,
For aw cannet reetly swally that cawd, nesty gingor-pop !
Didden't docktor Wawkor tell the', brandy, Sall, wad sewt us
    weel !

Fetch the bottil an' a tumlor ; Oh, hoo wake an' bad aw feel !
Lift us up ! there, noo ; that's canny ! gie's a kiss, maw bonny
     lass !
Noo, then, for a drop o' hivvin ; mind, Sall, that's a littil glass.

Oh, that's nice ! it's life an' sporrit tiv a man iv eigty five ;
Ef aw leeved te be a hundord, this wad keep me langor 'live.
A' things noo, thoo says, is reddy ; ne dispewt 'boot borryil brass,
Aw's deed sartin iv a fewnril ; that's a blissin' Sall, maw lass.
Te be borry'd like a pawpor wad hae rackt me sad an' sair ;—
Lie me doon, aw find aw's gannin'—let maw gran-bairns say a
     prayr.
Aw's contentid—Him thit meyd us understans maw wishis noo—
Lord forgie maw greet iffensis ; tiv His holy will aw boo !"

The winter snaw is on the grund ; the frost-prents on the pane,
Rawf lang had battil'd for his life, but grim deeth wan the main;
The stubborn aik lies law on orth—his snaw-croon'd branchis bare,
Leuk doon on Dagg, an' Jarra's brag, an' for yor doom porpare !

———

THE BLAGAIRD PITMIN'S LETTOR TO THE
" TIMES."

" Mistor Cockney, gobby scribblor, Roolor o' the modern
    "Times ;"
What's a' this thoo's said aboot us pitmen an' wor horrid crimes ;
Reel doon blagairds, thoo he's ca'd us ; scoondrils thit disgrace
    the orth ;
Black hart villins, wi' black feyces, spawn fra deevils, beyn an
   borth.
Had the' hand ! thoo thundrin leeor ! Jewpittor's thaw queer
    nick neym—
Ef aw had the' be the throppil, seun thaw inky jaws aw'd leym ?
But aw'll show the' greetor marsy nor thoo meets te colloyrs pooer,
Aw'll convince the' thoo's a leeor, an' the deevil's undorvewor.
Was Dick Torpin bred a pitman? bred a theef, mair like the mark !
Ewgeen Airim was ne puttor, tho' he mordored Adim Clark :

Thortill nivvor wis a trappor, tho' be him a Weer wis droon'd,
Covorseer, the bluddy flonkey, nivvor wark'd annunder ground.
Tho' Spen's wettors may be reeddish, what chance hae they wi'
    the Teymes ?
On hor banks thor's been mair mordors ivvor telt on be thor
    neymes.
Tawk o' pitmen been dip raskils, leuk it Cockney's butchrin'
    ·deeds !
Choppin' bonny bairns te peeces, cuttin' off men's legs an'
    heeds ;—
Whei the varry neym o' Lundin, wiv its Toowors an' Traytors'
    Brigs,
Speeks o' puzzins, rapes, an' mordors, borkin' rips an' pale-feyced
    prigs
Didst thoo nivvor heer o' Tyborn, where Queen Bess hung up the
    preests,
Where the vorjin Star iv Iuglind *quartord* gentilmin like beasts ?
Cockney Kings hes been ne bettor ; leuk it hump Dick i' the
    Toowor !
Mordrin' a' the bonny princes, just te gain a throne an' poowor !
Droonin greet Deuks mang wine-treekil ; stickin' sovrins in the
    back.
Ef pitraws showed sic transackshins, *then* thoo *weel might ca' us
    black.*
Tho' aw cannet praise maw marras for thor soborniss an' sense,
Seldim de they teyk the steemor it the govvormin's expense.
For yen blagaird 'mang us minors, hundrods 'mang the Cockneys
    leeves,
Whei, the honnist Bobbies tells us thit thor's skeuls for breedin'
    theeves !
Mistor " Times," thoo munnet fancy thit becaws thoo fills a rag
Full iv humbug, news an' speechis, that thoo hes a reet te brag
Boot the varty o' thaw pressgang, when, ef thoo the trooth wad
    tell,
Thoo's been flummax'd be the mobsmen, an' weel dredged oot,
    tee, the' sel.
Tuthor day, it Chortsey Races,—ne North pitmen's *there,* aw'll
    sweer—
Is wor Prince o' Wales wis stannin' backin' owthor horse or
    meer—
Frev his pockit wawk'd his tickor, thit he'd getten fra the Queen,

While the Cockney raskil chuckild, *Halbort Hedword's worry
    green !*
Noo aw ax the', wad a pitmin hailin fra the Weer or Tyne,
Tiv his Prince proov sic a scoondril ? Man, aw ken the ansor fine !
Wad the warst o' drunkin boolors, warst o' fightors, warst o' men,
Rob the bairn o' Queen Victoree ? No ! tho' he belang'd the
    Spen !
What dis thoo knaw 'boot us pitmen ? Hes thoo leeved aside
    wor Raws ?
Hes thoo ivvor hailed us cummin fra wor shifts is black is craws ?
Hes thoo keek'd inside wor hoosis ? seed the holy cumforts there ?
Hes thoo hord the littil dowpy stuttrin' oot his neetly pray'r ?
What can *thoo* ken 'boot us minors ? Ax wor marras, man an' lad,
Ef we ivvor shork'd wor dewty when a wife or bairn wis bad ;
Ef we torn'd the hung'ry beggors, *'speshly awd uns,* fra wor yett,
Ef we whupp'd a dog or deevil fra wor doors in cawd an' wet ?
Where's yor greet nobs 'mang the Cockneys, tho' thor up te
    French an' Greek,
Tho' they scribbil for yor papor, an' on eddycayshin speek,
Can, wi' trooth, show they oot-hew us in wor luve is man te man?
Or is man te wummin studdy ? Dash maw buttins, ef they can !

      *   *   *   *   *   *

Pollygize, sor, for the' leein' geyn us pitmen o' the North,
An' in fewtor, be mair cawshis what in prent thoo lets gan forth ;
Ne man in this warld is parfit, pitmen ne mair nor the rest—
Cookoo's eggs hes ne just tytil te the humbil Sheeley's nest !"

                   .

"MAW MARRAS, TEYK WARNIN' BE ME !"

" Maw shift in this warld nobbut lasts a few days,
    Then afore stairin' croods aw mun dee ;
It's a' on icconnt o' my wild drinkin' ways,
    An' poor Nell's, for she liked a drop, tee,—
Thit the rope o' cawd deeth seun ill stop Matty's breeth,—
    On a life-crushin' hang-gallas tree.
Drink, drink was maw bane, aw repeat it ageyn ;—
    Then, maw marras, teyk warnin' be me !

" Twelve eers syne wor Nelly was canny an' kind,
    Lads, aw nivvor fand fawlt wiv hor *then ;*
Becaws as wis sobor an' Nell nivvor pined
    For strang drink, nor the joys o' strange men.
But the meunleet o' luve thit shud marry'd life pruv,
    Torn'd te cloods an' te storms o' the sea ;
Bad words led te blaws, mevvies, oft wivvoot caws,—
    O, maw marras, teyk warnin' be me !

" Aw tried, biv a' fair meens hor fond ways te keul,
    But hor tung wis a snake hard te kill ;
Aw kep' off the lush just te show what a foul
    A daft wummin can be when she will.
Seun hor bad ways gat worse, an' maw life wis a corse,
    Se aw started te be a feul tee ;
Aw wark'd an' aw drunk ;—noo te mordor aw've sunk—
    O, maw marras, teyk warnin' be me !

" Eigt eers o' fair howstrow, sad mis'ry, an' strife,
    Aw pass'd, like a feend oot o' hell :—
Ef aw'd ony had sense te hae torn'd off maw wife,
    Aw wad teun greetor care o' messel'.
Tho' aw knaw'd she hid geyn iv hor drink wi' strainge men !
    Lads, aw still tcuk hor heym, de ye see ?
For its hard te forget a nawd bed-meyt an' pet—
    O, maw marras, teyk warnin' be me !

" Aw've threshed hor when drinkin', an' madniss wis mine,
    An' aw've pray'd hor te mend hor bad ways ;
An' when te be canny aw seed hor incline,
    O, aw gav hor kind coaxins an' praise.
But the lowe o' the lamp ouey showed the chouk damp,
    Bella Hall set maw wife on the spree—
Then aw vood biv a blaw she shud lie cawd an' law—
    Canny marras, teyk warnin' be me !

" On the sivinteenth day o' Dissember aw went,
    (Coaly-black was the day an' the deed !)
'Tiv Hopkinson's Pit, on a shuttin'-match bent,
    Oh, aw wish sic a match aw'd ne'er seed !

Aw gat blind, howin' heym,—nowt maw drinkin' cud teym—
   Aw wis maddor nor bull-dog can be ;
For aw cors'd an' aw swore, ranted, blasfeemed, aw's shoor—
   O, maw marras, teyk warnin' be me !

"Aw wis boilin' wi' strife, when aw seed Nell, maw wife,
   An' nowt for te gar me feel croose ;
Scairsh a spuuk i' the grate, an' ne suppor, ue bait,
   For te welkim Matt back tiv his hoose.
Noo, maw brains brunt like coal, in my breest wis a hole,
   Still wor Nell tawk'd is peert is cud be ;
It wor door she run oot wiv a jeer and an' a shoot—
   Canny marras, teyk warnin' be me ?

" Seun aw hawled hor back owor ; then started the stowor,
   That hes fetcht me to deeth's warst o' stengs ;
Nell's reed blud an' hor hair on wor brush was seed fair,
   An' blud-rust on the colrake an' teyngs.
Oh, aw cared nowt for aw thit Joe Whitfield cud say ;
   Aw wis mad is a mad bull can be ;
Poor Nell's carkish aw brayed tell iu deeth she wis laid—
   O, maw marras, teyk warnin' be me !

" O maw sentinse is just—but aw's weery o' life—
   Judge an' joory deels justis *this* time ;
Thor wis neboddy else laid a hand on maw wife,
   Se maw deeth is dissarved be maw crime.
Oh, fra drink, marras awl, keep away, is maw cawl—
   Leest, like Matt, for fool mordor ye dee ;
It's the last word aw say—*fra strang drink bide away*—
   O, maw marras, teyk warnin' be me."

THE HEYM-HANKORIN' PITMIN.

A RISSYTASHIN.

LANG's the road an' dip's the wettor ; what a kevvil, Mall, is mine !
Sixteen thoosen miles te travvil fra maw borthpleyce on the
   Tyne !

A' the way upon the oshin ; doon an' up, then up an' doon,
Nut a hoose te breek the jorney twixt Sheels bar an' Melborn
    toon.
Tawk o' warkin' i' the " Fanny," where for fifty eers aw've rowt ;
Ye hae solid grund te stand on ; ef yo're scumfish'd—whei, its
    nowt :—
Lang way better nor get droonded, an' chowed up be hungry
    wales,—
Sixteen thoosen miles o' dainjor ; nowt but sea, an' sky, an
    sails :—
Had yor hand, there ! aw's forgotten brustin' boilors, fyor an' tow ;
O, deer me, aw'll hae te gan tho', else thor'll be a bonny row.
Maw sun, Tom, is it the diggins—meyd his fortin iv a eer ;
See, he's sent wor passige-munny ! Mall, we'll hae te gan, maw
    deer !
O, the thowt on't gars me trimmil ; dash, ef aw like them Black
    Bawls !
Marsy on us, Mally, hinny ! we'll get blawn te bits be squalls !
Thor's tyfoenors an' sleclonors, an' thor's awfil wetterspoots,
Warse nor onny, horrykins thit teers up shipmasts be thor snoots.
Wheest ! them's Leymsley chorch bells ringin ! Bonny bells, aw
    like ye weel !
Sweet ye rung oot on maw weddin'; leet wis then maw hart an'
    heel ;—
Noo yor soon's gars mallincolly cuvvor owre maw sowl wi' care,
Tho' aw leeve te get te Melborn, Leymsley bells, ye'll nut ring
    there !
Littil bords, wild yaller yowleys, aw's nut like maw 'Straylyin
    sun,
Aw wad seunor heer ye singin' nor destroy ye wiv a gun.
Ef man's wings hid been i' fashin, aw wad flown away, like ye ;
On maw back aw,d teun wor Mall, an' been a land gull on the sea.
Cum here, Pinchor ! poor blind doggie ! thoo'il be left behint
    aleyn ;
Monny a howlin' neet thoo'll gie them when thoo fin's the' maistor
    geyn.
Back an' forrid te the collry, drack'd thaw skin wi' weet an'glair,
Thoo'll be seekin' me, poor beestie ; but thoo'll nivvor find me
    mair !
"Andro Swan" is on thaw collor ; let ne mortil rob thaw brass,
Till thoo gets the duzzy feevor, an' thaw hide lies 'neeth the grass.

Maw kinnairies ! yo're bispockin ! Breed away, aw wish ye weel!
Puss ! thoo's gannin' te the Cassil ; mind, behave an' divvent
    steel,
Else the ownor's undorkeepor thaw distruckshin will cumpleet ;
Keep thesel abeun the commin, an' fra clarts them velvit feet.
Bliss us a' ! hoo time gans fleein' ! On the mornin's morn we
    start
Be the train wiv a' wor luggige.   O this pairting breeks maw
    hart !
Fare the' weel, maw coaly rivvor ! fare the' weel, brave suns o'
    Tyne !
Coll'ry lads an' lasses bonny, wi' yor cheeks an' lips like wine !
Fare the' weel, maw stordy boolors ! Gud-bye Teem, where oft
    aw've fished.
Gud-bye, maw kind ownor's Cassel, where grand feests is offins
    dished.
Mally ! Mally ! whe's this cummin ? It's a flonkey wiv a box,
An' a lettor fra' the ownors ; hares and fezzins, hens an' cocks !
Lissen, Mally, what the note says, " Andrew Swan, don't go away.
"You have been a faithful servant ; cease to work, we'll send
    your pay.
"In the cottage where you dwell now, there remain, the rent is
    free ;
"Give the notion up entirely of th' Australian trip to sea !"
Andro Swan an' his wife Mally blaired till beyth wor oot o' breeth,
Then dittormind they wad tarry in thor prissint heym till deeth.
Tom heerd a' things fra the skippor iv a Black Bawl steemor line,
An' the awd heym-hank'rin' pitmin still leeves on the banks o'
    Tyne.

———

MAW GUD WISHES TIV A' MEN.

The bumlors fetch thor hunnypots frev ivvory bonny flooer ;
The lark scroos, like a gimlick bright, abeun the cloody booer ;
The rose grows modist is sum lass that knaws nowt hoo she's
    luved,
And Bewty thinks o' Varty's links, be hivvin itsel' appruved.

But wasps, thit shams the hunny blobs, ne sweetness ivvor
    knaws,
An' hawks, tho' fleein' nigh the stars, fin's blud-wark for thor
    claws ;
The puzzen-buds, the deevil's guds, leuks cumley, fine an'
    free ;—
Thor'e rank bad foaks wi' cankris harts thit ne'er can happy be.

Orth's cramm'd wi' rips o' monny sorts ; the hippocrit is *yen /*
He weers the robes iv innorsinse, an' cheets his fellor-men.
Rillidjin's elwis on his lips, while mischeef fills his breest ;
Ef black claes meyks a parfit man, awd Clooty beets the preest.

Sum creetors, swindlers born an' bred, the sporrit dodges tries,
An' in the dark, like Noey's ark, teyks in the fond an' wise.
The rope can save an' strangil beyth, the Davinports to me
Wor'e cheps thit meyd a lot o' feuls, an' scoondrils proov'd to
    be.

Troo Jeenis is a creetor rare, an' hard beset it times,
An' tho he dornet cheek the stage, he breeds the singors'
    rimes ;
What caws hes he the brains te steel iv empty, gawkey feuls ?
He caps a' mushrim jillissy, an' envyis paddick steuls.

The muck-flee thinks he meyd the skies becaws he feels the
    sun ;
The midgy fancies iv its pride its day 'll ne'er be deun ;
While Jeenis wiv a sowl o' flame teyks in air, land, an' sea !
Aw wish thit men wad nut be feuls, an' bother thoo an' me.

The soopor o' Newcassel streets may try a brush it Greek ;
The tallychandlor, wickidly, may Homor leern te speek ;
The rolleyman o' Carvor's croo may say he's Pollor's sun,
Becaws his horse ca'd Peggysis, hes pulled a Airmstrang gun.

But soopor, an' the greecy chep an' rollyman is wrang,—
Let ivvory creetor keep his pleyce, or bide storn wisdim's stang :
The waggor iv a cookoo clock wi' Time's wheels mun agree,—
Aw wish thit men wad nut be feuls is heer thor'e seed te be.

Aw wish thit reesin had hor seet iv ivvory mortil brain ;
Aw wish thit peepil wantin' sense wad let wise foaks aleyn ;
Aw wish thit ignorrins wad melt afore instruckshin's fires,
For' men thit nivvor play'd the harp can nivvor teun the wires.

Aw wish thit cheps be naytor meyd te dress a cobbler's last,
Wad te the lethor, an' waxend, an' awl, stick hard an' fast,
An' nut portend te cum oot Keens, an' stage-struck Hamlicks be ;
Sic men shud keek in judgmint's glass, an' then big feuls they'd
    see.

Noo, tho' aw dicktate te the world, remembor, aw's nut pure,
Slill brayin' cuddies offins tells the cummin' spate an' shooer.
The spotted paddick 'mang the grass meens summat biv his croak ;
The brightest lowe thit ivvor brunt forst beelt its nest 'mang
    smoke.

An' mind, maw sarmin issent ment te hit sum singil chep,
The brumstin pan aw've set te born mun cleer the hornet's
    skeyp.
Tho' shud the cap fit sum queer heed, let us the weeror see,
While the best wish iv maw aw'd hart's *may a' men happy be !*

NELLY O' THE TYNE.

WHEN maw sweet Nelly forst to me,
    Hor tendor luve confest,
Aw vood upon maw bended knee,
    O' fair yens she was best.
Aw kisst hor broo, hor cheeks, an' lips,
    An' claimed hor hart is miue ;
Ne lass te me can ivvor be
    Like Nelly o' the Tyne.

Hor teeth for whiteness sheymed the porls
    Thit in the oysters grow ;
An' sunshine danced amang the corls,
    Thit fell owre breest an' brow,

Whene'er she spak' twe roses seemed
  Te oppin iv a line ;
Ne lass te me cud bonnier be,
  Nor Nelly o' the Tyne.

Like lilies painted wi' sweet wine,
  An' varnished owre wi' dew,
Hor tapor fingors clung te mine,
  Wi' fond reliance troo.
Maw breest hove like a ship it sea,
  Te hear hor voice divine ;
Ne lass te me cud cannyor be
  Nor Nelly o' the Tyne.

She was a lady biv hor borth,
  But dark misfortin's blaw
Hid laid hor parints cawd in orth,
  An' left hor poor an' law.
But far afore the chink o' goold,
  Te me she did incline ;
Ne lass te me cud dearer be
  Nor Nelly o' the Tyne.

O sad the day an' dreer the hoor,
  When sickness seized hor hart,
An' tore me fra maw cumley flooer,
  An' bad' maw joys depart.
She lies amang the luved an' lost,
  For which troo harts repine ;
Ne lass te me can ivvor be
  Like Nelly o' the Tyne.

Sin' Nelly deed lang eers hae past,
  Still cumfort aw hae neyn ;
Fra morn te neet aw grane an' freet,
  For all aw luved is geyn.
Aw offins sit beside hor grave,
  While bittor grief is mine,
For till aw dee maw luve mun be
  Wi' Nelly o' the Tyne.

THE CONTENTED COLLIOR.

WHEN furst aw went a trappor lad,
   Amang the men o' Wear an' Tyne,
Aw teuk me seat, be day an' neet,
   Is ef the pits wis mine.
I the darksim shaft, aw spread an' lafft,—
   Aw nivvor glumpt it onny thing—
Aw ansort shift, an' kep' me drift,
   Is happy is a king.
When wark wis deun an' freedim won,
   Off heym aw went wi' dancing feet,
Where keyk an' tea wis meyd for me—
   Noo, wasent that a treat?
Aw wesht me feyce, pat on me claes,
   An' joined me meytes the coits te fling ;
Then bed aw sowt te dream o' nowt,
   Is happy is a king.

(CHORUS EFTOR IVVORY VARSE.)

     O it mettors not whate'er's yor lot,
       If ye te sweet contentment cling,
     Yor days 'ill pass is smooth is glass,
       An' happy is a king.

The time went by wivoot a sigh,
   An' then maw coortship aw began,
Aw howk'd an' hew'd, aw toil'd an' tew'd,
   An' seyv'd me brass for Nan.
Wor banns wis cried, the knot wis tied,
   An' prood maw cumley showed hor ring ;
Ne mair aw said, but went te bed,
   Is happy is a king.
Aw wark'd away an' gat me pay,
   An' seun wi' bairns wor love wis blist ;
Aw gat me share o' heymly fare,
   Me beer an' baccy twist.

Greet foax may torn their backs wi' scorn,
  It what a collior's wark can bring ;
But, spite o' rank, aw cum te bank
  Is happy is a king.

Maw bairns aw see aroond me knee,— .
  Lord bliss thor bonny feyces a'!
When aw sall fail te orn me kale,
  They'll lend a helpin' paw.
For weel a ken iv a' the ten,
  Thor's neyn but what will cumfort bring
They shape se weel, thit, oh, aw feel
  Is happy is a king.
Te skeul they hop, for that's the shop
  Te polish up the dullist heed ;
O ! leernin's load is weel bestowed !
  Yung brains shud hae thor feed.
It gie's thim sense te tawk wi' mense ;
  It trains for flite thor spurrits' wing ;
It meyks thim free o' land an' sea,
  An' happy is a king.

Aw've deun me wark afore the mirk
  O' wintry cloods sets owre the scene ;
Aw's not aflaid but aw'l be paid
  'Fore deeth sall close maw een.
Aw've till'd the grund, an' aw'll be bund
  But floor's o' love will roond us spring ;
O Nan ! maw sweet, maw joy's complete,—
  Aw's happier nor a king.
An' when maw days, like glim'rin' rays
  O' Life's dim Davey trim'ils law ;
When callor Deeth cums for me breeth,
  An' shuts me iv his Raw ;—
Let maid an' man thit kent maw plan,
  These words in Frindship's 'ritin' bring ;—
" Wi' life weel spent he sleeps content,
  An' happy is a king."

MAW HEYM ON THE TYNE.

O, AW want te get back te me awn native toon !
On the banks o' the Weer aw can ne'er win renoon ;
For me heed's tornin' gray an' in sorrow aw pine,—
O, will neyn bring us back te me heym on the Tyne !
Iv a seesin' o' dreed, when the fire on the kee,
Freetin'd a' the poor folks, aw wis feulish te flee ;—
O, aw wish thit mair sense i' the heed hid been mine ;
Noo aw lang te get back te maw heym on the Tyne !

Tho' thors mony kind sowls iv awd Sunderland here,
Maw fren's o' the Tyne is clean geyn wi' the Weer ;
Thors nut that form fren'ship—whei, hoo sud thor be ?
For what dis the people o' Weer care for *me* ?
Thor toon's verra weel, an thor lasses leuks grand—
An' thor docks is a' reet—an' the sea's close it hand ;
An' thor Park's verra bonny—thor Piers verra fine—
But gi'e me the Leezis an' Kee on the Tyne !

Huts ! the toon o' Newcassel's *me awn*, ye may say ;
There's the heym o' me yooth an' the pleyces o' play :
There's the canny awd Brig thit thor'e gan to pull doon—
O, aw ken iv'ry inch o' maw beautiful toon !
There's the bonny green meeddis ; the Hassicks an' Team,
Where aw've fisht, when a lad—lork ! it leuks like a dream !
Dear, dear, what a heart-brockin state noo is mine—
O maw fren's, fetch us back te maw heym on the Tyne !

Aw ha'e sung ye queer sangs tiv awaken yor glee,
Noo thor's grief in the heart, where it ivor mun be,
Ef me marras o' Tyne divent pity me case,
An' teyk us away te me awn native pleyce.
,O, aw's just like some link thit's been pulled frev a chain,
An' tosst i' the durt there a' rust te remain :
Is thor neyn thit will cawse fren'ships tether te shine ;
An' bind wi' luve's chain a poor bruther o' Tyne ?

Is the Tyne wis me borth-pleyce, noo, a' thit aw crave,
Let me dee on her banks ; let her grund be me grave !
Mang the daisies o' Jäismind contentit aw'll rest,
Like a lennert asleep iv its awn muthor's nest.
Maw spurrit cud *then* roond me canny meytes flee ;
Aw wad sof'en thor sorrow, or join in thor glee ;
An' when deeth whisport, " come !" they wad nivor repine
Te lay doon thor beyns side thor bard o' the Tyne !

LAMENT O' THE PUDLOR'S WIFE.

A TALE OF THE STRIKE.

Aw'll tell the' a tale o' sair grief,
    Ef thoo'll oney sit canny an' still ;
Tho' thoo cannet te me fetch relief,
    It's not 'cas thoo's wantin the will.
Oh ! Jinny, maw hart's fairly broke !
    Aw've had trubbils, but nivvor sic like,
Sin' the days when them delegits spoke,
    An' garr'd a' wor factries te strike.

Aw was norsin' wee Fan at the breest,
    An' chormin' some bee-a-baw sang ;
Aw fand then is prood is a preest,
    Nivvor dreedin' owt dowley or rang :
When Tommy cam' in wiv his brass—
    The yell five o' maw bairns wis abed—
" Bad news aw've te tell the', maw lass,
    " Wawkor's strucken for wages," he said.

His words wis like tar on the floor,
    That ne weshin can ivvor make clean ;
Maw singin wis stopp'd then, yore sure,
    For aw'd leev'd where sic strikin' hid been.

Then aw started te blubber an' blare ;—
  Noo, them's things thit the men dissent like—
Tom swore at us—hoy'd doon the chair,
  Bool'd oot, an' gat drunk throo the strike.

Aw still leev'd in hopes that the wark
  I' wore factry wad be is afore ;
For things noo wis gan past the mark,
  An' we cuddent get stuff fra the store.
We'd borror'd an' cadged it awl ens ;
  We'd pawn'd ivvory thing thit wad lift ;
And the warst on't what foaks *was* wor frins,
  Be this strike, lass, had a' geyn adrift.

What muthor can see hor bairns want,
  Ef a morsel she hes for horsel ?
God naws, but wor leevin' wis scant—
  We wor starvin ! the trooth aw mun tell.
That neet when aw lost little Fan,
  Aw raim'd like a creetor geyn mad ;
Oh, aw pray'd on maw nees te maw man,
  Te wark, tho' the wages wis bad.

"No, he waddent ! he'd dee forst !" he said,
  "He *dornet*, an' that was a fack !"
Oh, Tom, o' bad men thoo's aflaid,
  Thit hes roven the claes off thaw back !
There's thaw babby laid deed is a steyn ;
  Thaw laddies thoo set oot to beg !
Luck it me, thaw poor wife, skin and beyn !
  Thoo's a mord'ror—ef not a blackleg !

What mair aw wad say, aw naw nowt,
  For a blaw frev his neeve nock'd me doon ;
Te yor hoose be some foaks aw wis browt,
  While wor Tom in greet feer left the toon.
But is Consett hes geyn in, aw heer,
  Thor's sum hopes thit te wark he'll retorn ;—
Ef he dis, aw'll forgive him, aw sweer.
  An' ne mair boot this strike we need mourn.

THE COAL TRADE; OR, BEYTH SIDES O' TYNE.

Noo, drop yor tawk the time aw's singin',
A stave 'boot wor coal trade noo aw's bringin'.
O, lang hes the coal trade kep' us clivor,
Whei, it's been the meykin' o' wor awd rivor.
Thoosins iv ears it's been Tyne's sole trade,
An' kings meyd laws fornent wor coal trade;
It's the poor man's joy when winter's freezin',
When the pot boils ower, an' the coals is bleezin'.

CHORUS.

Then sing wi' me in a chorus clivor,
Beyth sides o' Tyne an' the coal trade for ivor !

Ef we had ne coals to bliss wor nashin',
For collier-lads thord'd be ne occashin ;
An' ef wor coal-fields raised ne crop, sor,
Whei, Inglin's jaws wad verra seun drop, sor.
Pitmen, then, might cadge for a crust, man,
Keelmen might feed on the huddick-dust, man,
Chimleys wad verra seun knock off smokin',
An' injins wad stick ef they gat ne coke in.

Wivoot the coal trade i' wor land, sor,
We wadn't get claes te leuk se grand, sor ;
We just might as weel be beers or monkeys,
Pillors o' sawlt, or frozin-up donkeys.
Wor hooses then, like graves wad be, man ;
Wor wives wad drop for want o' tea, man !
An' warse nor a', wor factories fine, man,
Wad a' be leyd in on the banks o' Tyne, man.

'Twis Adam furst, i' the Eden-drift, man,
For Lan'sale-coal sunk the Paradis' shift, man ;
He was howkin' for goold iv a greet, dip hole, man,
When he fand oot a seam o' Wa'send coal, man.

Adam an' Eve roastid teyties a' neet, lads,
Boiled a nelefint's trunk, an' stewed his feet, lads ;
Gat up the steam, an wi' spurits he stole, meyd
A jolly rum spree wi' toastin' the coal trade !

The coal trade keeps wor picks i' moshin ;
The coal trade covers wi' ships the oshin ;
Coals sends oot te war wor brave fleets steamin',
The coal trade stops the forrinors' scheemin.
The coals meyks iron, mowlds Airmstrang's cannon ;
Coals meyks the bawls for wor tars te gan on ;
Coals is wor country's best defence, sor ;
Killin' an' cuikin, it the seym expense, sor.

Then success tiv ownors, viewors an' shippors,
Colliers an' trimmors, wor tars an' skippors ;
May wor heyms leuk blythe be the ingle's bleeze, man,
An' the di'mins black gan seyf ower seas, man.
Lang may the Tyne, Wear an' Tees be meyted ;
May the seams pruv' gud, an' the pay furst-rated ;
May wor meystors an' marras pull hard for a whole trade,
Then the deevil cannet stop wor glorious coal trade !

THE AWD COLLYOR TE WOR QUEEN.

Cumley Queen, aw stand afore thee, just to tell thee what aw feel ;
Tho' thoo may dispise maw tawkin', still aw'll not the trooth
　　conceal.
Weel thoo kens aw's poor, an' stintid o' the leernin' biships get,
But aw's ritch in honist porpis ; aw'll nut teyk thee in, maw pet !

Poor foaks fin's this world a dessort ; still they ha'e te struggil
　　throo—
Still they ha'e thor tendor feelin's, tho' tho're not a' queens, like
　　thoo.
Tho' we weer ne croons nor septors, 'cept the croon on hat an'
　　heed,
We've a' sprung fra yen Greet Meykor ; we'll be a' alike when
　　deed.

Cumley Queen, maw awn Victorry, thoo hes sufford naytor's
    ban,—
'Twas the Foworteent o' Dissembor, Sixty-yen, thoo lost thaw man.
A' the world gat drest in mornin' ; teers o' greef dimm'd a' wor
    een,
A' thaw bairns wis brockin'hartid—what *thoo* felt, neyn knaws,
    maw Queen !

Paypors cam' oot a' deeth bordord, beyth fra forrin' an' fra heym,
Preechors oot frev ivvory pulpit teuk thor texts frev Albort's neym.
Albort is "the Good " wis corsend, an' the title weel he orned—
He hid rais'd the World's Greet Gethrin', an' the orth his mem'ry
    morn'd.

Marvil beeldins, marvil stattys, marvil pillors rose aroond,
An' his grave be flooers wis cuvord, an' be fame his greetniss
    croond.
Luve, respeck, an' vennorayshin, filled the sad an' sollim sceen,
While the world o' Pride an' poor foaks, morn'd beside thee,
    cumley Queen !

A' things ha'e thor times an' seesins ; Greef shud *sumtime* dry
    hor teers,
Noo, Royle Widdy, thoo's been, greetin' gannin' on for fowor
    eers !
Thoo's sair mist be Lords an' Commins ; thoo's gan past a' mense
    an' grace ;—
Diz thoo nivvor mair intend, Vic, on thaw throne te show thaw
    feyce ?

Be thaw lang-spun torm o' sorrow an' thaw absins fra thaw throne,
Thoo gars a' the highborn ladies, and the Lunnin mairchints
    groan ;
Thoo gans hykin off te Scotland, wi' thaw pipors an' the rest,
Ridin' on thaw heelin' sheltie, in thaw weeds o' darkniss drest.

Ef thoo stops a week it Winsor, like a pidgin thoo teyks flight,
An' we leern be sum Coort Jornil thit thoo's it the Ile o' White.
Thoo's been lateleys off te Coborg whair thaw canny man
    belanged ;
Thair thoo stript his last new statty—thair thaw bairns an'
    cronies thranged.

Thair thoo gat thaw footh a greetin'—ef thoo'll ivvor be content—
Thoo mun own a teery foontin, for its streems is nivvor spent.
O, cheer up, maw canny wummin ! Pull the black vail fra thaw
    broo !
Get thaw reed cloak put aboot thee ; don thaw stars an' sash o'
    bloo !

Get thaw croon stuck on thaw heed, lass ! Teyk the septor in
    thaw hand,
Then, yence mair we'll teyk the noshin we've a Queen o' Brittin's
    land.
Fetch thaw pages, yung an' bonny, for te lift thaw trailin' train,
Tell thaw blushin' maids iv honnor thoo's cum back te life ageyn.

Let thaw pallis lamps be leetid ; teyk thor bannors black away!
Let thaw coortors crood aroond thee, Deuks an' Lords an' Ladies
    gay !
An' when Joy shakes han's wi' Plisshor, an' troo grandor swells
    the sceen,
Let the ban's iv a' thaw ridgmints strike up lood, " God save the
    Queen."

THE CURSENIN' O' THE LITTLE PRINCE,

MAIRCH THE TENT', 1864.

MAW bairn, what a row thoo's creayted
    Sin' the varra forst day thoo wis born !
Whei, thoo cam' 'fore the time thit wis stayted,
    Like a heed o' sum furthorly corn.
Thor wis nowt i' the claes line meyd reddy,
    Nowthor bedgoons nor rowlors wis there ;
An' aw's warned thoo gae mooth, maw yung Neddy,
    An' squalled when thoo fand thoo wis bare.

But seun thaw royle carkish leuked bonny,
    Wi' new dresses a' goolden an' fine ;
For thaw feyther hes plenty o' munny
    Te gar his bit lad cut a shine.

Tho' thaw mammy wis varry sair bothor'd,
　　When she axed for te sookle her son,
To leern that iv Inglind wis smother'd
　　The luve wor forst payrints begun.

Maw bairn, tho' thaw blud may be reedor
　　Nor the pit-bairns thit's born i' wor Raw,
Still thaw muther's white breest's nut thaw feeder,
　　A strainjor mun settle the' craw.
Nivvor heed, for thoo'll get shuggor-candy,
　　Minty claggum, black bullets, an' spice,
Reed corrils wi' sillor-bells dandy,
　　An' goold Peetorwaggys se nice,

An' when thoo grows up, thoo'll hae gartors,
　　Bath-ribbons, an' crosses, an' stars ;
Thoo'll be meyd heed o' govvormint startors,
　　An' a cheef that need nivvor smell wars.
Thoo'll be Scotch wi' thaw fine sillor thrussel,
　　Thoo'll be Paddy wi' collor o' goold ;
An' wi' Mickey and Geordy thoo'll whussell,
　　For thaw luck-steyn can nivvor be booled.

But tell us aboot yor grand curs'nin',
　　An' hoo yor royle bairnship behaved—
When Lord Airchy forst started his norsin',
　　Is ef thoo wis gan te be shaved ?
Did the wettor fra Jordin nut freeze the',
　　When he sloosh'd the cawd drops i' the' feyce ?
Did a greet kink o' laffin' nut seeze the',
　　When thoo pulled the reed nose iv his Grace ?

But aw heer that thaw princeship wis sleepin',
　　Mang thaw robes, like a teyd iv a hole ;
While the kings, lords, and leddies wis keepin'
　　Thor watch roond the Groom o' the Stole.
Noo, the Belgyum King wis the man, sor,
　　Thaw godfeythor pick'd oot te be ;
But wor Queen wis the lass thit meyd ansor,
　　Is thaw godmuthor clivvor shud de.

Hinny, bairn? wi' grand neyms thoo's weel fettled,
　　Thoo can gan wi' yell fowor te bed :
ALBERT VICTOR wis twe thoo forst ettled,
　　Then eftor cam' CRISTIN an' NED.
Then, mind, ef thoo leeves, what thoo's deein',
　　An' divvent thaw curs'nin' disgrace,
Else thoo'll nivvor be fitted for fleein',
　　Or rain i' the GUD ALBORT's place.

Be thoo VICTOR 'mang a' the temptayshins,
　　Where thoo's sartin throo life te be led ;
Be a CRISTIN, an' proov tiv a' nayshins
　　That yor fit for the throne o' King NED.
Tho' thoo cannet be King iv a horry,
　　For monny lang 'ears thoo mun wait,
Gan' thoo on Briitins fayvors te corry,
　　An' let Time rite thim doon on his slate.

For the seyk o' maw sovrin Victorey,
　　For the seyk iv hor husbind ne less,
Leukin' doon fra the seet iv his glory
　　The'sel' an' thaw payrints te bless.
Aw'll elwis pray Grace may sorroon' the',
　　An' thit Wisdim thaw futsteps may guide,
An' thit Honor an' Vartey may croon the',
　　Till thoo lies be thaw grenfeythor's side.

WOR TOON AN' TRADE.

CUM, lads thit nivver felt dismay
　　I' times o' deeth an' dreed ;
An' sing wi' me a strain o' glee,
　　Aw's shoor the sang 'ill speed ;
For roond wor toon cheps weers renoon,
　　Biy Honor's neethud meyd ;
O, neyn need pine on banks o' Tyne
　　Te chant wor Toon an' Trade.
On beyth sides wor rivvor glides,
　　Hor Commerce a' things yeels,

Hor lines o' rail an' fleets thit sail,
   Fra Tyne Brig doon te Sheels ;
Wor factorys thrives, industry's hives,
   Whair fortunes quick is meyd ;
Wor mines o' coal what can control ?
   Nowt bangs wor Toon an' Trade.

Newcassel streets meyst pleyces beets,
   Wor shops is full an' grand ;
Whair croods gans in wi' lots o' tin,
   For Banks is close it hand.
Wor markets, tee, is lairge an' free,
   For Sundor dinnors laid,
Whair butchers bluff provides the stuff
   Thit feeds wor Toon an' Trade.
The foontins play an' lassis gay
   Wawk free fra clarts an wet ;
Whair haggish-wives wi' tubs an' knives
   Shoots, " Buy nice puddings het !"
O, Grainger Dick thoo did the trick,
   'Twas thoo wor markits meyd ;
Oh, neer a man teuk wisor plan
   Te raise wor Toon an' Trade !

Alang the kee just gan wi' me,—
   The sun shines elwis thair—
What croods o' foaks an' cheps wi' pokes,
   An' clarks iv ivvory chare.
Fra morn te neet full cairts ye meet,
   That i' the thrang yo're stayed,
Yo're put aboot, an' wundrin' shoot
   " Lord, what a Toon an' Trade !"
The wharfs is cramm'd, the ships is jamm'd,
   An' steemers, what a lot !
Wi' guds for sea an' plisshor, tee,
   Tiv ivvory airt an' spot.
But leuk up thair ! weel may ye stare !
   Nowt puts yon in the shade !
Wor Levvil stuns a' foaks it once,
   An' stamps Tyne's Toon an' Trade.

Ef war shud roar aside wor shore,
    We hevvint far te run,
We hev a spot for cassin' shot,
    An' Airmstrang hes a gnn.
The banks o' Tyne can fettle fine,
    Se neyn needs be afraid,—
Wor Ryfils brave wad dee te save
    Wor peepil, Toon an Trade.
Then wor Mare, *he* wad be thair
    Wi' thoosens it his heels,
For weel aw ken we'd seun get men,
    Fra beyth the canny Sheels :—
Hoots! tawk o' war when at the bar
    Greet Tinmith guns is laid ;
Ye may depend we wad defend
    Newcassel Toon an' Trade !

THE RIFLEMAN SOWLJOR.

Thor wis tawk iv invayshin in wor Raw,
Ov nowt but fightin' foaks wad jaw,
Sowljors, they said, they'd meyk us a,'
And send us off for slawtor !
" What's to be deun ?" says Mall to me,
" For thoo a sowlijor noo mun be ;
" Eigh, seun thoo'll be leevin' thaw canny wife grievin'.
" An' cockin' thaw gun it the eneme !"

KORIS EFTER IVVORY VARSE.

Thin cock up yor rifles an' peppor away,
    Fame an' glory's noo afore ye ;
Nivvor ye mind what feuls may say,
    Thor's nowt like a rifleman sowljor.

Aw'll nut hae te fight ageyn me will,
Ef neboddy cums for me to kill ;

Aw'll just hae te wark an' mind me drill,
   An' that's a rifleman sowljor.
Leern for to mairch an' stand it eese,
Torn oot me toes an' flatten me nees,
Leuk up te the sun an' shoothor me gun,
An' get te be corpril be degrees.

Oh, a rifleman sowljor's sartin te shine,
Drest iv his claes se smart an' fine,
The lassis wi' luve is bund for te pine
   When they keek it a riflemen sowljor.
Trampin' alang te the big drum's beet,
Trig is a lennert fra heed te feet ;
Gun ower his shoothor, wi' bullits an' poothor,
Freetint o' nowt o' creayshin te meet.

We'd seun let ye see sum feets iv airms,
Ef yence the drums bet war's alairms,
We'd seun set Brittin free frae hairms,
   Wi' wor Tyneside rifleman sowljors.
We'd gie thim the cawshin, just for fun,
We'd show thim the force o' the Airmstrang gun,
Wi' scroo-an-breech-Billy we'd knock them a' silly,
An' gar thim, like cats, fra the Tyne te' run.

But ef on the feeld aw shud chance te fa',
Biv' a cut on the heed or a nick o' the jaw,
The Queen wad be kind te wor Mall aw knaw,
   For the sake iv hor rifleman sowljor.
A pillor o' marvil they'd beeld for me
On the top o' the " Levvil" for foaks te see,
An' the deeds o' yor pitman, in goold wad be rit, man,
   I' the beuks o' *Newcassel Historre.*

   Thin cock up yor rifles an' peppor away,
     Fame an' glory lies afore ye ;
   Nivvor ye mind what feuls may say—
     Thor's nowt like a rifleman sowljor.

DEETH O' THE CAT, OR FLOGGIN' NE MAIR.

WHEN aw was a lad aw wis fondish o' leernin',
   Aw raimed on me muthor te send us te scheul ;
But me feythor wis bent on increesin' his earnin',
   He telt us a scholar wis warse nor a feul.
But me awn canny muthor gae list te ne bothor,
   Seun te scheul wiv anuthor we wandort a pair ;
But the maistor-man thumpt us ; he doost an' he dumpt us,
   Se aw left, for aw wadent be hammord ne mair !

Then te pit-wark aw went, an wis entort is " trappor,"
   But nowt aw can praise i' the coal-winnin' line !
Ef owt went amiss aw wis sartin te nap hor,—
   Aw wis verra seun seek o' the toils o' the mine.
Frev a tub yence aw tum'eld—the men swore an' grum'eld,
   Becas aw layd hum'eld, an' startid te blair ;
Aw wis thresht be the laddies, an' kickt be thor daddies—
   Se aw voo'd in the pits aw'd be hammord ne mair !

Next a sailor aw torn'd i' the ship " Harryhadme,"
   But the skippor wis warse nor the Lang Benton bull ;
Tho' aw elwis wis ready te de a' things steady,
   He seun meyd devolopmints new on me skull !
Aw hid neyn te defend us, or 'sistence te lend us,
   Man, he *liked* te rope's-end us an' leave me back sair ;
Gox ! aw lowpt i' the sea, mun, aw cared nowt te dee, mun,
   For then aw'd be free, mun, an' hammord ne mair.

Noo, a man-o-war's croo i' thor jollyboat spied me,
   An' hoisted me in like a fad o' wet straw ;
They gov us fresh claes, an' wi' sea-beuks they tried me,
   But they fand aw nawd nowt, se they bumm'd us belaw.
Aw've been offins in battle, 'mang slawtor, like cattle,
   Maw beyns they did rattle,—but what de they care ?
O, them cat-an'-nine-tailors is deeth te poor sailors !
   Will the day ivor cum when thor's *floggin' ne mair ?*

O wor airmy an' navy's disgrac'd an' degradid!
   What reet has the "cat" wi the Reed an' the Bloo?
We ken that the Blackies in floggin' hes traded,
   But the neegors hes getten the pull ov us noo!
Whei, wor Queen may think sheym on't—for *she* gets the bleym
   on't—
   Te let her brave subjics be haggisht se sair!
De we leeve amang Neros? Speak oot, maw bowld heroes!
   Say the word, bonny Queen, an' thor's floggin' ne mair!

Noo aw hear that i' Lunnin some leddy hes foondid
   A hoose for poor collies, the maingey an' leym,
But aw think, that is Inglind be *cats* is sorronndid,
   She wad dee a grand job ef she ga'e *them* a heym.
O, them "cats" is past beerin'—the sowlgers' backs teerin',
   An' scorin' poor sailors, like pork at a fair!
But the time's surely cumin', wivoot ony hummin',
   When Brittins shall brag that thor's floggin' ne mair!

LEMENT O' THE AWD TYNE BRIG.

MAW doom is fix'd, maw day is owor; tho're 'gan te pull me
   doon!
Me thit's se lang been coonted is the glory o' wor toon;
Afore that lang-shank'd monstor there wis ivvor browt te leet,
Aw wis the brig, beyth strang and trig; eigh, ivvoryways cum-
   pleet!

Dissent Newcassel foax think sheym te hoy me 'mang the muck?
Diddent aw fetch maw heeldors fame, an' lads o' Tyneside luck?
Hevvent aw been a' trusty frind tiv a' the country roond?
Be neet or day, hev aw gi'en way, te gar the foax get droond?

Yon irin-feul at Sunnorlin ne'er showed sic pluck is mine,
When she torn'd cranky, she gat keukt be Stivvysin fra Tyne;
Hor Rowley Bordin's barril-breest wis levvil'd an' meyd plain,
But *me*, they sweer they cannet mend, se treet me wi' disdain.
Me, thit ne'er sconnord it the storm, nor trimmild it the flud;
Pooer me, thit like the Tinmith rocks, hes elwis formly stud;

Eigh, me, thit's kep' the kee-dews reet, an' meyd the towl-geyts
    pay,
Te be dung doon in maw awd age—it issent spiff—aw say !

Aw've been a canny, deesint brig ; aw nivvor did owt rang ,
Aw've fed the beggor fra maw breest, an' nors'd the sons o' sang ;
The blin'd man and his dowly dog kenn'd weel maw flag o' bloo,
An' te the wives wi' froot an' ware aw nivvor proov'd untroo.

When Vairge-Day cam', an' thoosins rush'd an' clim'd upon maw
    back,
Gat on maw heed, the gam te see, whe says thit aw leuk'd black?
Wassent the vairges then maw pride ? The Corporayshin's boat
Sail'd grandly through maw oppin legs—the Mare wis then
    afloat !

We hae ne Mares just noo, aw think, like Brandlin,' Bell, an'
    Reed,
Or, de ye, mawgin aw'd been doom'd te deeth ?   Nut me indeed !
Seuner nor seed me levvild law for sum new-fangl'd pairch,
They'd put me on a crinnorleen an' stopp'd destruction's mairch.

What de ye want wi' new laid brigs ? Ye say aw's owor law,
Feuls sweers aw's doth'rin' on maw pins, an' that aw's shoor te
    fa' ;
Is thor ne doctors noo alive, ne maysins bowld an' free ?
Ef they ken owt aboot the airch, then bruthors let them be.

Its a' ne yewse ! thor's Lockey Harle, thor's Brysin, Cail an'
    Yure,
Dettormind aw shill wawk the plank ! maw life they'll nut in-
    shoor.
Aw's beuk'd for deeth, se aw mun dee, like uther things iv
    worth,
When they hae deun the best they cud te bennyfit this orth.

Fareweel, awd Tyne, maw bonny streem ! aw cannet stop maw
    teers !
Aw'l nut be hung ! that's yen grand job, aw's sentins'd be maw
    Peers :
Like kings aw'll suffor on the block—mair pity—tho' less sheym,
An' leeve te Tyne's porstority maw blessin' and maw neym !

WOR BOBBY THE SAILOR.

WHEN wor Bobby left Jarra for sea,
Thor wis groans an' sawt teers in wor hoose ;
Tho' aw browt me wife baccy an' tea,
Thor wis nowt thit cud make her leuk croose.
She wad nowthor drive, hopple, nor leed,
If the wind chanced te roar i' the neet ;
An' she blaired, like a bairn wantin' breed,
When the rain geyn the panes chanced te beet.

She wad leeve me it heym be mesel'
Wiv a bairn scairshly torned a munth awd,
Thit cud screem 'beun a bit aw can tell,
Tho' wi' boiley aw stuffed the poor lad.
Tho' aw oppint the dore o' wor clock,
For the crile the brass-waggor to see ;
Tho' aw showed him the chawk chucky-cock,
Hoots ! he waddent "bawbuntin" for me !

Then the traps thit belang'd te wor Bob,
Garr'd wor Nanny te freet an' te blair ;
His awd jackit, his cap, an' his fob—
But the warst wis a corl iv his hair !
Aw wis forced for te hide thim, ye knaw ;
Tho' aw blubbord mesel' on the slee—
When his pictor aw teuk fra the wa',
An' thowt boot maw bairn on the sea.

When aw cums frae the pay wi' me brass—
Aw've been 'custim'd te hev a drop beer—
Aw begins for te coax me poor lass,
But she leuks on me feyce wiv a teer.
Aw gets angort, an' lowps up te gan—
'Sides me marras is waitin for *me* :—
But she says, " Divvint leeve yor poor Nan,
" An' aw'll nut tawk o' Bob nor the sea !"

But the ship an' wor lad's cumin heym,—
O ! aw wish canny breezis may blaw !
Dash, wor Bob 'ill nut leuk like the seym,
For black whiskors he'll weer on his jaw.
But aw'll nut hae te welt him aboot,
Is aw yewsed 'fore he teuk te the sea :
Caws aw's warn'd he'll be boorly an' stoot—
Had yor hand ! but he'll, mevvies, thresh *me* !

Marsy me ! that's the laff o' wor Bob !
Lucka ! thondor he cums wi' wor Nan !
Black moosecatchors hings owor his gob ;—
" Gie's a wag o' thaw daddle, maw man !
O, Bobby, we've lang leukt for thee !
Man, se dowley thoo left the awd hoose !
But thoo'll get a spice fizzor for tea,
An' yence mair we'll be morry an' croose !"

HISTRY IV ORTHELLO BIV HISSEL'.

Noo, marras, heer me sing, maw storey seun aw'll tell, oh,
Ov Veenis aw's the King, maw reet neym is Orthello ;
Aw went te seek a wife, luve swalleyd me, like Jonah,
Se te cumfort me throo life, aw marry'd Desdymonah.

When Desdy's dad fand oot she'd teun me tiv hor truckil,
He chuckt his claes aboot, while Des. did nowt but chuckil ;
He swore aw was a witch, a hell-cat in maw moashins ;
A deevil black is pitch, a cunj'ror wi' rank poashins.

He stampt, an' shoothord airms, hawled me afore the mare, tee
Aw proov'd aw yewsed ne chairms, but coortid Desdy fair, tee.
She wis a sheemale brick, she coo'd hor fethor's rantin ;
She voo'd te me she'd stick, then on maw neck fell pantin.

E. Aggor wis maw chum, wi' lees he lyked te fill us,
He telt us storeys rum, an' seun he'd torn'd us jillis.
Boot honnisty te me he preecht a bleth'rin sarmint,
Then teuk luve's lock and kee, an' plundord me—the varmint !

A hankorshor aw had, a spottid Cassil-Garthor,
'Twis gien me, when a lad, be furtin tellin' Marthor.
Says aw, " luve, keep this snug, thor's mawjick in the web on't,
Aw's shoor te crack thaw lug when thoo feyls te wipe thaw neb
    on't."

But heer lies a' maw fash I, oh! wi' Des. an' luve supported—
Whe'd thowt thit Mickey Cash I, oh! wi' maw fair lady sported?
The trooth aw seun fund oot when aw gat Mickey fuddild,
E. Aggor still'd a' doot thit Mickey maw wife cuddild.

Maw blud boyl'd het is fleymes, an' skootid fra' me smellor,
Aw cawd me wife bad neymes, an' swore aw'd stick hor fellor —
Aw grippt E. Aggor's throat, an' garr'd him shoot an' groan, ah!
Te set sutch lees iffloat boot maw sweet Desdymcnah.

"A hankorshor," says E. " yor mistress had—'twis spottid,—
Wi' Cashy oft aw see,—tis nesty noo—an blotted,
He telt us, when abed, aneeth his heed he'd stowed it ;
"Its heer, me lad," he said, then on't his beek he blowed it.

Aw voo'd, aw ranted, swore wi' puzzin full te fill hor,
Aw'd kick hor to the door, an' wi' me sword aw'd kill hor ;
An' yit te spill hor blud mite humbugs fetch a futhor,
Se then aw thowt it gud, the faithliss witch te smuthor.

Poor Desdy went te bed an' tawk'd aboot a willor,
When in aw poppt me heed is she lay on hor pillor ;
She spak', just like a bairn, is aw stud glow'rin' at hor,
" O, luvey, hoo yor'e stair'n!—maw duckey, what's the mettor?"

Says aw, "just shut yor trap, yor weedlin' gob is awl craft "
Oh, aw's a warsor chap, nor that neck-stritchin' Cawlcraft !
Aw clickt the pillor wite, an' spite iv a' hor strugglin ;
Aw snapt hor, like a kite, wivoot won groan or gugglin !

A kickin' it the door roosed me in wild disorder,
Maw Desdy diddent snore—she slep' in airms o' Mordor?
Noo the reel trooth cam' oot, E. Aggor proov'd a villin,
An' for a raggy cloot, maw missis aw'd been killin.

Ne mair can aw find peece, maw conshinse is a' pickils,
Maw mind aw *mun* releese—aw'll gan te Captin Nickills—
An' ef the rope aw share, aw'll warn each marry'd fellor
Iv leeors te beware, an' think on black Orthello !

HAMLICK, PRINCE O' DENTON.

PAIRT FIRST.

Ov a' the lads o' Denton Burn,*
　　Young Hamlick had ne marrow,
He'd put or hew, an' take his turn
　　To drive the rolley-barrow.
His feythor kept a corver's shop,
　　His mothor teuk in sewin' ;
But, man, they say she liked a drop,
　　An' drunk gin like a new un,

Noo Hamlick had a sweetheart, tee,
　　Oh, Feeley, she was canny !
The weddin'-day was seun to be,
　　For Feelly lov'd her manny.
The furnitary a' was bowt,
　　The chairs wis polished bonny,
A German chep the clock had browt,
　　An' the bed wad challinge onny.

But iv a suddent a' was stopp'd,
　　Misfortin' cam' se cruiket—
The marrige meetin' seun was dropped,
　　Awd Ham had kicket the bucket.
An' what was queer, afore a week,
　　The widdy wed agyen, man,
The deed un's bruthor had the cheek
　　To coax her, it was plain, man.

* Denton Burn is a small village near Newcastle.

Noo boony gam' there was, aw sure,
    Yung Hamlick swore like Hector ;
He voo'd he wad his muthor cure,
    If biv hersel' he neck'd hor.
An' Clawdy, tee, might chucky oot,
    His jaws he'd surely plaistor ;
Whei ! if he did'nt gar him shoot,
    Then Ham wad own his maistor.

'Twixt twelve an' yen—the meun was sma'—
    As Hamlick hyem was gannin' ;
Just comin' past awd Denton Ha',
    He seed a white thing stannin'.
Tho' freetin'd sair, says he, " Whe's there ?"
    His neebeyns nack'd thegithor ;
It answered wiv a groanin' blair,
    " Oh Hamlick ! aw's thaw feythor,"

" What thoo ?" says he, " it cannit be !
    " Aw seed thee fairly barried ;
" But, feythor, tell us what to de,
    " For muthor to uncle's married ?"
" Then listen, hinny, for the cock
    " Aw's flaid 'll seun be crawin' !
" Ye ken it's lang past twelve o'clock,
    " An' yen mun stop maw jawin',

" Ye'll mind that neet aw wan the pig,
    " Aw went heym like a lammie ;
" Tho' Gurty sairly run her rig,
    " An' shameful used her Hammy.
" But warse, me lad—thaw uncle Clawde,
    " Bowt ars'nic fra thaw cussin,
" An' mix'd it wi' some fat he had,
    " An' aw lick'd up the puzzen.

" Ah, man, aw cud some queer things tell,
    " But the deevil's varra jellis ;
" Tho' aw've a fairish place i' hell—
    " Aw's heed man at the bellis.

"But, wheest! the banty's craw aw hear,
　"Come, shake hands wi' yor daddie ;
"Thou'll mevies cuik thaw uncle's beer ;
　"Ta, ta—ta ta—maw laddie !"

When Hamlick stuck his daddle oot,
　To grip his feythor's paw, man,
He gov a kind iv a' croopy shoot,
　To find the cawd steyn wa', man.
The ghaist was geyn—but sic a smell
　Was fand, like awd beuts burnin',
That Hamlick's niver been hissel',
　Sin yen o'clock that mornin'.

PAIRT SECOND.

Some strolin' folks to Denton cam',
　A' riding on thor donkeys,
An' conj'rin' cheps wi' nowse but sham,
　Spy-shows was there wi' munkeys.
The actors fand young Hamlick oot.
　An spun him sic a yarn, sor ?
Says Ham, "The gentleman can spoot,
　In Lissy Lampton's barn, sor !"

The play was made biv Hamlick's sel',
　His muthor's sowl to press, man,
The scene was laid by Barley Fell,
　The lingo was Bosjesman.
"The Blighted Boœr ; or Puzzen'd Pluck"—
　The folks a' flock'd to see, man ;
An' Feeley i' the front was stuck,
　Wiv Hamlick' on her knee, man.

Up went the cloot—the crood sat mum—
　A pig-fyec'd thing appearin' ;
Upon a' fowers 'twas seed to cum—
　By gox, it was a queer un !
It grunted thrice—thrice wagged its heed—
　And hadded up his paw, then ;
Then meyd believe that it was deed,
　By droppin' doon its jaw, then.

In popped a wife an' blubbered sair,
  Aboot her gissy's fate, then ;
" *Wise pigs*," says she, " *takes better care,*
  " *Thou's lick'd a puzzen'd plate, then ;*
" *Aw'd seuner loss my man, the Turk !*
  Aw wish that mine's was taken ;
" *Thaw pluck to neet sall de the wark*—
  " *There's ars'nic in thaw bacon.*"

Ham's muthor dothor'd like a duck,
  " Oh dear ! oh dear ! aw's drop noo !
" Divent ye hear aboot the pluck ?
  " Howay ! aw winnit stop, noo !"
An' fra the play like mad she flew,
  The crowd a' geypt an' won'er'd,
" Ho, ho !" shoots Ham, " the ghaist spak' troo !
  " Play-actors for a hun'er'd !"

Next pay, Ham's feythor 'peared ageyn,
  I' th' spot he elways hawnted ;
" Oh Hamlick, Hamlick ! tell us when
  " Aw'll get maw wishes granted ?
" Thaw heart's like withered haws or hips ;
  " Revenge thaw feyther's deeth, then ;
" Ta, ta !" Ham's een was i' th' eclipse,
  He geyp'd clean out o' breeth, then !

To Feeley's house, wivoot a stop,
  Thro' peuls, cross progly ditches,
Young Ham ran peltin', neck an' crop,
  His sark ootside his britches.
He brak the door, an' smashed the glass,
  Spanghewed poor Feeley's feythor,
An' teuk the coal-rake tiv his lass,
  An, jaw'd a heap o' blethor.

The pollis cam' wiv a' thor speed,
  But whe dore Hamlick teyk, then ?
The crooner sat upon the deed,
  A verdick clear to meyk, then.

Noo Feeley cam' in rantin' mad,
   Wiv a guese's thropple screemin' ;
She cawd her Ham, " her bonny lad,
   " That set her daft wi' dreamin'."

Hor heed was dressed wi' docken leeves,
   Stuck round wi' cabbage caskets,
An' milky thrustles in hor neeves,
   An' rasher caps an' baskets.
The crooner bad his men gi'e pleyce,
   To let hor view hor feythor :
She smack'd the forsman on the feyce,
   Then chow'd some bits o' leathor.

She leeved on grass an' paddick's steuls,
   Dry-asks and teyds she chorish'd ;
An' Tommy-lodgers, fra the peuls,
   Iv' blacking pots she norish'd.
Yen day she plodg'd to catch a duck,
   A soomin' seiz'd hor heed, there,
An' in the sleyk poor Feeley stuck,
   And "Cuckoo" fand hor deed, there.

PAIRT THORD.

The winter efterneun was dark,
   The winds, like bairns, was cryin' ;
The fun'ral folk had left the kork,
   Where Feeley cawd was lyin'.
Yung Hamlick lowped oot frav a dyke,
   Seiz'd fast o' Feeley's bruthor,
An' Ham was Larty gan to strike,
   When up cam' Hammy's muthor.

" For sheym, ye feuls, on sic a neet,
   " To set yor neeves for boxin' !
" 'Twad sarve thee reet, Ham, vera reet,
   " To stick thaw shanks the stocks in !
" Thoo hes ne chance wi' Larty's fist,
   " Thoo kens he was a ring-man ;

" He'll let the day-leet to thaw kist—
" He is a second Spring, man !"

The match cam' off at Throckley Fell,
   Ham's uncle own'd the field, man ;
His muthor, te, cam' there horsel',
   Ham's fate she thowt conceal'd, man.
To wark they went, Ham droo forst blood,
   Tho' Larty ken'd the science ;
But Hamlick like a terrier stood,
   An' grinn'd a bloo defiance.

Hoot, Larty, hinny's, fairly blawn,
   His breeth comes thick and shorter ;
But what's that stuff Clawde's sleely thrawn
   And mix'd amang the porter ?
But Larty's deun, the time is ca'd,
   Ham's muther seems a' queer, noo,
She grabs the glass, an' drinks like mad,
   She's drunk the pussin'd beer, noo !

" Oh, hinny, Clawde, what's this, maw lad ?
   " This porter's queerly fettled."
Clawde blair'd out, " lass ! put doon that glass"
   Poor sowl ! her hash was settled.
Smack at his uncle's jaws struck Ham,
   Doon went the teystril sprawlin',
Doon went his puzzen'd mistriss flam,
   The crood for help wis bawlin' !

Up stackered Larty for a blaw,
   Fair on Ham's jug'lar nibb'd him,
But Ham swung round his iron paw,
   An' wiv a deeth-thraw fibb'd him.
The victims bodies iv a dray,
   To their last heym was sent on ;
Oh ! mourn for Hamlick neet and day,
   For he was Prince o' Denton !

A MIDNEET CRACK.

THE POTE.

Is aw wis stannin' yen fine neet upon Newcassel Kee,
Aw seed the Tyne waves slidin' past an' slippin' te the sea ;
The m'yun l'yuk'd like a lewnytick, wi' laffin jaws askew,
Mang skies like Tyne-bred Pollissis—them dark lads drest in
    bloo—
Suddent the awd Brig gov a groan—assmattick she's been lang—
Then on the air aw heerd hor blare wi' roopy voice an' strang.

AWD BRIG.

Maw days is short ; Life's span aw've stritch'd—YURE's gan te
    ding us doon !
Me thit wis yence the keelmin's pride an' glory o' wor toon !
That greet lang monster there aw bl'yem, that t'yeng-leg upstart
    Levvil ;
Aw wish thit he wad t'yek a fit an' tummil te deeth's bevvil.

HIGH LEVVIL.

What's that thoo says, thoo bowleg stump ?   Dore thoo g'yen
    me te rail ?
The Keelmin's pride !   Mair like his *corse* whene'er he low'rd his
    sail ;
Ef aw'd been born when thoo wis m'yed, nut only *keels* but *ships*
Wad scuddid throo maw legs like fun, wi' nowt te spoil thor trips.
Aw's Robbort Steevsin's Monnymint i' spite iv a' ye say !
Yo're d'yun an gannin' te the cats—*aw nivvor can decay !*

GREY'S MONNYMINT.

An' what is aw, thoo Levvillor ?   Hev aw nut stud the storm ?
Yor beeldin's ment for *sleepors* man ; maw Monnymint's RIFFORM.
The warkin' man is maw delite—a' foaks is prood o' me ;
Aw gae the world a Bill o' Reets—*pay tuppinse an' ye'll see !*
Climm up maw steps an' keek it seets thit ivvory een mun dazzel,
Maw n'yem is Grey, aw'll last they say far langor nor the Cassel.

THE CASSEL.

Thoo pillor o' sawt ! Thoo'll nivvor see a quartor o' maw time!
Thoo's but a lollypop o' st'yen, stuck up wi' mooldy lime.
Aw leeved 'fore T'yelyors i' maw Garth wis ivvor 'lood te stop,
Afore John Lynn it maw Black G'yet o' whiskey seld a drop.
Lang fore the Tellygrip wis knawn or guttor porshor shoos,
An' lang afore Joe Cowan cam' te *chronicle* his news.
Aw's awdor nor Sin' Nicklis Chorch—an' strangor nor the steepil,
For *that* sum day is shoor te fa' au' scumfish a' the peepil.

SIN' NICKLIS CHORCH.

There, that' eneuff, thoo braggy f'yul! Lie doon an' gan te
     sleep !
Thoo ca's theesel a *Cassel*—whei thoo's but a Dungin Keep !
Thoo's but a *scrap* o' what thoo was—see thoo shud had thee
     tung ;
Is thoo like me, aw've m'yed kings pray an' s'yevd rips getten
     hung.
Maw Lantrin Toor, maw nobil Spyor thit gars a' nayshins stare,
Sh'yem on them cheps thit winnet gree te keep me in rippair !
Hundords iv eers maw Bells wis hord 'fore Peersin pulled a rope,
They ring me noo for onny f'yul, aw've oft peeled for the Pope.
When greet men dee maw Major towls wi' dowly soons o' sorror,
Tho' lang may Cornil Porkins leeve, the mare o' this awd borror,
Aw seed the forst brig owor the Tyne.

THE CASSEL.

Aw seed that weel is thoo ;
An' owor me heed greet cannins fyord till a' the Garth l'yuk'd
     bloo.

THE M'YUN.

O had yor jaws 'boot what ye've seed an' divvent raim an' spar,
The awdist on ye's but a bairn, yung cloods aside a star !
Ye've a' been beelt for sum gud end—it mettors nut the when—
The Chorch to pleese the Preests, aw's warn'd the Cassel for
   · brave men.
The Awd Brig wis a New Brig yence, an' thowt a strucktor clivvor,
Till the High Levvil startid up an' dwarft it on wor Rivvor.

The Monnymint wis beelt te show Rifform hid yence its day,
An' tho' it breetins when aw smiles, it elwis will be *grey*.
Drop fightin' then, an' be like me, for when aw's in the clipse,
Or in the *wane*, aw hides me heed, an' nivvor opes maw lips.
When *full*, aw's like a reel John Bull, aw govorns land an' sea ;
Noo, hinnies set yorsels to sleep, an' silent dreemors be.

THE TIPTOP WIFE IV ENGLAND.

A SKETCH FRA LIFE.

THE tiptop wife gans tiv hor bed when warkmin hes te rise,
An' gets up frev hor silky loll is day dissens the skies.
Hor sarvint dressis up hor hair an' tells hor smutty t'yels,
Consarnin' sum queer ackshins d'yun be Fashin's neetin'g'yels.
She hes hor lunch an' glass o' wine or mevvies O.D.V.,
Then oot she gans wi' hor smart tygor dryvin' swells te see.
Away she skuttors in hor coach te millinors for dress ;
But as for vissitin' the poor te lesson thor distress
She nivvor dis ; hor *tendor* heart wad brick in peeces too.
Hor littil gam' is gamminin' the unsuspecktin' joo.
Then off ageyn te don hor skin wi' plaistor, paint, an' puff,
She h'yemword drives, an' florts wi' cheps thit tells hor bawdy
    stuff
Boot things a deesint countory lass wad blush like bricks te heer ;
But then she is a tiptop queen worth thoosens ivvory ear.
Te bawls she gans, an' dances thair wi' swells thit squeeze an'
    kiss,
An' is hor feelins bleeze like f'lems thor's nowt they de amiss.
Then what wi' drink an' flortin' ways she's fairly spent an' dyun,
She cums h'yem in hor carridge grand it rysin o' the sun.
She t'yeks a fancy te be bad—hor favorit docktor cums—
He's singil, yung, an' hansim tee ; she win's him roond her thumbs,
Ef his inclyned te wildish ways, he hes ne bothor thair,
She puts horsel', an' vartue tee, beneath the docktor's care.
Or when she heers a parsin, yung an' moddist, preech an' pray,
She gans te chorch for little but te leed the preest astray ;
An' ef he's nut o' form, sturn will, its dickey wiv his n'yem,
The flash-up lady s'yun destroys his sowl an' preechin' f'yem.

The flash-up lady's life is m'yed o' nowt but godliss spree ;
Nowt holy ye can fin'd in hor, she's bewty g'yen aglee.
Hor pitty's but a m'yek beleeve—she's hipporcrissy's slave—
She nivvor thinks aboot a life thit starts beyont the grave.
Laizy, is laizyniss can m'yek hor, loongin' in hor bed,
Be thowts an' acks, an' sowless facks, an' senshyil noashins
    fed.
She's marryd tee ; but, is a wife. she is ne gud te *him ;*
Hor banker is hor best gudman, that she in lust may swim.
She is the mother o' fine bairns, but *she* cares nowt for *them ;*
She's like sum hollor humlick grown a' puzzin te the stem.
Gasleet she likes mair nor the day thit shows hor faded cheek,
Thit shows hor teeth, a' false an' wite, an' a' hor bewty week.
She's Rachelized an' plaistord owre wi' stuff fra forin pairts ;
A female libortine in life, a moosetrap for f'yuls' hairts.
She dyes her eyebroos, paints hor lips, an' lets hor breests be
    seed,
That awd fyuls may be tysed te luve, an' honor'd in thor need.
Plisshor's the oney god she naws in dissippayshin's world,
Sin, like a peece o' gilty lace, it is elwis roond hor forl'd ;
She envies a' the bally-queens thit flee aboot the stage,
She'd show hor legs wi' them, for spite, the yung men tiv
    engage.
Hor eyes gloats on the men in luve, or lawliss, lewd dissire,
She's like a silvor buttorflee neer sum haystack on fire.
O, Lord be praised, that wife o' mine, this picktor dissent fit,
Else aw wad skrush the wanton like a bit o' cookoo's spit !
Then let us pray thit we may keep frev a' sutch ladies fine,
An' leeve alang wi doose, kind, wives that grace the banks o'
    Tyne.

THE PITMIN'S ADVICE TIV HIS MARRAS.

CoME, hinnies, marras, list to me,
An' drop yor gam' an' feulish spree,
While aw blaw oot a veaise or twee,
    The best way that aw can.

We're not just monkeys or baboons—
Beers, cockatoos or mad racoons—
Or sec-like beests they show i' toons—
    Here ivery chep's a man.
Tho law's wor lot iv yearth's wide spot,
We hae wor chance to rise ;
Wor reasons hae ne reet to rot—
    'Cas feuls wor words despise.
Then colliers, lissen to maw sang,
Aw'll tell ye nowt aw think is wrang,
But what may keep ye fra life's stang,
    An' meyk ye clivor men.

Noo, a' ye lads aboot to wed,
Be cawshus whe ye teyk to bed ;
Be not biv rings an' trappins led—
    For dress will stop yor scran ;
But teyk a cliver lass an' stoot,
That winnet send yor weshins oot,
That sarks can meyk an' hoggers cloot,
    To gar folk leuk like men.
A wife that sings, and warks, an' brings
Fat bairns yor hoose to bless,
That wiv kind speech your hearts can reach,
    When toil an' troubles press ;
A wife that keeps her awn hearth-steyn,
An' lets her neebor's fawlts aleyn,
That watches weel her husbin's gain,
    An' luves her canny man.

Let honest labour boil yor pot—
Teyk care o' what be toil is got—
An' tiv a farden pay yor shot,
    For debt's the deevil's den.
Stop a' the chalks ahint the dore,
An' niver meyk a yell hoose score ;
Let nivor drink yor senses flore,
    But a' be sober men.
Be always croose aboot the hoose,
An' nowthor sweer nor fret—

An' when ye dine ne'er twist nor twine
  For things ye cannet get.
An' if yor marrow be's hard up,
Refuse him nowthor bite nor sup,
'Tis Friendship fills his empy cup,
  An' helps his fellow man.

Wiv fightin feuls ne'er meyk a row,
Ne'er teyk a lazy man i' tow—
Anuthor's keyk ne'er try te chow,
  Nor cowp yor neebor's can.
Wiv pollytics ne'er fash yor heed
Nor bleym a marrow for his creed—
But follor him that teyks the leed,
  To teech reet ways to man.
An' let ne meyte hae caws to hate
Yor interlowpin' ways ;
Be kind tiv a', baith leesh an' sma',
  An' divent cadge for praise.
Walk steadily an' honestly—
Yor awn an' maister's intrest see,
An' let a' useless sticks a-be,
  An' stick to wark like men.

Remember, tee, yor bairns to guide :
Keep a' yor lasses free frae pride—
An' divent drive them frae yor side,
  Els they bad geytes may gan.
Leuk te the weelfare o' yor wives—
For they're the bumlors i' luve's hives—
Its them that cheers the colliers' lives,
  An' meyks them happy men !
Let ivery bairn his Bible leern,
There's penny scheuls galore—
That when yor'e awd—each lass and lad
  May sheym keep frev yor dore.
Wark hard, an' elways be content—
Be croose, but not improvident—
An' meyk reet use o' blessins sent—
  An' ye'll a' be stunnin' men !

REET CHEPS I' THOR PL'YESES.

WHEN forst Newcassel Toon wis m'yed,
  Awd fashin'd styles wis ganin ;
Awd fashin'd l'eyns o' bricks an' st'yens,
  An' Chares an' Streets wis stan'in ;
An' iv'vry street wis kursin'd reet,
  Like horses it wor races ;
Thit things an' men, like noo, is then,
  Might pick thor propor pl'yeses.

Leet ships sailed up te Ballist Hills,
  P. D's Keel Entry stay'd in ;
An' Stella-Bar showed monny a star,
  When sharp lads leeved it Blaydin.
Then Airtists went te Paintor H'yuff,
  An' Locksmiths sowt the Key, man ;
Then Grindin-Chare had Millors there,
  An' trav'lin Cutlors, tee, man.

The Carpintors t'yuk Joinors' Ha',
  The Skinnors' Born t'yuk Tannors,
The Dancin-maistors, yen an' a',
  Gat hoosis be the Manors.
Sum pitmen claim'd the Fightin-Cocks,
  Thor crowdy-mains te pitch in ;
But Gallas-Gate, aw's bund te, state,
  Retorn'd thim te Hell's Kitchin.

The Harmits stopp'd i' Pilgrim Street ;
  Then Monks gat their desires,
When vargin lasses used te meet,
  I' Nun's Street wi' the Friars.
Tripe-cleanors liked the Butchor Bank,
  Is weel is Puddin Chare, man ;
But Dog Bank, tee, wis famed for spree,
  For piemen a' flock'd there, man.

The Sinkors s'yun fand Pitt Street oot,
    Where Coll'yors kep' thor staishins ;
While on Parade the sowljors stayed,
    Queen's Square defied a' nashins.
Te Sallyport the Rifles run,
    Te Nelson Street the Sailors ;
While Masons stuck i' Lime Street muck,
    Cloth Market bore up Tailors.

The Joolors rentid Silver Street,
    Tho' Close wis oft thor dwellin ;
They liked the Pandin-foaks te meet,
    When tickits they wore sellin.
Te Shakspur Street Play-actors wawk'd ;
    Tiv Hood Street went dry joakors ;
The Street o' Dean hid elwis been
    A harbor for white chokors.

Lord Judges weel liked Eldon Square,
    Tho' Clayton Street l'yuk'd bonny ;
Man, 'torneys ye'd see flockin there,
    They liked the law'yor, Johnny.
Shoe-blacks te Blackett Street wad gan,
    Vine Lane fit oot Wine-dealors ;
An' Sandhill's Cort m'eyd clivvor sport,
    For prigs an' Tyneside Peelors.

The Bums gat wark i' Bailey-g'yet,
    Tiv Hare Street went the Shaivors ;
The Stock Bridge garr'd the Brokors fidge ;
    When St'yenny Hill gat Paivors.
The Brooers stuck te Barley Moo,
    The Chorch Wawk fed Deeth-huntors ;
Wor Dairymaid te Coog'yet stray'd,
    While Hogg's Cort fed the Gruntors.

Tiv Haddick's Entry wi' thor kreels,
    Thrang'd a' wor canny Fishwives ;
I' file an' rank te Pott'ry Bank,
    Cam' Muggors' an wor Dishwives.

The Sweeps it Chimley Mill wis seed
   Te sew thor poaks for luck, man,
But Bellas-mendors kep' the lead,
   Iv a' it Windy N'yuk, man.

But lor! aw cannet tell ye hawf
   What foaks thor streets silectid,
But a' wis reet an' fair cumplete—
   Newcassel stud dissected.
An' noo, aw think, aw've said en'yuff
   Aw'll imitate Jack Hornor;
Just sook me thum's—for, see! here cums
Maw Clark frev Amen Cornor.

THE BOBBIES AN' THE CLAES LINES;

OR, THE WESHORWIVES' RIVVENGE.

Wor Tyne Lysint Fudlors for lang had been sweerin'
G'yen Bobbies, in plain claes, on Sundors appeerin',
An' fetchin' thim up for wor mawgistrates' heerin',
   An' puttin' on Tommy wi' cairt-loads o' fines.
But the cheef o' wor pollis is droppin' his raid
G'yen the Fudlors an' Beer Shops thit manidged te trade,
In spite o' the bothor thit thorsty cheps smuthor;
   Noo the deevil's te pay wi' the claes-dryin' lines.

The time aw rimmembor when Croft, Forth, an' Spittil
Wis spred wite wi' claes for the poor, big an' littil;
Where a chep cud, in public, the shift-watchors kittil,
   An' nowthor feer Bobbies nor mawgistrates' fines.
Noo the Forth, Croft, an' Spittil ne langor is seed,
For wor kind corporayshin seez'd awl in thor need;
Thor's nowt bnt the Leezis, an' the Toon's Moorish breezis,
   Or the Wesh-hoose, for paymint,—an' them's hardish lines!

Noo wor Back Streets is handy an' fit for claes dryin',
Still mindin' wor k'yukin', an' stoppin' theeves pryin',
Content, thit for cumfort, an' cleenlyniss tryin',
 We get up wor husbins, lads, spiff, te the nines.
But a blite's on wor weshins when Silvestor speeks,
For the pollis, like dogs, up wor back lonnins sneeks ;
He hawls doon wor hippins, wor goons, shifts, an' slippins,
 He clarts wor grand weshins an' humbugs wor lines.

Uz wives is mad raygin' ag'yen wor tormentors ;
Wor angor is coppy'd in dayleys be printors ;
But wor cheef o' the Mannors is like stiff dissentors,
 Te stick tiv his bylaws he stubborn inclines.
A' wor gobbin' ag'yen this m'yest sh'yemfil abewse ;
A' the warst o' bad wishes, or pleedin's ne yewse ;
He says, "be yor chimley dry a' yor duds nimley,
 " Ef ye divvint, maw skrubbors, away gans yor lines !"

Noo, te dry in wor hooses a fortneet's big weshin',
Is a law o' the deedlyist sort iv oppreshin ;
Cawse it leeves aigeys, feevors, an' deeth in porsesshin,
 An' for sartin the hilth o' wor bairns undormines.
The steem o' the wet things hings ower thor bed ;
Be the cloods frae hoose-dryin' consumpshin is fed ;
Then a coff brings a coffin thit s'yun tho're hawled off in,
 An' awl for te stop the Back Street Dryin' Lines !

A chep thit leeves close te the heed o' Bath L'yen, sors,
For us poor weshorwives hes a spite an' disdain, sors ;
Se he thowt sum greet praise for wor cheef he wad gain, sors ;—
 Is a coo-keepin' cairtman, this bizzy Dick shines.'
Five lines o' wet claes he spies oot in Oak's Street ;
Says he, "Pull thim doon, else thor reck aw'll compleet !"
Away gans this cairtman, wivoot luve or hairt, men,
 An' clarts a' the claes is he rives doon the lines !

But the wives wis dittormind to m'yek him rippent it ;
They swore they wad plaistor his jaws—an' they ment it !
Cooshairn, be the pailfuls, they raked up, contented,
 For s'yun to reel slawtor us wimmin inclynes.

He cam' doon the street iv a rush an' a horry,
When us Cooshair Sharp Shuttors commenced a deed worry ;
We hit him, we fit him, we collord an' bit him,
    An' gov him green jollip for smashin' wor lines.

Noo, wor pollis, t'yek warnin', an divvint mislist us,
For a' wor gud-men hes swore thump they'll assist us ;—
We oney want fairplay an' weshorwives' justis,
    Se let wor cheef constybil drop his dissines,
For is sartin is deeth, ef wor claes is hoyed doon ;
 We'll giv his Bloo Bobbies a cooshairney croon,
An' we'll nail the cheef skippor, an' giv him a nippor,
    Se he'd bettor sing sma' 'boot the claes-dryin' lines.

SILLILLYKWEE FRA MACBETH.

A TYNESIDE TRANSLAYSHIN.

" Is this a Bobby thit aw sees afore me,
  His staff aim'd for maw beek? Cum ! let me crush thee !
Is thoo nut sensybil tiv a crackt skull ?
Or, is thoo sum Bloo Robbort's ghaist thit gans
His roon's te hunt for pie 'mang greesy keuks?
Thoo's heer ageyn ; an' on thaw jaws an' trunshin
Black-puddin' skins, thit wassent thair afore.
Thoo wags me on the road aw just wis gan.
Here nût maw clogs thoo awd an' craizy stairs,
An' divvint cheep tiv owt aw's in for scran,
Or else the cats 'ill wowl wi' black rivenge.
But while aw stand, maw lass may pig te bed,
An' then aw's flummaxd ! wheesht ! the tinklor's soondin'!
Heer it nut Bobbies, ye thit's sweet on Nell,—
Aw heer hor whussil ! Oh aw'll gan messel' !"